THE BEST TEEN **WRITING**
OF 2020

Scholastic Art & Writing Awards

Alliance for Young Artists & Writers

For information or permission, contact:
Alliance for Young Artists & Writers
557 Broadway
New York, NY 10012

artandwriting.org

Cover: *Emiree No. 2*, Photography by **Anna Schooley**, Grade 12, Langham Creek High School, Houston, TX.

ISBN13: 978-1-338-71595-8

Table of Contents

Dedication

The Best Teen Writing of 2020 is dedicated to Scholastic Inc. and its visionary founder, the late Maurice R. Robinson, in celebration of the company's centennial anniversary.

Robinson, who was known by his friends as "Robbie," had a bold idea—to help build a future in which creativity, artistic expression, and a greater appreciation for art, literature, and "things of the spirit and of the mind" would become intrinsic American values. In 1923, a few years after the founding of *The Scholastic* magazine for motivated and intellectually engaged high-school students, the Scholastic Awards were born.

This enduring vision remains, having touched the lives of millions of creative teenagers and their families, teachers, and communities. Countless past Awards recipients have forged new paths in the worlds of literature and art, as well as science, politics, activism, business, and design. As important, our alumni have acquired, in Robinson's own words, "a feeling for beauty, which will color their entire lives, and the lives of those about them. There lies the great encouragement."

Today, the Awards are presented by the Alliance for Young Artists & Writers, and Scholastic Inc. and the Maurice R. Robinson Fund remain the Alliance's staunchest supporters. The Alliance proudly and gratefully dedicates this publication to the transformative nature of the Awards and the leadership of Maurice R. Robinson and the company he founded 100 years ago.

About *The Best Teen Writing of 2020*

The Best Teen Writing of 2020 features selected National Medal–winning work from the 2020 Scholastic Art & Writing Awards. Since 1923, the Scholastic Awards, presented by the Alliance for Young Artists & Writers, have identified teenagers with exceptional artistic and literary talent. The program celebrates these young artists and writers with opportunities for recognition, exhibition, publication, and scholarships.

This year, more than 1,100 works won National Medals in writing categories. The works selected for this publication represent the diversity of the National Medalists, including grade, gender, geography, genre, and subject matter. The selected works also present a spectrum of the insight and creative intellect that inform many of the submitted pieces.

Visit **artandwriting.org** to view online galleries of all nationally awarded works of art and writing. There you can also learn how to enter the 2021 Scholastic Art & Writing Awards and ways you can partner with the Alliance to support young artists and writers in your community.

About the Scholastic Art & Writing Awards

Since 1923, the Scholastic Art & Writing Awards have recognized the vision, ingenuity, and talent of our nation's youth and provided opportunities for creative teens to be celebrated. Each year, increasing numbers of teens participate in the program and become a part of our community—young artists and writers, filmmakers and photographers, poets and sculptors, video game designers and science fiction authors—along with countless educators who support and encourage the creative process. Notable Scholastic Awards alumni include Andy Warhol, Sylvia Plath, Cy Twombly, John Baldessari, Ken Burns, Kay WalkingStick, Richard Avedon, Stephen King, Luis Jiménez, Paul Chan, Marc Brown, Truman Capote, and Joyce Carol Oates to name just a few.

Our Mission

The Scholastic Art & Writing Awards are presented by the Alliance for Young Artists & Writers. The Alliance is a 501(c)(3) nonprofit organization whose mission is to identify students with exceptional artistic and literary talent and present their remarkable work to the world through the Scholastic Art & Writing Awards. Through the Awards, students receive opportunities for recognition, exhibition, publication, and scholarships. Students across America submitted nearly 340,000 original works during our 2019 program year across 29 different categories of art and writing.

Our Programs

Through the Scholastic Awards, teens in grades 7–12 from public, private, or home schools can apply in 29 categories of art and writing for a chance to earn scholarships and have their works exhibited and published. Beyond the Awards, the Alliance produces a number of programs to support creative students and their educators, including the Art.Write.Now.Tour, the National Student Poets Program, the Scholastic Awards Summer Workshops and Scholastic Awards Summer Scholarships programs, the GOLDEN Educators Residency, and many more. The Alliance features art works by National Medalists that received our top awards in *The Best Teen Art*. Additionally, we publish a collection of exemplary written works in this anthology, *The Best Teen Writing*, and a chapbook that features works from the National Student Poets. These publications are distributed free of charge to schools, students, educators, museums, libraries, and arts organizations across the country.

2020 National Writing Jurors

Sean Cho A.

Rasha Abdulhadi

Tolu Adeyeye

Opal Palmer Adisa

Marissa Nicole Ahmadkhani

Dilruba Ahmed

Nadia Alexis

Hanna Ali

Ignatius Valentine Aloysius

Yasmine Ameli

Eloisa Amezcua

Rayshma Arjune

Joseph Tyler Arnold

Louisa Aviles

Lucas Baisch

Quenton Baker

Joan Bauer

Jumoke Adeola Bello

Danielle Bennett

Sarah Boudreau

Kate Brandes

Amy L. Brewer

Kristine E. Brickey

Ryan D. Brinkhurst

Kathryn L. Brohawn

D. Winston Brown

Laynie Browne

Camryn L. Bruno

Eisha Buch

Lorea Canales

Cortney Lamar Charleston

Karissa Chen

Erica Christensen

Brandon Ray Christophe

J K Chukwu

Darin Ciccotelli

Ian Clarke

David Clawson

Ian M. Cockfield

Jaed Muncharoen Coffin

Gerald L. Coleman

Miles Collins-Sibley

Abigail B. Colodner

Britny Cordera

Paige Cornwell

Sylvan Creekmore

Molly Cross-Blanchard

John Darcy

Barbara Darko

Hílda Davis

Marissa Davis

Jade Dee

Michael J. DeLuca

Trace Howard DePass

Adebe DeRango-Adem

Anna deVries

Julio Cesar Diaz

Tarik Octavio Dobbs

Miranda Lynn Dubner

Jennani Durai

Summer Edward

David Ehmcke

Philip Elliott

Enoch the Poet

Rachel Ewen

Tanis Franco

Michael Frazier

Kim Fu

Lanxing Fu

Mark Galarrita

Jonathan Francisco Garcia

Lauren Garretson

Alexa Garvoille

Alison Granucci

Harold Green

Cassie Guinan

Gary Hawkins

Adilene Hernandez

Marcelo Hernandez Castillo

Sara Holbrook

Ravi Howard

Heather K. Hummel

Emily Hunt

Glen Huser

Jennifer Inglis

Vida James

Victor Jatula

Cordelia Johnson

Fred L. Joiner

Ellen Jones

Zeyn Joukhadar

Seelai Karzai

David James Keaton

Oonya Kempadoo

Saba Keramati

Aryaana Khan

Chelene Knight

Michael H. Koresky

Talia Kovacs

Dr. Debra R. Lamb

Meghan Lamb

Sonya Lara

Rich Larson

Brett Fletcher Lauer

Evan Lavender-Smith

Amanda Lechenet

Jennifer Dominique Lee

Winona Riley León

Andrew G. Levy

Maurisa Li-A-Ping

Chip Livingston

Corinne Logan

Rebecca M. Luxton

Sandeep Mahal

Charles J. Malone

Racheline Maltese

Halimah Marcus

Wilnona Marie
Suzette Mayr
Trapeta B. Mayson
Chris McKinney
Pat McLean-Smith
Katya Mezhibovskaya
Richard Michelson
nelle mills
Brad Aaron Modlin
Danielle Mohlman
Anthony Moll
Tracie Morris
Vynetta A. Morrow
Da'Shawn Mosley
Doug Murano
Walton Muyumba
Yvette Lisa Ndlovu
Dr. Kerry Neville
Will Niedmann
Jennifer A. Nielsen
Marc Nieson
Biljana D. Obradovic
Uche Okonkwo
Jose Olivarez
Karl Otto
Anne Marie Pace
Angelique Palmer
Elsbeth Pancrazi
Elissa Ann Parker
Eric Thomas Parker
Dustin Kyle Pearson
Sara Pirkle
Nathan Jordan Poole
Shaunwell Ramon Posley
Joy Priest
Dr. Adam Prince
Monica Prince
Alice Freeman Quinn
Shazia Hafiz Ramji
Anna Duke Reach
Jessica Reino
Luke Reynolds

Linda Rodriguez
Rollo Romig
Chris Rosales
Jonah Rosenberg
Rachel Youngeun Rostad
Alanna Rusnak
Vasantha Sambamurti
Kevin Sands
Luc Sante
Robert Reese Sawyer
Eleanore J. Scott
Kate Elizabeth Lu Sedor
Paul Seesequasis
Christopher Donshale Sims
Daniel Sklar
Charles R. Smith Jr.
Maggie Smith
Matthew Ross Smith
Nell Smith
Zoe Elizabeth Smolen
John Elizabeth Stintzi
Francisco X. Stork
Allan Stratton
Ben Stroud
Virgil Suárez
Jarvis Subia
Kaushika Suresh
Jeffrey Sweet
Dante C. Swinton
Glenn Taylor
Janessa I. Terry
Anah Tillar
Paul Tobin
Laura Tohe
Katy Diane Towell
Vu Tran
Derek Updegraff
Anne Ursu
Jessica Verdi
Adam Vines
Asiya Wadud
Richard Wallace

Kevin Waltman
Deshaun Washington
Elissa Washuta
Jemimah James Wei
Brian Phillip Whalen
Aaron Wiener
Carmin Wong
Tobias Wray
James Yeh
Hari Ziyad

Foreword

This book celebrates the creative accomplishments of the exceptional teens whose works received National Medals in this year's Awards. Our National Medalists are part of a tradition that dates back to 1923—one focused on recognizing young people who represent the future of American art and letters.

On behalf of the entire Awards family, we congratulate all of this year's Medalists. We would also like to acknowledge the extraordinary educators and supportive family members who have helped to nurture the voices and visions expressed in this year's national award-winning work.

Since their founding, the Awards have grown to become the country's largest, longest-running, and most prestigious recognition program for creative teens. This is possible only because of our dedicated Affiliate partners, who oversee more than 100 regional programs across the nation; our expert jurors at both the regional and national level; and our generous supporters. And of course, none of our programs would exist without the leadership of our Board of Directors and the yearlong efforts of our exceptional staff. We are grateful to this extraordinary community for all they do to support our shared mission.

Dr. Hugh Roome
Chairman of the Board
Scholastic Art & Writing Awards

Christopher Wisniewski
Executive Director
Scholastic Art & Writing Awards

Special Achievement Awards

Political commentaries and civic engagement. Climate change. Love and loss. Teens have a lot to say about life and the world around them. Every year, we partner with dedicated individuals, foundations, and corporations to offer creative scholarship opportunities to teen artists and writers whose experiences and ideas help shape the communities around them.

Portfolio Awards
- Gold Medal Portfolio
- Silver Medal with Distinction Portfolio

Other Special Achievement Awards
- American Voices Medal
- Best-in-Grade Award
- Civic Expression Award
- New York Life Award
- One Earth Award
- Alliance/ACT-SO Journey Award

Selections of Special Achievement Award writing works are included in the following pages.

His Hearth

SHORT STORY

SAM BOWDEN, Grade 12, Wyoming High School, Wyoming, OH. Keith Lehman, *Educator*; Art Academy of Cincinnati, *Affiliate*; Gold Medal Portfolio

SCHOLASTIC INC. WRITING PORTFOLIO

You have a twin brother named Thaddeus, apparently. When you heard the knocking on your door you assumed it was the Girl Scouts—it was, after all, cookie season. You were sitting in your Lay-Z-Boy watching a History Channel documentary about Eddie Rickenbacker; the front door, wooden and peeling, was a room's length away. You told the Scouts to piss off through the door. You live alone. You cannot cook for yourself and the Girl Scouts seem to know this because they keep knocking and offering sweets. The TV goes off just as the trenches become clotted with grainy mustard gas. You cross the dry and crusted shag barefoot. Your toe strikes an old Bud Light can you didn't see. You wince in pain. You almost walk away but then the knocking comes back. You've gotten this far, and you feel a little embarrassed now, so you open the door.

It is not a Girl Scout. Your eyes were tilted down, expecting some pigtailed and skirted blonde. You are now staring at the crotch of a man in weathered black dress pants. He greets you by name. You look up. He looks like you without the beard. He's smiling. His teeth are white and straight. He says his name is Thaddeus, that he heard about Mom dying, that he's very sorry and he'd like to come in. You aren't sure if he's bullshitting you or not. You watched this show from your Lay-Z-Boy once about people who go door-to-door and try to get reactions out of people. You thought it was a little funny but mostly disturbing. There is no cameraman over Thaddeus's shoulder. You ask him—cautiously, though—if he likes the History Channel.

You sit across from each other in the living room, which you're now beginning to realize smells like beer and smoke. The blinds are drawn. The light is pale green. You ask Thaddeus if he wants a Bud Light. Thaddeus tells you he doesn't drink. He's looking around the living room like a small boy at a zoo. There's a photo of Mom sitting on the TV stand. He points to it and asks if it's her. You don't say anything.

Listen, Thaddeus says, I understand perfectly if you don't want to tell me, so I have the birth certificates in the car. Yours and mine both.

You don't buy it. You grill him. You ask him Mom's full name—he answers, correctly. You think for a second, then ask him what her full name was before Ellis Island, her Swiss name, before the Americans cut the name down so it would fit through the gates. He gives you the full six-syllable family name without missing a beat. You purse your lips.

Thaddeus tells you Mom didn't have the money for twins so she put him up for adoption. He thinks Dad flipped a coin to decide which boy to keep and which to send away—how else but by chance, that impartial god, could they decide? Thaddeus talks like that a lot. You notice he likes big words and talking with his hands. You're looking at his perfect teeth again. A rich British family took him and raised him in the Hyde Park Residential. He has been surrounded by money and pristine trash all his life. You ask him if he shits into golden toilet bowls and gets his feet rubbed by French maids. He sighs. No, he says, I don't. Most of them are from Puerto Rico.

He goes on to say he's been keeping checks on his birth family. He uses the word *hearth* a lot, as if you and this cruddy-looking living room somehow represent something to him. As he says this he starts to seem more familiar. Have you seen this guy before? Have you passed him on the street? You thought the man who delivered your pizza Friday kind of looked like you too. And the taxi driver who took you to the A.A. meeting on Saturday. Suddenly Thaddeus has become every person you've interacted with for the past few weeks, and you're so lost in this idea that you almost miss what he's saying: that he tells you that he read about Mom in the obits in the newspaper, that he couldn't make it to the funeral because of a business trip. He turns away from the picture of Mom and stares at you and for just a second you get the feeling that Thaddeus is deeply, deeply sad, and not just because of Mom, but because he's seeing what he could've become in you.

Thaddeus asks if you'd like to come with him to the cemetery a few miles away. Mom is fresh in the ground there, in a tiny cardboard box. You cremated her because it was cheaper. He offers to drive. He looks a little guilty.

You aren't quite sure what to think of all this. It's a bit much and like you always do when confronted with something a bit much you shut down and withdraw yourself. You imagine all the nasty things Thaddeus is thinking about you. Thaddeus asks to go to Mom's grave together again. Maybe you didn't hear him the first time?

In the end you submit and climb into Thaddeus's car. It is a Mercedes. That gets you thinking about the guy at the A.A. meeting who told everyone a few meetings back he was driving his Mercedes drunk and totaled it on the side of the highway and hit and killed a whole van of Girl Scouts. The Girl Scouts were on their way to a campsite. There were five of them in the car and a mom, and you think the mom died too but you aren't sure. It was this big, horrible thing, all over the news for a day or two. All you can think of as you slide into the front seat is the dead Girl Scouts and the Mercedes. You feel like you're dirtying the cream-leather seats, the dash, but when Thaddeus takes his seat beside you he says it doesn't matter. He's just so happy to see someone from his hearth again. Oh, this wonderful day.

You ask him a lot of questions in the car, but these questions are less about trying to prove Thaddeus is who he says he is and more about Thaddeus himself. Yes, he is some kind of actor or something. He won something called a BAFTA, which you think is like an Oscar but you won't ask in case you'll look stupid. Thaddeus has two kids, both girls, adopted like him. He has a husband. He is a queer. You think this is strange, but he's family too—hearth, you think, feeling strange—so you act comfortable. Thaddeus can probably tell how you really feel anyway. The Mercedes growls under your legs like Eddie Rickenbacker's SPAD XIII. You like the smell of the seats. You watch Thaddeus start to make a wrong turn, then correct him, reaching over.

As the two of you pull into the cemetery through rusted, open gates, Thaddeus starts asking his own questions. Mostly they're about Mom and what she was like and how she did after Dad ran off with some high-school girl he met at his janitorial job. You answer each question slowly and carefully, trying hard to remember; you don't want to get anything wrong. Thaddeus stops the car. There are polished gravestones that shine with dew spectating the Mercedes silently. You tell him that this is the place, that she's right there, right on the top of that hill ahead.

Thaddeus doesn't speak again until you're both out of the Mercedes and approaching the hillcrest. He asks how you're handling it all. The death, he means. You're the last one left in the family. You did not marry because women were too much, too scary, too different from Mom. You have been alone for sixty-odd years—at least, that's what you told yourself. But now Mom is gone and you're truly alone and god dammit it hurts to imagine. You tell this stranger-family-brother Thaddeus some of these things but not all. Thaddeus says you're not alone. Thaddeus says he's there for you and yes he knows you probably hate him for just showing up out of the blue like this and yes he knows you have every reason not to consider him a part of your family but still he says he's there. You do not have to be alone. I want to know my family again, he says, hands in his pockets. If you're all I have left? Then you're all I need to know.

You arrive at the top of the hill. A little heap of reddish dirt is clumped beside your feet. Mom's name—Americanized—stares up at you and Thaddeus from the ground. You paid an extra fifty dollars to put ""Beloved Mother" under her death date.

So, Thaddeus says, this is her. Yeah, you mumble, it is. Thaddeus has no flowers, nothing to lay at her stone. He just stares at her name and the back half of it that used to be his. He's doing that thing where he purses his lips again. His hands are balled up in his pockets. So are yours. You two stand in the exact same way, one fused shoulder hunched, eyes on the ground. All of this like two sides of a mirror, one side dirtied and greased and still a little drunk. Thaddeus is in a black suit. You wear sweatpants and a fraying yellow tank top that was white when Mom was alive. His hair is clean. Yours touches the back of your neck.

Thaddeus tells you to come over to his house at Hyde Park. Dinner, tonight. His husband makes the most fantastic beef roast. Please. He wants to get to know you better.

You open your mouth but don't quite respond. Mom is watching from under your feet. You realize Thaddeus has her eyes.

Thaddeus asks if you heard what he said. You say yes. Yes and you would love to come for dinner. You'd like to get to know him too. You're nervous as you say it but you mean it, don't you? How come you've always been afraid? Of change, of something new? You raise your head up from the grave and see with half-weeping eyes across the cemetery a group of Girl Scouts kneeling at a row of five fresh gravestones, leaving decorated cookie boxes stuffed with flowers. ∎

Aubade on Rainy Sunday

POETRY

EMORY BRINSON, Grade 12. South Mecklenburg High School, Charlotte, NC.
Deborah Lee, *Educator*; Charlotte-Mecklenburg Schools, *Affiliate*; Gold Medal Portfolio

THE MAURICE R. ROBINSON FUND WRITING PORTFOLIO

Rainwater collapses through dense breath;
damp laminate and lacquer:
Trembling droplets settling and
Father Jones bows his head, I say
pray like breaking dam and
give the parishioners an illusion—
of grace.
Voices trill and twist together
sunlight feeding through throats
We are enclosed in a holy body of work.
Summertime always bleeds burning
tempers.
and even God must fall prey to the humid urge,
humans stumbling to false confession.

Fruit flies take refuge during collection where
Old-Man-Charles dropped two teeth &
87 years of memories,
Bones rattled with coins; pennies and thoughts—
swimming together for the pastor
to swallow.
the sermon,
spirit of giving too much like
When the drowning happens
these empty words will line hungry pockets

Rain slamming into open palms.
a believer baptized in sacrificial blood
This God, he is giving and taking
yes, but always,
keeping

I wish the pews would splinter me into
the wetting of desert throats.
all of us: drowning on dry land.
maybe if I swallow the sparks of lightning,
drink down the deluge he will
forgive my sins in the flood
We become ants in search of crumbs
for communion
as we give up flesh and blood;
He counts coins; my fingers find bits of her—
skin. This is the season for hurting
I am bruised, bursting
giving in to the anger and lust sending
Fire of sin swelling in my belly.

I almost left my sin in the tin pot, but
I dropped my bible, hand-me-down,
instead.
I collect hickeys and lipstick stains
for prying eyes
She is the fly on the stained glass,
the air in my gasping lungs,
the bible verse in ink on my father's wrist.
bury me in the rain barrel,
away from hallowed ground.

I am saved child spewing holy water
on slick vinyl tile.
she is the storm banging on the door,
tempest hiding uneasy worshipper—
from his bitter gaze. ∎

Seoul Haibun

POETRY

ISABELLA CHO, Grade 12. North Shore Country Day School, Winnetka, IL.
Frances Collins, *Educator*; Writopia Lab, *Affiliate*; Gold Medal Portfolio

THE HARRY AND BETTY QUADRACCI WRITING PORTFOLIO

i asked for home in this city, sold my tongue to the fisherman un-teething pol-
lock in the lip of the monsoon. *bad weather,* he said, brandishing his knife slick
with red film, *bad weather to sell the sea.* i asked for home and was given meat
wrapped in cellophane, the muscle-thrash of fin still warm in my palms. the
man said *eat,* slipped the ocean's welled tear in my throat.

*

there is no repentance here. instead, my tongue welling with blood, culled of
syllable. back home in america telephone pole cordons my teeth, makes meat
of my hands. back home there is hamburger grease on my chin and the denim
makes it hard to breathe. back home i cannot hear my grandmother—*when
you coming back?*—over the lawnmower sliding its teeth over pansies, over the
picketed lawn, the violence of it. but not here. here i watch boys pocket drag-
onflies in their mouths and say *aya aya aya* as asphalt peels their knees. here
i steal glances at the girls scrawling pictographs over their pale arms—*moon,
daughter, hunger hunger*—under camphor, catch their immaculate pronunciation and let it add skins to my mouth.

*

my mother told me i used to run open-mouthed through these parks. at night
she read me stories, traced her hands over symbol-studded pages, watched as
my tongue moved worlds: *there is a rabbit on the moon.* i'd clamber over steel
jungle gym, claw at the blue air. *i want that rabbit i want that rabbit i want that
want that that.* back then, i hadn't learned to economize want. back then, the
buildings were so close they felt like skins made of turning walls. back then,
there was a way to salvage what i'd lost in the fish bones xylophoned through
my lips smeared in cheap gloss. back then, there were words for the person i
wanted to be: *powerful, intimidating. well-spoken. ambidextrous. two-tongued.
two-tongued. two-tongued.*

*

at the lakefront, the city bristles before turning away. my tongue lodges against
the slums of my teeth: a foreign root. esophagus darkens with spit and i cack.

the muscle slips, blue and wild, onto my palms, stirs like child like dog like rainwater maddened by teeth, moves as if mouthing hymnal. and the fisherman knee-deep in black water mistakes my posture for praying. and i blister animal under the moon. and i beg for home and this, this is what is left to be given: the city turning its back, souls collected in its limbs like a forest. and my tongue shifts in my hands, looks into my eyes as if to say *chase*

me as if to say *you*

never owned me as if to say *goodbye*

now as if to say *gone gone.* ∎

Museum of My Own History, Age Sixteen

POETRY

JEFFREY LIAO, Grade 12. Livingston High School, Livingston, NJ.
Mary Brancaccio, *Educator*; Newark Public Library, *Affiliate*; Gold Medal Portfolio

COMMAND COMPANIES WRITING PORTFOLIO

EXHIBIT I: EXCERPT FROM DIARY ENTRY: OCTOBER 19TH, 2013
"It wasn't until today, when Nathan from school squinted his eyes at me
and told me to go back to my dirty country, that I realized how it felt
to be ashamed of my own skin."

EXHIBIT II: PAIR OF BROKEN GOGGLES
The ocean was my first mother. She made me tsunami.
She made me revolution. I am a product of radio static, of immigrant dreams
thawed by the slow of summer, of a native tongue silenced by a bullet wound.
I still have the scars of a sunken geography etched into the fissures
of my palms. I still wear the misshapen syllables of my parents' broken English
like a second name. When I was ten, I butchered my own throat
and tossed out the mangled organs of my old language,
swallowing my accent to baptize my tongue clean.
For years, I tried to navigate the learning curve of a new hemisphere
by undressing myself of my yellow phantoms,
the way you must first learn how to float
before learning how to swim.

EXHIBIT III: GHOST OF MY THIRTEEN-YEAR-OLD SELF
In eighth grade, I waged a war with the boy in the mirror.
I was a reckless arsonist, dousing the almond-slant of my eyes in gasoline,
setting fire to the constellation of pimples strung
along my face. I became of the scorched earth,
wasting futile hours attempting to destroy every cell of my being,
aching for all-American blue eyes the size of saucers, for the
sunflower-blonde hair and porcelain skin I saw in magazines.
I prayed to a broken faith for the type of transformation
they sang of in the movies. For the day I saw my body

as anything other than a cemetery. Under the bruised glow of moonlight,
I spent sleepless nights researching ways to win the battle,
then the war, failing to realize there is no way to win a war
in which the enemy is yourself. Sometimes, though,
I still want to fight.

EXHIBIT IV: CONVERSATION BETWEEN MY GRANDMOTHER AND
HER NEIGHBOR, CIRCA 2015
"What's it like being a communist?"
      i am not.
  "Do you eat dog?"
      no.
  "Jeez, are you always this uptight?"
      my english not good.
  "Is it a cultural thing?"
      i sorry. i don't know.
  "What? I can't hear you! Speak! Do you know how to speak?"
      i do speak. just quieter.

EXHIBIT V: YELLOWTAIL
In a market stall in New York's Chinatown, where the fish outnumber people,
I am a foreigner among my own blood. I breathe in exhaust fumes like the air
in heavy monsoon season: a toxic alchemy of smoke, fog, and dust.
I do not remember the language of my birthplace,
but I do know the language of the body, of being Chinese-American—
the way mothers push past each other in order to get the last pound of gutted
mackerel,
the way children complain of rice-swollen bellies to ignorant ears,
the way fathers hunch their shoulders inward as if to make themselves invisible.
The portrait of a nation hardened by silence, so used to being unheard that we
do it to ourselves.
A kaleidoscope of fish stares back at me, hollowed out like a thousand corpses.
I imagine the fish drowning in air, their fins convulsing
like snakes, bulbous eyes wide and unseeing, full of trauma instead of light.
I wonder if I am like their eyes: unable to see past my own reflection, which
is to say,
I cannot love myself but hate my own yellowness, which is to say,
I do not love either of us yet.

EXHIBIT VI: LIST OF SLURS I'VE HEARD THROUGHOUT MY CHILDHOOD

chink. tai-chink. ching chong. slit eyes. coin slot. squint. dog-eater. eggroll. gook. grasshopper. ninja. fresh off the boat. yellow boy. chinaman.

EXHIBIT VII: TELEGRAM

"it's just a joke."

"i don't think that asians, like, face actual discrimination."

"how are they so good at math?"

"are they all this awkward and shy?"

"your parents will probably beat you up if you don't get an A."

"why are asian guys so feminine?"

EXHIBIT VIII: MY BODY

My body is a tired thing. Even now, it is bleeding from self-inflicted wounds, and I do not know how to heal them. My body is an abandoned wasteland. A ghost town. I tell it to leave, to pack its belongings and find another boy to haunt. I want my body to take the contagion it inflicted upon me and toss it into the sea. But my body always stays. It is the only thing that holds me at night, when every dream I have is a montage of my body's funeral. It is the only thing that admires my own nakedness, because it too knows how to be unwanted and androgynous, how to carry the impossible burden of never being enough.

EXHIBIT IX: PHOENIX

Sometimes, I feel the lost syntax of my mother tongue clawing at my throat, hoping to reclaim her son again.

EXHIBIT X: RAILROAD TRACKS

In 1869, Chinese migrants built the transcontinental railroad,
a bridge connecting the East with the West,
the spark that propelled America into modern civilization.
Thirteen years later, the government prohibited Chinese immigration
so that even our own victories were not ours to enjoy.
I never meant to write this story into tragedy, never meant for us to be
written off as yellow weeds in a white garden. Sometimes, I
imagine my life as a series of railroad tracks, no clear end in sight.
I can only hope for the version of the story
where my Chinese is the destination instead of the roadkill, the version where
I run toward it with open arms, shouting, *I am here, at last.*
I've come home. ∎

Crashing into the Hood of the Free World, After Willa Carroll

POETRY

LUZ MANUNGA, Grade 12. Douglas Anderson School of Arts, Jacksonville, FL.
Liz Flaisig and Tiffany Melanson, *Educators*; Region-at-Large, *Affiliate*;
Gold Medal Portfolio

THE NEW YORK TIMES WRITING PORTFOLIO

Miscalculates the legitimacy of the illegitimate driver's license,
caught, hands behind back,
air parting from his lungs
answering to punches—
gut spilling out from knuckles,
hurt slams into shins.
He sees fifty stars against blue sky & opened car door,
it's at a strange angle, tethered to the hinges,
my father crawls on his belly
to call for help. He has my sister on the phone,
asks for an English dictionary from her
for the cop asking his name—the one on his license
stole, and ruining the birth name against his tongue
that is trying to speak a language of
war, pride, strong white men marching from an immigrant
they smugly crushed between the meat of their palms.

From his studio apartment, bandaged, he calls me half-
expecting ICE on the other end of the phone, and cries
America broke my legs. ∎

Beyond Brains

PERSONAL ESSAY & MEMOIR

AYUSH NOORI, Grade 12. Phillips Exeter Academy, Exeter, NH. Christina Breen, *Educator*; the National Writing Project in New Hampshire, *Affiliate*; Gold Medal Portfolio

THE NEW YORK TIMES WRITING PORTFOLIO

This summer, I held a human brain in my hands and wondered which grieving grandson let the neuropathologist cleave it from his grandmother's cold corpse. This 3-pound mass of dead, gray tissue was a relic of signals sent by synapses long since strangled by the tangled proteins which invade the brain in Alzheimer's. In our lab at MassGeneral Hospital, thanks to the generous sacrifices of dying patients, there is no shortage of severed brains—freezers full of frozen memories which I diced, sliced, and stained with esoteric antibodies, probing the diseased neurons and listening for their dying secrets. These are the processes—simple, sterile, and surgical—which, since antiquity, scientists have used to single out therapies, treatments, and cures. Scanning the cortical sections with fluorescent lasers, I converted webs of proteins, tendrils glowing in myriad colors, into echelons of ones and zeroes, black and white, clear digital code. This unique capacity to carve away the unknown and reveal the singular truth—intricate and interwoven, yes, but ultimately ordered and undeniable—secures my steadfast faith in modern medicine.

My grandmother's neurons have been pillaged by the same proteins under my microscope. As neurodegeneration ransacked her memories, it also stole memories that should have been mine—my Nani and I belting happy birthday, baking cookies, or bursting into laughter as I barreled into her arms for a warm hug. The imagined echoes of these missing moments leave only surging anger in their wake. Instead, I curate an arsenal of prescription pills and prepare her favorite hot chocolate at 2 a.m., gently mopping her mouth with my sleeve as it dribbles down her chin.

My Nani is bound to a hospital bed, and I know that her cold, callous brain will soon be in the hands of someone like me, who will dice, slice, and stain. Modern medicine marches on, and martyrs like my grandmother surrender their cerebrums to our scalpels and scopes, so we may forge ahead, step by step, towards the cure. In some ways, this crusade brings me closure.

When your ringtone trumpets at 1:34 a.m., it's either a nervous beau, a scammer from India, or a harbinger of something much worse. That sultry July night, my inordinate optimism was no use when the attending pulmonologist at the Stanford Hospital intensive care unit declared that my grandmother would not survive the night. Her atelectatic lungs would inevitably collapse, the frail labyrinth of alveoli and bronchi flooded by viscid fluid. Within four hours, I left the research lab and boarded a flight to Palo Alto.

I have now deep sympathy for flailing fish, plucked from the ocean and suffocated by air in a genocidal massacre by merciless fisherman. If, like a fish, you gasped for oxygen at sixty breaths a minute, one mighty heave every second, how long would you last? Seven minutes? Two hours? Enough time for an airplane to traverse 3,107 miles? Flummoxing physicians and defying the conviction of countless specialists, my grandmother maintained a respiratory rate of 60 for nearly one week.

Each night, Nani played tug-of-war with death. As she slept, her retching lungs languished as the noose of mucus constricted in her chest. At ungodly hours, I wakened to code blues and prayed for miracles as platoons of medics, armed with IVs and resuscitators, forced air into her bleeding trachea. Conjuring lifeblood with each raspy cough, my grandmother repelled the impending last stand. This infernal ritual—our midnight tradition—continued unabated for nearly one week. When dawn kindled the firmament, we heralded her seeming resurrection, a lease of life until the next night.

In a desperate bid before their death, Chinook salmon rocket from the shackles of the river and soar upstream, braving the maws of grizzlies and smothering their gills for a transient moment of peace. Witnessing this annual spectacle helped me understand why, for perhaps the last time, Nani wanted to experience life beyond ambulances and without ICU wards. Once her condition stabilized, the stunned doctors hesitantly obliged. One week later, alone together at the summit of a rocky precipice on the California coast, Nani and I confronted the cold Pacific Ocean. It was risky—the shoreline was a warzone, a terrible collision between the firm, fertile earth and the swirling, murky water. Salvos of resentful swells beat the boulders, and churning currents of sand, silt, and salmon carcasses shot up the cliff face. It could not reach us. With each labored inhalation, sweet and clean breeze surged into Nani's lungs, breathing blood into her fractured body, a bulwark against the rising tide. As tendrils of fog were born from the spray, the horizon melded with the gloomy mist until we opposed an infinite wall of gray. One could never be quite sure what lay beyond.

Mumbling with her mouth and signing with her stiff fingers, my grandmother asked me to return to my research. Above the clamor of the surf, she murmured into my strained ear, "Find me the cure." Though silent she may be, you cannot quarrel with Nani. I was simply transferred to another front of the fight, where we use antibodies instead of Ambu bags, microscopes instead of moxifloxacin, lasers instead of levodopa. As the airplane ascended into the roiling clouds, I gazed down at the coast. My grandmother's wheelchair is still perched on that cliff. Amidst this raging battle, this constant and ceaseless conflict, she stares at strange, beckoning forces past the gray horizon, shooting rays of God and brilliant flashes of green. She inches closer to the edge and gouges her heels into the ground.

I learned from my Nani that humans have dying secrets too, superpowers which we summon from spaces between our cells. She was determined to survive, to fight for the right to create more memories, to breathe, and banter, and bake, to celebrate my birthday with me. This determination, faith, and belief transcend the confines of modern medicine. I am comfortable with this contradiction. More than ever, I believe that medicine is our future. Yet, conclusions of clinicians cannot explain how a 3-pound lump of limp tissue, a jumble of jumpy neurons, becomes something more. On the morning of my birthday this year, I cut my cake, then called my grandmother and sang happy birthday while she listened. ∎

The Old Rice Cooker Under the Counter

POETRY

VITORIA SANA PEREZ, Grade 12. New Orleans Center for Creative Arts, New Orleans, LA. Anya Groner, *Educator*; Greater New Orleans Writing Project, *Affiliate*; Gold Medal Portfolio

THE HARRY AND BETTY QUADRACCI WRITING PORTFOLIO

The household most often has living within
the underbelly of its kitchen counter an old and clunky
rice cooker. No matter how many times the thing is washed
and no matter what dish soap is used in it, rice-colored
flour-like dust always seems to accumulate within its bowl.
The rice cooker boils while I finish my prayers, the sound of
its sizzling where the overcooked rice hardens into the hot
metal following each ear as I turn my head to give salaams
to the angels on my left and right.
The rice cooker burns my hand—
and I recoil. ∎

The Blue Umbrella

SHORT STORY

JIEYAN WANG, Grade 12. Moscow High School, Moscow, ID. Robert Bailey, *Educator*; Boise State Writing Project, *Affiliate*; Gold Medal Portfolio

COMMAND COMPANIES WRITING PORTFOLIO

Yesterday, when the autumn rain was particularly hard, I became my mother's blue umbrella so I could watch her childhood self. From my seat above her head, I saw her walking home alone from school for the first time. This was before my grandmother became wrinkled; she was still in her twenties. My mother carefully stepped around the puddles on the streets in her squeaking yellow boots. Her backpack sagged around her shoulders in the rain. She breathed in the wet air and the sound of the whirring cars. It was then that she realized that she was lost.

She stood there for a minute, clutching my handle in her hands. Scared of speaking to strangers, she sat on the doorstep of a convenience store. As she watched the men and women in heavy coats walk by, she counted the minutes on her pocket watch. One. Two. Tick. Tock.

It was fifty-eight minutes before my grandmother noticed that she had not come home and called the police to find her. That night, my mother returned home in a white-and-black police car. When my grandmother asked what had happened, all my mother did was shiver.

* * *

I turned into my mother's blue umbrella to witness my mother and my grandmother eating dinner five days after my mother got lost in the streets. From my corner in the dining room, I could see what was on the table: two plates of mashed potatoes, both half-eaten. The rain had slowed outside. A few rays of sunshine broke through the clouds.

My mother put down her fork and said, "I don't understand. Why can't I just walk back with you? Yesterday, I almost got lost again."

"You still found your way back here," My grandmother replied, scooping more potatoes into her mouth.

"You used to always walk me back. What's different?"

"You'll be fine."

"What—"

"Eat your potatoes."

My mother opened her mouth and then shut it again. Many years later, I asked my mother why we never visited my grandmother. My mother answered that she was born when my grandmother was too young. Carrying this living weight all through her youth, my grandmother eventually became tired of taking care of my mother. So, she stopped walking my mother home from school and instead left her in the rain.

However, my mother did not know this as she finished her dinner, eating mouthful after mouthful of potatoes in silence.

* * *

I became my mother's blue umbrella to sit next to my mother as she gazed into the fireplace in my grandmother's home. My canopy was still wet. It was only one hour after my mother's fifty-seventh walk from school alone.

My mother closed her eyes to listen to the crackle of the flames. She thought about how empty the house was. It was only her and my grandmother, who was tucked in away in the bedroom on the opposite side in their home. Often times, my mother went several long hours after school without ever seeing my grandmother. On those days, she sat in front of the fireplace, thinking about how lonely the word "lonely" looked with its two tall "ls" standing far apart from each other.

As my canopy began to dry, I wondered what it would be like to be one of the raindrops clinging on to me. During a storm, there were thousands of them falling towards the ground. But now, in the heat of the fire, they were all disappearing one by one as if they had forgotten that they were once together in one cloud.

* * *

I was my mother's blue umbrella on the day that my mother became an adult and left my grandmother's home. It wasn't raining. So, my mother folded me up and put me under her arm. As she walked under the bright sun, she wasn't sure where she was going. She just wanted to find a place in the world that wouldn't feel empty and cold.

She ended up going to many places, working many jobs. Once, she served as a waitress in a restaurant next to a cow farm. Another time, she became a wide-smiling salesperson for a vintage clothing store. She had that same smile on when she met my father in a café on a weekend.

The first thing he said was, "Do your cheeks not hurt from smiling so much?"

"I've gotten used to it. I could smile all day if I wanted to," she replied.

"But still, doesn't it hurt?"

"If it does, I don't feel it."

My father could tell that my mother was lying. It hurt her to grin, but she believed that if she smiled enough, she could eventually remember what a real smile felt like. For the rest of the day, my father and my mother talked with each other in the café. He asked her about her smiles, and she turned the topic towards the rain. In a long ramble, she said that she sometimes wanted to drench herself in a storm so that she could ask the water in her clothes whether it was alone or not. This was what she wanted to know: the number of ways someone could feel solitude.

My father listened to her the whole time, and by the time she was done talking, it was already nighttime.

* * *

I became my mother's blue umbrella to witness the moment when my father first held the umbrella. Several years after he first met my mother in the café, they moved in together. My mother retrieved the umbrella from her closet and handed it to him.

When he closed his hands around the handle, he almost dropped it. The metal shaft was frigid. The iciness spread into his arms. Still, he held on to it, feeling the temperature drop in his veins. Outside, the rain slammed against the windows. The pounding raindrops vibrated through his bones.

A decade later, which was a few years after I was born, my mother explained to me why my father continued to hold on to the umbrella. It started with his life story, which turned out to be a sequence of deaths: his father died in his childhood, his mother in his teens, then his grandparents, and then his aunts and uncles. From that day in the café, my father recognized in my mother the same loneliness that dwelled inside his ribcage.

Now, as he held the umbrella, he felt the coldness that flooded inside both of their bodies. It was a full minute before he handed the umbrella back to my mother. In the sky above them, there was a bolt of lightning. The thunderclap that followed rang through their ears.

* * *

I became my mother's blue umbrella so that I could watch my mother cradle my infant self. It was the summer. Sunlight poured into the house. My father was mowing the front lawn outside.

As my mother sung me a lullaby, she wondered what kind of child I would become. Every day, she rubbed my hands between hers to check to see if they had gone cold. She put her ear against my chest to see if a hole was growing there. My father suggested that she was being paranoid, but secretly, he was also worried. Both of them never quite got rid of the empty spots in their bodies. They pondered about whether or not I had been born with the same hollowness that haunted them.

* * *

I turned into my mother's blue umbrella to be at my mother's side as she watched my childhood self play on the playground. In the distance, I spotted the little girl that was once me rocking back and forth on a swing set. The sky was still a light blue. But there were heavy gray clouds gathering above us.

My mother placed her hand on the umbrella's shaft. As her fingers wrapped around it, I could hear what she was thinking. For a moment, she contemplated leaving my childhood self in the park. She would pack up her things and walk away. Then she would have dinner with my father, and only decades later, when both of them were old, would they remember me again.

Before she could make a decision, my childhood self was done playing. She clasped her hand with my mother's. My mother wondered if her grip was strong enough to keep hold of me. If I ever left her, she wanted to be the first one to let go. So, she was always prepared to see me drift away and disappear from her sight. Twenty minutes later, we arrived home. She released my hand and went to her room, shutting the door behind her.

* * *

I was my mother's blue umbrella on the day that it became my blue umbrella. On my eleventh birthday, she gave it to my younger self as a gift. My younger self ripped apart the gift wrap and stared at the tattered, faded umbrella.

"What is this?" My younger self asked. She wanted many things—toys, books, clothes—but not a used jumble of fabric and metal.

"It's an umbrella. It was mine. My grandmother gave it to me when I was about your age," my mother said.

"I thought you were going to get me dolls."

"Next birthday, maybe. You're a big girl now. You can walk alone now. Even in the rain."

"Why isn't the umbrella new?"

"It was mine. Now it is yours."

The questions that my younger self didn't know to ask at the time: How long would it take for my mother to find me if I ever got lost in the streets? Was her giving the umbrella a sign that she wanted me gone, like my grandmother did? Or was it mere resignation, a realization that she couldn't hold onto me any longer?

My younger self kept the umbrella in her closet until the autumn rain came, when she walked to school with only the canopy over her head.

* * *

I did not become my mother's blue umbrella to listen to the song that she sang to me last Thanksgiving. My parents and I were sitting at the dining table with whole-roasted turkey. The storm clouds blocked out the sun, making the world dark. Breathing in the windless air that came before a downpour, we carefully forked the meat into our mouths.

My mother sang to break the silence. The melody was quiet, almost inaudible. But I listened to it. In the few minutes after she finished, I almost believed that her words had stopped the rain that still hung in the sky. My parents and I talked through the evening about everything from the weather report to gossip about the new neighbor three houses away. By the time we were finished, the sun had sunk below the horizon.

The thunderclaps came that night. I pressed my hand against the window in my room to feel the raindrops rolling down them. Even though my fingers went numb from the coldness, I tried to remember what it felt like at dinner. The talk. The sudden closeness. The fleeting belief that we could stop the voids inside of us.

* * *

Today, as I wake up from becoming my mother's blue umbrella, I am about the age where I should be leaving my parents' home to find a new life for myself. Every day, when I look at the umbrella leaning against the corner in my room, I wonder how lonely I will be when I walk out of my parents' front door for good. I wonder if I am lonely right now, and if so, how long it will last.

On some days, I put my hand on the handle, waiting for the time when I feel the iciness rush through me. Then I will know that the holes in my parents' chests have passed on to me. I will go through life grasping onto people, recognizing that my fingers are not strong enough to make them stay.

When that time comes, I will learn that the best thing I can do is to let go. To watch the people in my life vanish as the raindrops do when they meet the earth.

But for now, the handle is not frozen yet. The sun is coming over the horizon. I sit in my bed and feel the warmth of dawn on my face, in my chest, through my heart. ■

Murmurations

SHORT STORY

CAROLINE CONWAY, Grade 12. Charleston County School of the Arts, North Charleston, SC. Francis Hammer, *Educator*; Region-at-Large, *Affiliate*; Silver Medal with Distinction Portfolio

Watching the ribbon of the Thames pass below her, Alice tried to list all the things that might be able to crash a plane: clouds, hail, drones, flying saucers, lost balloons, the occasional bird. Starlings—she had heard that sometimes birds crashed planes, tumbling out of their sprawling flocks and into engines, everything halted with a blur and a puff of suspended feathers. She turned from the window, pushing the rough plastic shade as far down as it would go. Her hand fumbled for the silver button on her right armrest, and she slowly reclined her seat, a faint sigh issuing from the unseen passenger behind her. Looking at the white paneled ceiling, Alice eyed the no smoking sign with resentment. She had been clean for over a year now, doctor's orders, but the little cigarette light still made her mouth feel strangely empty. Restless, she put her seat upright again, raising the window shade. The woman to Alice's right re-adjusted her eye mask and turned away. Soon, Alice knew, they would pass over Brighton and the English Channel. She wondered if it was still light enough to see the starling murmurations by the pier. Pressing her hand against the cold plastic, Alice smiled to herself. She liked the idea of all those starlings flowing beneath her, safety in numbers, swarming in a patternless mass as though searching for a hidden blueprint. It had been almost exactly nine years since Alice's last visit to Manchester Airport, though that time she had been the one fading into twilight, pale in the shadow of those great, metal wings. It suddenly occurred to Alice that she could not remember her soon-to-be son-in-law's first name. She withdrew her hand from the window and reached for the rumpled magazine in the seat pocket in front of her, sure that something in there would jog her memory. The rest of the cabin seemed to be various stages of asleep. Across the aisle, a silver-haired man in a sweater vest drooled into his wife's hair as she slept on his shoulder and he on her head. Alice had to loosen her seatbelt slightly but was pleased to find she could still reach the light button above her. Crossing her feet and quietly humming "New York State of Mind," Alice flipped the magazine open to an article about ocean currents. Alone in her artificial sunbeam, she started reading, imagining that with each word she drifted farther across the Atlantic and closer to Sophie.

Two hundred miles—it was the farthest from Sheffield Sophie had ever been. She had expected that they would take a bus to Brighton (they always took the bus), but just this once Alice had surprised her with a light blue train ticket, hole punches running down the sides like little tracks. For five hours now Sophie had been bouncing in her seat, watching various towns and rivers fly by to the rhythm of the engine. Half-timbered houses blurred together into one great, wooden checkerboard. Half tenth birthday present, it was the best Christmas holiday she could remember. Time passed with the aspen trees, and the brilliant white of the snowdrops outside the window faded as Sophie's eyes slowly, slowly thudded shut.

Sophie woke up to the acrid smell of cigarette smoke and a somewhat dodgy rental car. She bolted upright, pressing her hand to the car window. In gaps between the houses, Sophie spied a shimmering expanse of dark water.

"Is that the Celtic Sea, Mum?" Sophie imagined glimpsing rolling Irish hills from some stony beach.

Alice took a long drag from her cigarette, then delicately balanced her wrist on the edge of the car window. "No, love. That's the English Channel."

In Sophie's mind, she swapped the green hills for French vineyards. "Can we swim in it, Mum?"

Alice laughed, briefly taking her eyes off the road to smile at Sophie. Sophie held her breath to avoid the cloud of cigarette smoke that inevitably followed her mother's smile.

"You can, love, but I don't reckon you'll want to." Alice took another drag, gazing at a disheveled resort house as they drove toward the pier. "Not this time of year, anyway."

Sophie spent the rest of the drive looking at clouds and deciding if they looked more like jellyfish or parachutes. She had been to the North Sea several times because it was closer to Sheffield, but they never visited in summer because of the price difference, so Sophie had never swum there either.

As Alice parked, Sophie cracked the car door, holding the handle tightly as she inhaled the smells of salt and fried fish and sunscreen. She had imagined wading to the channel through a sea of wild grass but instead found a line of houses where sand dunes should have been. She wondered if people could cannonball into the ocean from their balconies at high tide.

In a mere five minutes, Sophie was dipping her toes in the channel. She tried to gasp at the cold, but found that she couldn't make a sound, as if the channel was gasping for her, foam sucking at her toes.

"Alright?" Alice grinned at Sophie.

"You're right about swimming, Mum." Sophie tiptoed back onto the beach, trying to dig herself a warm pocket of sand. Alice stepped into the ocean, walking until the water lapped at her ankles.

"Sophie, love, I think the channel wants to say hello." Alice whirled around, leaving one hand in the channel so that Sophie was hit with a freezing wall of water. Shrieking, Sophie rushed to reciprocate, fumbling for handfuls of the rhythmic waves. After a minute, they both grew still and stared off into the distance. The sun was setting to the right, leaving a blinding trail in the water as if the star had been skipped to its current position.

"If we could swim out to that shiny part, Mum, would it be warm just there?"

Alice cocked her head and eyed the golden trail. "Maybe, love." She looked at Sophie with a sudden expression of gleeful mischief. "But we're not going swimming today. We have other things to see."

Alice held out her hand, but Sophie had hardly reached for it when Alice snatched it away again. Alice crouched so that they were on the same level.

"In two months, you will be 10 years old," Alice whispered fiercely. "You're getting all grown up on me. We're about to go see something amazing, but first I need you to show me you can fly. Can you do that for me?"

Sophie nodded, eyes wide.

Alice winked. "I'll show you how it's done, love." With an inhuman shriek, she sprinted toward the pier, holding her arms out at her sides and dipping this way and that. She wheeled around and sprinted back, circling Sophie several times before coming to a gradual halt, flapping her arms a few more times for good measure. She grinned at Sophie.

"What do you think?"

In response, Sophie gave a shrill cry of her own, running away as her mother gave chase. The sun continued to set, and Alice and Sophie took turns scaring couples on their evening beach walks. Panting, Alice stopped and picked up a shell.

"Hello? Sophie, can you read me?" She changed her voice so that it sounded like a man from a black and white spy movie. "This is Alice, coming through on my shell phone. I request an immediate escort to the pier. Can anyone read me out there?"

"I copy!" Sophie whirled around and skipped to join Alice. Taking Alice's hand, she started dragging her toward the pier, making chirping sounds as they went.

"Sophie, have you ever seen a starling?" Alice asked.

Sophie frowned. "I dunno. I think, maybe? Are we going to see any tonight?"

Alice playfully pulled at Sophie's ponytail. "Love, you've no idea."

"Peanuts?" Sophie's voice suddenly sounded much deeper and more insistent. "Peanuts?" she chirped. "Peanuts? Peanuts?"

* * *

"Peanuts?" the flight attendant asked Alice. Alice groggily rubbed her eyes and sat up, knocking her bag over on the floor with her foot as she shifted. She sighed.

"No, thank you," she muttered, bending down to reach her bag. They had spilled out across the airplane floor, all 18 postcards (two a year) and the wedding invitation. The woman next to Alice raised her eyebrows but said nothing, sleep mask very much gone. Alice tried not to feel guilty as she unceremoniously stuffed the cards back into her purse, realizing a moment later that she was missing a postcard. She glanced at her feet. *Did you know there's a Brighton in New York, too?* Sophie's handwriting asked her. Alice snatched the card and shoved it in with the rest.

"So you're going to a wedding, huh?"

Alice started at the New York accent. "Um, yes. My daughter's, actually."

The woman's face scrunched up so tightly that Alice worried it might implode. "Aw, your daughter! I still remember marrying off my first. She thought I was overbearing with my flower suggestions and all, but she liked them in the end. Oh, did you cry when you saw her in the dress?" The woman bit her lip.

Alice opened her mouth to respond that no, she hadn't actually seen the bride-to-be in nearly a decade, but the woman was already going again.

"And oh my *gosh* the vows, the music, the sermon!" She sympathetically placed a hand on Alice's arm.

"It's gonna kill you, it really will."

The woman leaned back and looked up at the fasten seatbelt sign, shaking her head. "And then, of course, you'll keep thinking of how she's a *Mrs.* now. It's the strangest thing. You have the actual event photos on your bedside table, but the strangest part is that every time you go to write her a letter, you have to white out the "Ms." or try squeezing a little "r" in there somewhere. Of course, you're sure you'll just remember next time, but you won't, you really won't."

The woman looked back at Alice and smiled. "Is this your first?"

Alice cleared her throat, trying to avoid direct eye contact. "It's my only."

Again, the woman's face threatened to implode as she gave a squeal of delight.

"Oh, your little baby! Well isn't that just *wonderful*. Oh, it really is. So you did cry when you saw the dress, then? I've heard it's so much more emotional with only children. Is it true? Do you think it's harder for you?"

Alice stared at the woman, at a loss for words. "I really couldn't say," she finally sighed.

"Oh, but you're being modest," the woman mused. "Of course it's harder, how could it not be? You know, when I got married, my mother told me—"

"Excuse me," Alice said firmly. "I need to use the restroom."

"The fasten seatbelt sign is on," the woman objected importantly.

"So is my bladder."

The woman pursed her lips, pulling her feet in so Alice could get into the aisle. Alice walked briskly and didn't look back. When one of the bathroom stalls opened up, Alice locked herself in with a sigh of relief. She hated talking about Sophie. She pressed the faucet to turn the sink on, splashing the too-hot water on her face. She wondered if Sophie went to many New York beaches. The faucet automatically turned off, and Alice irritably pressed it again. Eighteen postcards and one wedding invitation in exchange for an annual Christmas card—and the kind without a picture. She took a deep breath and pressed her forehead against the dirty mirror as she exhaled.

"Alice, you idiot," she muttered. She looked in the mirror. "You are going to pretend to sleep in your seat for the next three hours, and then you are going to escort your favorite marine biologist down the aisle, and that's that."

Alice started to unlock the door. "Carlos! Good God." She slid the lock, making a mental note to write down her son-in-law's name as soon as she was back in her seat.

* * *

Sophie and Alice lay flat on their backs above the uneven wooden slats of the pier, shoulders pressed together like two girls at a sleepover. Only a breath of sunlight was left now, and the starlings were beginning to stir. Then all at once, they were in the air, forming one fluid shadow that seemed to twist and stretch, a scarf, blowing, knotting in the wind.

"It's lovely," Sophie breathed. In the darkness, it was easy to forget about the other spectators, and Alice imagined that it was just the two of them, the pier, the channel, and the starlings. As if the wood had splintered where the pier connected to the beach, and the structure had simply floated off with the current and the shipping boats. As if it was an island all to itself, isolated and cozy and alive. As if they didn't have a train to catch that same night.

The only sound was a strange rustling like hands rifling through straw. Alice found Sophie's hand and squeezed.

"See, this is why we practiced flying," she whispered. "We needed to be able to appreciate the technique."

In response, the starlings rotated like pinwheels, a dozen flying saucers hovering over Brighton Beach in the dead of winter.

"Imagine if all these rustling noises are whispers. What if starlings are merely great gossips? See, I bet they fly all around like that because they're excited by their own rumors." Alice paused. "Did you see those humans flying earlier?" she asked in her highest voice. "I think they've discovered our secret!"

Sophie fake gasped. "Golly, Petunia, you're right!" She collapsed into a fit of giggles, then suddenly grew very quiet.

"I don't want to be home again tomorrow."

Alice searched the starlings for a response. "You're not going home alone, love."

* * *

"Welcome to New York, folks," the overhead announcement blared. Alice raised her window shade, giving up on her sleep facade. The Big Apple loomed beneath her. The Empire State Building was a domino she could flick over with her pinky finger if she so chose. In the dark, the city was lit up by thousands of tiny lights, some moving, some flickering, some steady. It reminded Alice of one of Sophie's calls. She had been talking all about microorganisms and bio-luminescence, how sometimes a person could rake their fingers through ocean water and leave moondust in their wake. Alice imagined the plane turning, its tip grinding into the ground, all the sparks and lights and fire. She thought of stony beaches and loopy handwriting and imagined a combination of the two, the strangeness of addressing a card from Brighton Beach to some distant *Mrs.* Alice turned away from the window and fumbled in her purse for the wedding invitation. It had an underline in the form of a wave, and Alice traced it with her fingernail, wondering about the flower arrangements. She looked out the window again and imagined starlings converging in the air beside the plane, speckled wings alarmingly close and stunningly delicate. The birds seemed undeterred by the danger of the situation, falling into their familiar flow, stretching as a flock like saltwater taffy. Alice closed her eyes, banishing the imagined birds. *Lord, I don't want this plane to crash.* ∎

When I Was Your Age

POETRY

BRENDEN DAHL, Grade 12. Germantown Friends School, Philadelphia, PA.
Anne Gerbner, *Educator*. Philadelphia Writing Project, *Affiliate*; Silver Medal with
Distinction Portfolio

We didn't have *allergies*
There was no *gluten* to be *free* of

We drank our soda straight from the *source*
We didn't worry about cups and bottles and cans
We turned on the hose and guzzled sweet candy water
Until our teeth turned gray

Curfew was the town screamer
Us kids would be outside, playing *Shoot the Indians* all day, no parents in site
Until the town screamer would run around screaming
Then it was time to go home

Our bearded grandfathers taught us how to hunt
Not with *guns* or *bows,* with *flamethrowers* and *poisoned darts*
But first we'd pray to the demon Romulus
And organize our blood jars

If you wanted to climb a tree, you climbed it
We had no *knee pads* or *safety nets*
You'd check to see if there were any tree elves
If there were, you'd say "excuse me Mr. or Mrs. Elf, I'm climbing this tree,"
And then you'd just climb it

When I was growing up
We said no to the candy men in clown suits
We murdered our fathers when they said *please*
We understood what it meant to *bury a bone in the dirt*
We didn't believe in "object permanence," or "the linear passage of time"

What is it with kids these days

With their iPhones
And their Adderal

What happened to respect?
What happened to decency?
What happened to *community horse executions?*
Those were the best Saturdays

Today is nothing like when I was your age ■

My girlfriend burns her hand trying to make soup

POETRY

A-MEI KIM, Grade 12. Conestoga High School, Berwyn, PA. Cyndi Hyartt, *Educator*; Philadelphia Writing Project, *Affiliate*; Silver Medal with Distinction Portfolio

& the handle hit the floor with a clatter.
We had just woken up. I sat at the kitchen table,
calculating how many days before we had
to pay rent, and how many days until
my cold would break, and if we needed
to buy more lettuce. After, wrapping the gauze
around your palm, I noticed you had a mole
on your left pinky. There are things we know
but don't speak of, like how we can't sleep
without the windows open. Last night, you pressed
your hand on my forehead, placed
a thermometer under my tongue.
Outside, I watched the light rise, pale
and hungry against the neighborhood
trees, but I never even saw the sun coming
until I was there. ■

Games We Play

PERSONAL ESSAY & MEMOIR

POPPY ROSALES, Grade 12. Interlochen Arts Academy, Interlochen, MI.
Brittany Cavallero, Joe Sacksteder, and Mika Perrine, *Educators*; Kendall College of Art and Design, Ferris State University, *Affiliate*; Silver Medal with Distinction Portfolio

Tag:

My cousins, Michael and Alexis, and their parents come over to our house for a cookout. They come over often in the summer after kindergarten, and we fill up on grilled hamburgers and my grandma's homemade fries. After lunch our parents begin to talk about "adult things" and send us away. We don't really care, preoccupied by the notion of being outside, and quickly begin a game of tag. We run up and down the yard, our bare feet on the grass, and every so often on the surface of the wooden play set. Our bodies bump into each other, and I run aimlessly until somebody's hand slaps into my arm and it's my turn to do the chasing.

Comforter:

I go to my room, back when I had bedtimes, to find my sister cradling herself on the floor. *What's wrong?* I ask. *I don't know. I don't know. It's Michael.* She sits up, drinks a glass of water and pushes her hands into the carpet until the carpets design imprints on her palms. *This is what he did to me.*

   She stands up and pulls me to my feet, snuggles next to me in my bed. I cradle her head, though she's older than me, and she hides us under the blankets. She repeats *this is what he did to me*, and she takes off her outer layer of clothes to show me. I giggle under the blanket, not understanding, and pretend to be asleep when my parents check on us later.

Tattoos:

In first grade my sister tells me about the moon cycle: about how beautiful it is, how poetic. She tells me how the moon is romantic and that people can travel there. *All the way there?* I ask, and she smiles, *Yeah, all the way there.* In the evenings when the sun begins to set we sit on towels in our backyard and watch the sky: we study the moon, and fight about whether a moving dot is a shooting star or a plane. She tells me stories of werewolves and vampires, tells me of how she'll learn to read the constellations. She draws stars on her arm with yellow highlighter, and between them a little crescent moon—every day she retraces the images.

I want to match my sister, but I can't draw like she can, so I press my fingernails into my arm until little crescent shapes appear. I do it again the next day while she retraces her picture. My arm bleeds, heals, reopens with my nails the next morning, bleeds, heals, etc. When our obsession with the sky fades, the highlighter quickly washes from her skin, but little dots stay on mine.

Art:

My uncle moves in with us when I'm seven, into our new, new house (the fifth one we've had). There are only three bedrooms and five of us, and my sister and I were promised our own rooms if we moved again, so my grandma lives in the unused half of the laundry room, and my uncle stays under the basement stairs. *Why's he living with us?* I ask my parents, and they respond, *He needs a place to go.* I smile and eat lunch while my mother flips through the TV channels.

My uncle comes up a bit later, says he's finished bringing his stuff downstairs, and sits on the chair across the room with a pencil and sketchbook. We watch TV, he draws, it goes on like this for a while. Later on he shows us what he's been drawing, a beautiful angel with tinted wings, and I am in awe. *I want to learn how to draw.*

The next day while my parents are at work I sit across the table from my uncle, and he tells me I must start small. I draw the alphabet in bubble letters, block letters, and sketch a cartoon dog that I later repeat in my notebooks at school methodically. I add spirals, neon shades of colored pencils—morph them into chaotic designs until one day my uncle picks up my notebook, shakes his head and drops it on the table saying, *This isn't what I taught you.*

It's not until he's lived with us for a few months that I start venturing into his room under the stairs, blocked off by hanging sheets and clothesline pins, to watch him draw in the mornings. He draws cartoons at first, like me, and then he begins with pianos, stars, naked women. I sit crisscrossed on the basement floor and he explains to me how he draws, why he draws, why he keeps a collection of nylons in a box under his pillow: *To remind me of fun nights and to stay positive.* His hands run up and down my little legs, callous and dry on my inner thighs, and I stop going to his room because even though I'm too little to understand why, his touch makes me tense.

Redecorating My Room:

I get obsessed with the sky again, this time on my own, and ban darkness from my room. I cover my ceiling in green and yellow stars that glow if you shine flashlights on them before you turn off the lights. I put some of the stars on my fan so that I can watch them spin, put some in shapes of constellations, and scatter others above my bed. I hang up miniature plastic planets, the biggest one the size of my palm, in order from Mercury to Pluto, and paint the moon with glow-in-the-dark nail polish. I lay on my floor and cover my body in my blanket until just my head pops out and wait for someone to find me.

Dry Skin:
When I was eight I had terrible eczema. The outsides of my hands turned bright red, cracked in a million places until it looked like alligator skin. Little dots of red would leak onto the surface between my fingers, and I would press it carefully onto Kleenex just to see what it looked like. It would burn, and I would sit cross-legged, placing my hands on my thighs like I was meditating, concentrating on how the pain felt. It was sticky, like lemon juice on a paper cut, and I would pretend for a moment that my hands were pincushions. When I concentrated long enough it would hurt too much and I would sit down next to my mom while she blew on the dry skin. *Come here*, she said one day, and turned the sink water warm. It wasn't hot, but to my already stinging hands it felt like it, and I placed my hands under the water anyways, crinkling my eyes until the pain stopped. I felt nothing for a second, then for a minute, and then for a few. However, after some time had passed I would start to feel a small prick, like a loose drop of water right before the rain really starts: when the pain returned completely I would run to my sink and burn my hands again ∎

The Farewell

POETRY

KELLY HUI, Grade 12. Lexington High School, Lexington, MA. Taylor Liljegren, *Educator*; School of the Museum of Fine Arts at Tufts University, *Affiliate*; Silver Medal with Distinction Portfolio

Nai nai died for a long time. The hurt pulled the memories
away, bone-thin, bare bloodshed. Everyone back home says
she gave birth to my father in a river, eighteen hours knees
pressed against a bed of dirt. He came out like a fish,
they say, slick & untouchable. He swam away & never
came back. Sometimes I think I see him: here, there.
A still-life of my father leaving forever. My nai nai dying
forever. In the end maybe every man was her son. Every river
a birth story. My father visits, finally, wet and rust-smell.
He tries to hold her hand but slides away. Back in America
I swallow blood like rainwater, a river refusing to flood.
Every old woman I see my grandmother. ■

Goring the Torero

POETRY

OLIVER MOORE, Grade 10. Pittsburgh CAPA School, Pittsburgh, PA.
Mara Cregan, *Educator*; Western PA Writing Project & the University of Pittsburgh
School of Education, *Affiliate*; Gold Medal, American Voices Medal

Bulls can't see red;

they're colorblind.

So when the cape is flung,

the crowd is electrified,

and the behemoth

of a thing

(muscle and bone and lightning)

flies forward with such

intense and unstoppable rage,

it is not the scarlet fever

driving it.

It is the torment and bolts of static

that have sparked

    between its horns.

It is the single quivering man

Standing alone with a cape.

It's his vulnerability.

It's the 4th grade

lunch room,

the classmate

who charged

across the yellow tiles

and gored the torero,

smashed his

head against

the tiles,

dyed them red.

The boy went to therapy, sat in the couch,

let his shoulder slump, face fall.

The woman across from him asked

why he'd done it, asked why he'd tackled

the torero; he shrugged,

sighed, paused

for a second and said

he'd been Shocked one too many times—

Someone had to be struck

by lightning and the boy with the cape

was standing alone. ■

The Woman Wading in Yellow

POETRY

AMINA ADEYOLA, Grade 10. Appomattox Regional Governor's School, Chesterfield, VA. Gail Giewont, *Educator*; Visual Arts Center of Richmond, *Affiliate*; Gold Medal, American Voices Medal

Today you're an artist
Painting white space
With golden brown
Giving life to the breathless
You pencil in large eyes
Trace the bridge of nose
Color in every piece of
You are to be seen by all

//
A woman walking next to a river
Her light steps waver on wet rocks
A dress the color of a rising sun dancing
In the wind behind her bare cocoa butter feet
Yellow paint chipped against nail beds
Henna flowers her full arms and circles fingers

Her lips touch the warm water, whispers a prayer
To Oshun, Allah, anyone who will listen
The river holds the ends of her hijab
Embroidered with words of every slur
Every joke taken too lightly
With each Bible quote poured down her throat
Wrapped around her neck and over her head
She kisses her hand and pearls drape against brown skin
When jewelry slips to water, it turns into gold

//
Etch the woman until there are lips
Parted, smiling, filled with Ebonics
And rebirthed Arabic
Breathe her life, add the final stroke
See yourself appear from nothing ■

Ballerina Boy

PERSONAL ESSAY & MEMOIR

JOSHUA TORRENCE, Grade 12. George Washington Carver Center for Arts and Technology, Towson, MD. Rebecca Mlinek, *Educator.* Baltimore Office of Promotions & the Arts, Inc., *Affiliate;* Gold Medal, American Voices Medal

I've always been a dancer. Throughout my childhood, I would shake my hips, wear my mother's high-heeled shoes, and pretend I was Madonna. I'd sing "Material Girl" and imagine myself with gemstones glittering off my sequined skin. My father tried putting me on the soccer team one year. Maybe he was holding out hope that there was something manly still hidden within his only son. Each game, though, he'd watch in horror as I'd steer clear of the ball and make a stage of the field, shimmying through the grass like the performer I knew I was. No, sports were never for me. I've been taking dance lessons since then for eleven years.

I've also always known that it's strange for a boy to dance. There's something different from the tights that principle dancers wear at the ballet and the span-dex players put on at a football game. I learned it from my father first. I learn it again and again, every day.

I learned it from a friend of mine once. He told me I couldn't beat him in a race because he played baseball and I danced. Maybe I could, maybe I couldn't, but it wasn't like dance was the root of my supposed physical inferiority to him. Just because he threw pitches when I did pirouettes didn't mean that he'd reach the finish line before me. He didn't stop there. The short of what he told me was that tights were gay, dancing with other men was gay, ballet was gay, ballet slippers were gay, but no, I myself wasn't gay because he wouldn't be friends with me if I was. The whole time, I kept asking myself why "gay" was such an insult. The whole time, I kept asking myself if he'd ever danced before in his life.

Dance is not a determination of one's sexuality. There is sensuality in it. There always is in art. Dance is performance, acting, focused, precise angles, lines, arcs, a mathematical formula injected into the body and fused with blood, muscle, marrow, and bone, to make each movement beat with feeling as the heart does.

And where is the feeling in masculinity? Men must wear baggy, ill-fitted clothes, pants sagging to the knees. They must walk with their hands in their pockets, laid back like cool boys. Not ballerina boy. Unlike them, he must wear tight clothes and leotards. He has a rhythm to his walk as his feet fall to the pounding of drums in his head. Combinations whir around in his brain, dervishes of *pas de chats, battements, coupes, assembles,* every movement laced with the softness of lilies and the electric power of thunderheads. Boys like my friend don't have that in them. No hugs to give, just fist bumps and handshakes. No smiles in pictures, just straight faces. It's gay to do otherwise.

I look at them and thank my parents for taking me out of soccer all those years ago. They opened my soul like the sun opens tulips in spring to the love of the sky, to the blue beauty of passion. I have the freedom now to wrap the world in my hugs, to tell men I love them without putting "no homo" at the end, to dance like no one's watching anywhere I want, all because I can feel emotions in a world where men's egos are hot air balloons popped if women ever see them cry. Dance gave me the gift to cry, to laugh, to love, without shame. I will dance until I die. This is a promise.

I smile when I think of the cage my old friend is trapped in now. I've beaten him in this race. While he sits brooding behind the unbendable bars of boyhood, I *glissade* and run and leap, feeling manhood's breeze that whistles in my ear, *you are a man not because you can't feel, but because you can* ■

Pappy

PERSONAL ESSAY & MEMOIR

VICTORIA CHOO, Grade 11. Milton Academy, Milton, MA. Indu Singh, *Educator*; the School of the Museum of Fine Arts at Tufts University, *Affiliate*; Gold Medal, Best-in-Grade Award

I sat on the beach listening for the ocean's peaceful lull to lurch me out of my head and throw me back to myself. The sun had just reached that point when it dipped parallel with the horizon illuminating everything cotton-candy pink: one last shebang before sleeping for the night. I didn't remember driving here. I didn't know how I ended up here. Somehow, I just always came back to the beach.

Hours earlier, I whipped into the rehab center my pappy lived in. I began the long walk through the double glass doors, down the beige hallway, and through the common area. My keys swung in my hand—a foreign feeling that my fingers had not quite gotten used to yet. The man in the wheelchair stared at me as I walked in. His beard dangled past his chest and his eyes continued to follow me as I walked past. I went straight through the common area and into my pappy's room.

"Mr. Choo!" His caretaker yelled. "The second daughter is here!"

In case you are wondering, that is I. I am the second daughter, the nameless girl that visits him almost every day on her way home from school. And today, like most days, Pappy was refusing to eat.

I got up close to his bed, shaking him awake. His eyes splintered open, fighting through the thick crust that formed around his eyes. At this time, the routine begins.

"Oh, you lovely, lovely girl," he says. He tells me how much he loves me. He tells me how proud he is of me. He tells me how smart I am and how beautiful I have become. I remind him that I am leaving for China in three days. He grows solemn—both of us do.

I plopped grapes into his mouth as he tried to talk—poking them in through his chapped lips, ignoring his screams. No, it was not nearly as violent as you think it was. I was not torturing him—I was *saving* him. Pappy is almost 92 years old and he weighs less than his age. Each day he eats fewer and fewer grapes, slowly disintegrating into dust.

I watched as his eyelids began to droop back down, caving in towards his wrinkles. He gripped my hand as he slept. Sometimes, I think Pappy is afraid to be alone. His fingers trembled as he squeezed my arm. The skeleton of his once firm hand clattered as it fluttered against my wrist. I waited there a while, watching him sleep. The internal clock in my head kept ticking louder and louder, and I knew if I didn't leave soon, I probably never would.

I escaped back through the common room. The wheelchair man gawked at me as I tiptoed through the commotion of mealtime. His eyes expressed something deeper than interest. Curiosity, maybe? After all, I have been coming here for months, and I have never seen another child in there. Maybe it was my backpack? Was he was reminiscing about his days at school? I flashed him a polite soft smile and continued walking, embarrassed by the attention I attracted.

I needed to get out of there. In a way I cannot quite express to you, I needed to leave. That deep feeling of "I do not belong here" sunk in, and I bolted. I drove over the bridge, past the river, and somehow ended up on the beach. I sat in my car that night waiting for the sun to set, but it never did. The sky hovered in an orange haze for eternity but never quite landed. I drove home.

* * *

Two days later, I sat on the beach, again. The sky was a purple fuzz that soaked deep into the darkness of the ocean. Each drop of color plunged farther and farther down until only scrapes of light remained crawling across the sky. I drove here through the light mist of my own crystal eyes. I listened to the sound of my gasping for air and calmed knowing I could still breathe.

Hours earlier, I sat in the chair of my pappy's room. I shook him, but the haze around his eyes won. He talked to me quietly. Nothing short of the routine. It was all "I love you" and "I'm proud of you." He fought his eyelids as he tried to speak. No grapes today.

"I'll see you tomorrow," he said.

"No, Pappy. I am leaving for China tomorrow."

Everything inside of him collapsed. He knew. I had told him every day for months that I would be leaving. I think a part of him did not register that I would actually go. He wanted me to stay there with him, feeding him grapes, forever.

"Pappy," I said. "You have to promise me you'll eat while I am gone."

"I promise," he said.

"I need you to be here when I come back," I said.

"I will be right here waiting for you," he said.

"I know," I replied.

Both of us were lying. Neither one of us wanted to be the one to admit that we would most likely never see each other again. Both of us too selfish for our own good: my leaving and his refusing to stay. A constant battle between self-interest and love. The thing about goodbyes is you never know it is your last one until it is too late. The problem with this goodbye was that I knew it was my last, and I chose to leave anyway.

I walked out of the rehab center that day. The man in the wheelchair continued to stare. For the first time, however, I realized that that look was not curiosity nor fascination: it was jealousy. Jealous of my youth. Jealous that I would get to walk out of there on my own two legs and not two wheels. Jealous that I could leave.

I drove away in a fury. The sun was setting and the sky pumped bright red across the city like the heartbeat in my chest. I needed to get to the beach. I needed some piece of me to float away.

I drove.

I drove.

I drove.

I did not make it. By the time I flew into the beach parking lot only the dust of purple fogged my vision and the grey of night dangled over me like a loose tooth. That's the problem with the sun: it doesn't ask when it is convenient, it just sets.

* * *

The doctor at Boston Medical Center greeted me warmly upon my arrival. "You are the famous granddaughter we have been waiting for," she said. She was not alone. Everyone was waiting for my return: the hospice woman playing the guitar, the young nurse checking his vitals, the priest coming in to pray, even the woman changing his bedsheets.

Before even going home, I went to the hospital. In that little room, I sat for hours hoping for a response. At this point he had long decayed. The tiredness spewed from his body like the brown guck that seeps out from your feet after stepping into mud. He was no longer the man I left behind. The grapes were gone. Somewhere over the course of that month they had been replaced with an IV. I thought of the irony that the splitting of a needle into his bruising skin somehow provided the nutrients his body craved. I guess not all love is gentle. I guess not all care is love.

The city seemed small. You don't notice how much bigger the world is until you see it. The skyscrapers of Boston shriveled next to the redwoods of Shanghai. Everything had changed when I got home, or maybe only I had.

The skyline was indifferent. The Prudential Building, city hall—all buildings my pappy helped design—suddenly were not enough for me. After seventy years as an engineer in Boston, he built this entire city, and I was so quick to leave it behind. It was more than the city I left behind.

"He was sick when I left," I tell myself. "There was nothing I could have done."

After hours, I finally went home.

They unplugged him.

I learned what everyone was waiting for.

Correction: I learned *who he* was waiting for.

* * *

The man at the flower shop gave me a rose. He told me I was beautiful—he *meant* it. He was three times my age; his kids were my senior. And before you judge, he was not perverted. He was just a nice, middle-aged man at a flower shop who was entertained by my youth. Before I left, he asked me if I liked flowers.

"Of course," I replied.

"What kind?" he said.

"Anything yellow."

He went to the back room and cut me off a yellow rose. The teardrops from the sun melted into my hand, and I paraded around Boston with this shy flower. The most beautiful things in life do not just come to you; they need to be found, and this sheepish flower reeked "come find me."

I walked into my pappy's hospice center. He looked at me with two eyes searching for light in his dark world. The language he used to speak so well got caught on his tongue, and even the air he breathed seemed to reject him. Everything about him drooped: his wrinkles, his fingers, his hair. All searching for a healthier body that would nourish them properly. Their current host was too weak to preserve the type of maintenance they required—and by maintenance, I mean food and water.

I entered the solemness of this hospice room, parading my yellow rose. Proud of not only its beauty but also my means of acquiring it. His room harnessed nearly no light, and the beige paint job doused the room with cardboard-box vibes. The lone flower became the sun in this dark and miserable tunnel heading towards the train's last stop.

"Pappy, the man at the flower shop gave me a rose," I said.

The sound of his muffled breaths responded to me as if to say "I am awake, I can hear you." He was not lost yet. His body might be crumbling to time but his mind was very much cement.

I tucked the rose in bed with him. One last reminder that there is happiness in this dismal world. One last touch for when I am not there.

* * *

I returned looking for the rose. The mellow flower with roots robbed from her feet only to be found planted on a dying man's chest. She assumed her responsibility now. Her beauty must be enough for the both of them. There is nothing beautiful about death, but somehow, this rose made dying look like dancing in the wind.

I went to look for a vase. I needed to put the flower in water.

I realized that would not be needed. He will never make it long enough to watch that rose die. Both of them can wilt away together, slowly starving their way back into the ground. Misery loves company, and I found solace knowing they would not be alone. The flower and the man can enter their new world together, two beautiful souls, robbed of more time.

She loses a petal. It drifts onto the pale blanket cocooning my grandfather. A final indication that even the beautiful crumple. Another reminder that even the sun sets.

* * *

I found Pappy in the funeral home days later. He was lying the same way I left him, this time, however, he seemed at peace. The walls were no longer beige—instead, they were covered in floral wallpaper. The TV now illuminated a slideshow of memories. And most of all, he was surrounded by baskets of yellow roses.

* * *

His grave was on a little patch of grass that overlooked a little pond. The weeping willow tree danced in the soft breeze, and the waterfall trickled down the rock like teardrops. Everything was at peace: the grass perfectly cut, the flowers at full bloom, my pappy finally laid to rest.

His casket sat above the hole anxiously waiting to be filled. Hovering over the spot of ground that would become his home for the rest of eternity. He was covered in flowers. Each one brilliant in its own respected color.

We sat in rows waiting as the pastor spoke. His beard's bright red hue laughed at the brilliant scarlet roses. He preached what he could, fumbling over obstacles like remembering my pappy's age and that my pappy was divorced. When he was done he welcomed all of us to place a rose on the casket. I waited as everyone got up, filing in from the back. I was the last seat in the first row. I waited as dozens of people rose to plop a flower onto the casket. With each flower, the casket grew taller, slowly margining up to the skyscrapers.

I was the last to go. The last embrace my pappy will ever receive. I walked up to the casket and placed my yellow rose on top, tucking it in like a child to sleep. One last reminder that there is happiness in this dismal world. One last touch for when I am not there. ∎

After the Floods

SCIENCE FICTION & FANTASY

YUCHI ZHANG, Grade 10. Middlesex County Academy for Science, Mathematics & Engineering Technologies, Edison, NJ. Dorothy Simon, *Educator*; Newark Public Library, *Affiliate*; Gold Medal, Best-in-Grade Award

The man's face was inches above the waterline, his skin bloated and pale. Camila tightened the bandana around her face before paddling towards the carcass, silently evaluating it for freshness and disease. When times were bad, people in the Floats would eat anything, even each other. For a moment, she considered. The man hadn't drowned; his body would have been devoured by fish and bacteria otherwise. Camila reached into the corpse's pants, searching the pockets for a wallet or tablet. Nothing. Whoever killed them had already stripped them clean. Disappointed, Camila shrugged and left the man's body for the raucous gulls now circling above her.

Her tiny canoe was crammed with metal scraps, leaving barely enough room for her to sit. Camila paddled it through the wide avenues of the Bedford-Stuyvesant neighborhood. Here, where the flooding hadn't been as bad, the water was only about eight feet deep. Brownstone houses still stood, lining the nonexistent streets. Most of them had been long abandoned, their inhabitants fleeing to higher ground as the waters crept ever closer. Some of the structures had completely collapsed, succumbing to the constant ebb and flow of the tide. Few humans still lived here, choosing between the dry land beyond the Wall or the upper floors of residential skyscrapers in former Downtown Brooklyn.

Camila gave a few halfhearted paddles before yielding to the current, letting it carry her across the uninhabited remnants of the vacant neighborhood. She began sifting through the growing pile of salvage that sat at the back of her canoe. It was the product of a week's work, picking through disused warehouses and flooded offices for anything that could be of use. She obsessively scraped at the dried mud caking a large drone battery, hoping that it would still hold a charge.

When the first blackout occurred in 2067, Camila still hadn't been born. Instead, she was raised in the tumultuous years that followed, in a world burdened by natural disasters and extreme rationing. Order quickly dissolved in Puerto Rico, as hurricanes and tsunamis demolished infrastructure as quickly as it was rebuilt. Her parents fled to New York City, where they had family. They weren't faring much better. The East River swelled, its roaring waters tumbling over levees and makeshift barriers, transforming the Big Apple into a canal city overnight. The Wall was built to keep the water out. The towering concrete barrier stretched across Manhattan Island to Queens.

Her family had moved into its shadow, fighting for space in that congested strip of land. Behind the Wall, New York continued to grow, reveling in endless wealth and splendor. Construction never stopped for an instant, demolishing and rebuilding skyscrapers in an endless cycle. Meanwhile, the old city outside the Wall was all but forgotten. The flooded landscape of the Floats remained unchanged and unlit, its inhabitants left to fight over fuel and water and shelter.

Before her father died, Camila had expected to live her entire life in the New York City behind the Wall, where industry thrived and civilization prospered. She had never once considered life beyond, up until her uncle had gone into the Floats and vanished. They never knew what became of him until Camila and her mother were forced out of the dry land as well, once they could no longer afford the rising rent. They had lived in the ruins of old Brooklyn for well over eight years now.

Signs of life began to appear in the dead city around Camila as she made her way downtown. Hastily constructed bridges stretched between buildings, covered in barnacles and algae. Boardwalks ran alongside waterways, linking blocks together instead of crosswalks. Market stalls floated alongside her on inflatable rafts, their inhabitants hawking their wares while casting greedy glances on her stash of salvage. Grabbing her paddles, Camila deftly steered the canoe down a series of winding alleyways, avoiding winding eddies and banks of pulverized rubble. She scanned the damaged walls of the buildings around her until she finally found what she was looking for: the rough image of a coquí frog, graffitied with bold black paint.

The heart of the Coquís' territory was a cluster of high-rise residential buildings near the East River. Snipers prowled across the rooftops and automated drones hovered overhead, competing with the seabirds for airspace. Armored guards manned checkpoints, the laser sights of their automatic rifles casting red dots across Camila's arms as she continued paddling. She made her way toward a large office building, where a pier had been constructed in the open plaza before it. She eased her canoe in between two hovercraft, whose black hulls bristled with fearsome machine guns. She clambered onto the pier, standing alongside the others that had come to pay tribute. Her eyes caught a familiar figure nearby.

Camila's uncle stood at the other end of the platform, hands folded behind his back as his piercing eyes scanned the crowd. When they inevitably landed on Camila, they twinkled with pleasure. Her uncle's scarred face twisted into a crooked smile, and he stepped forward to beckon her with a friendly wink. With curiosity tugging at her soul, Camila cast a cursory glance at her canoe and obeyed.

Her uncle looked far worse than he had been before going beyond the Wall. Gruesome scars ran from his forehead to his collarbone, and his left eye was clouded with milky cataracts. Nonetheless, he beamed brightly as he ran his fingers through Camila's hair.

"*Mi sobrina*, what have you brought your *tío* today?" Camila's uncle asked as he bent to inspect her canoe. He waved away a group of enforcers, reaching for a small cardboard box carefully tucked into the pile. He examined the package, gently running his fingers over the label on its side. "Antibiotics?" he inquired, reading the sticker. His grin widened even further, exposing chipped and yellowed teeth. "How'd you manage to get your sticky fingers on these beauties?"

Camila remained silent, staring towards nothing at all. Her uncle simply laughed. "Best not to ask, eh?" he exclaimed jovially as he slid it back into the pile. Then his expression hardened.

"There was something I wanted to talk to you about," her uncle said, clenching his jaw. "Your mother." Camila nodded absentmindedly.

"No, listen to me. I need to talk to you about that woman," her uncle repeated urgently, his eyes flashing in brief rage. "I need you to leave her. It will be better for the both of us if you do."

Camila shook her head firmly. "Children don't abandon their parents."

"She's not *being* a parent. She's a useless junkie, and she has never helped you with the tributes. Join *me*, Camila. We're still family. I need your help." Camila looked into her uncle's eyes and saw the sudden anguish reflected in them.

"You're recruiting, then? And you want me to join as a soldier? Where have you *been* all this time?"

Her uncle scratched at his head in agitation. "I'll make sure you can become lieutenant before you ever see activity. You won't ever have to kill anyone with your own hands. I'm earning money again. We'll be able to return to dry land very soon. Just *promise* me you'll do it."

Camila shook her head again, feigning dejection. "I can't leave my mother. She won't survive without my help." His uncle sullenly looked away, becoming despondent. He removed a slender vape from his pocket and inhaled a lungful of aerosol. Then he straightened his back and began to chuckle.

"You're scared, *niña*. Believe me, I was too." He continued to smoke the vape, his cheerful manner returning as he patted Camila on the shoulder. "I'll be here tomorrow, if you change your mind."

When Camila and her mother had moved to the Floats, there were not many options. Most surviving buildings were missing floors, ceilings, and walls. Some were susceptible to rain, while others were prone to flooding. Everything became soaked within a week of settling down. Her mother managed to find an ancient apartment in Bushwick, built long before the floods had begun. They lived on the second floor, which wouldn't flood even when the tide was high. Here, Camila had helped her mother hoard fuel and clean water, creating a rough semblance of life behind the Wall.

The sky was streaked with bands of purple and orange by the time Camila arrived at her doorstep. The setting sun burned red behind a dense curtain of smog. She exited the canoe and securely tied it to a steel pole. Unlocking her front door, Camila stepped into the apartment.

A smell of mildew and rust lingered throughout the building. Camila heard loud snoring emanating from one of the rooms. She peeked through the doorway to see her mother sleeping on the rotting carpet, wrapped in their best blanket. A small bottle, half-filled with purple pills, lay beside her on the ground. Camila scooped the bottle up, carefully counting the pills left inside before placing it into the family safe. Four had disappeared since yesterday. Her mother wouldn't be moving for at least another twelve hours, and Camila would not dare to wake her up. Instead, she changed out of her waders, soiled with silt and washed-out sewage.

Nights in the city were cold, especially without a functioning heating system. Camila's teeth still chattered, even after she had bundled herself into a tight ball. It was impossible to sleep, so she could do nothing but think. Her stomach protested another forgotten dinner as she reconsidered her uncle's words.

Although united by their plight, the people of the Floats refused to remain together. Instead, they splintered into their own separate factions, forming gangs and clans. Water Rats, Tiburones, Copperheads, and Coquís. To join a gang meant dubious safety from one while inciting almost certain retaliation from the others. Yet, it could be better than having nothing at all. Camila had considered it more than once, especially her uncle's group, the Coquís. It meant having people to count on when times were tough, which couldn't be said of her own mother. In a way, she was already a part of them, paying her weekly tribute in exchange for uncertain protection.

Her uncle had joined and wanted her to be member. Camila couldn't remember a time when she had been needed so dearly. She might even have the chance to return to her old life behind the Wall, something she would never achieve with a mother that spent half their earnings on narcotics. It might be her last chance to escape. The next morning, Camila had made up her mind.

Turf wars occurred even behind the Wall, although they were decidedly rarer there. Camila's father had purchased a rifle in case they ever happened a little too close for comfort. As a child, the weapon used to terrify her, and her father kept it on a tall cabinet, out of her reach and sight. Now, it lay next to the safe where her mother kept her drugs, loaded with ammunition in case of a robbery. Camila grabbed it, hanging the sling across her shoulder. She caressed the barrel and stroked the trigger, fully aware of its fearsome power. Death in an instant, inevitable and unstoppable. She would need such certainty in a firefight.

Her mother was still asleep when Camila headed out of the apartment door for the last time. She untied her canoe and grabbed its paddles, seized with sudden vigor. She didn't look back as she rode the current, concentrating on the path ahead. The water lapped against the sides of her canoe, creating a melody she had never noticed. It filled her ears as she dove down familiar shortcuts, leading her towards a different life.

Just as he had promised, Camila's uncle was standing on the pier the next morning, priming another vape as he waited to welcome her with open arms. ■

The Role of Black Girl Magic in Intersectional America

CRITICAL ESSAY

TIFFANY ONYEIWU, Grade 11. Meadville Area Senior High School, Meadville, PA.
Kristy Porter, *Educator*; Region-at-Large, *Affiliate*; Gold Medal, Civic Expression Award

Black women are the single most disenfranchised beings in the United States. Historically, the effects of discrimination against Black women manifested disdainful stereotypes in society. This illustrated a counterfactual narrative of Black females. Black women took upon themselves a commitment to alter these misconceptions for their counterparts, which had the additional effect of altering the cultural atmosphere of the nation. The duality of race and sex further limit Black women in society. Although necessary, it becomes difficult to maneuver life through these enigmas. The instrumentality of tools to solve such problems is imperative to the successful integration of Black women into society. The social movement of Black Girl Magic is one mechanism used to combat these issues. Black Girl Magic in its sincerest form is essential to navigating the systemic inequities of social and political hegemony of intersectional society.

Systemic inequities blatantly disadvantage Black women. In the context of inequity, "systemic" refers to inconspicuous issues, institutionalized disparities in society's workings. Systemic barriers prevent equality from being enough because it awards varying degrees of privilege. The Black woman is barred from America's public and private institutions (e.g., segregated schooling, restaurants) and denied basic rights granted to all other citizens (e.g., voting) not only because of her race but also her sex. Equity focuses upon the belief that equality is inadequate, especially in the case of minorities. It is necessary for more marginalized groups of people to receive additional support. Considering the beginnings of members of minority groups is an important element of equity. The general varying differences in the environments of people due to privilege necessitates varying differences of aid. Equity is "[all individuals] getting what they need to survive or succeed—access to opportunity, networks, resources, and supports—based on where [they] are and where [they] want to go" (Putman-Walkerly). "Striving for the equality of women across all fields has its drawbacks. It fundamentally leaves no room for issues which are particular to [some] women" (Abdul-Kareem). For example, the needs of White women to survive in society will ultimately differ because the Black woman deals with the additional effects of racism on top of sexism and the White woman does not. Discrimination due to systemic inequity has hampered Black women from societal progressions.

Intersectionality "shows how people who are categorized in two or more ways can experience these things together rather than separating these experiences from one another superficially" (Mayblin). In the 1970s, Kimberlé Crenshaw, now a Columbia law professor, was inspired to illustrate the means of oppression for persons of more than one identity by the 1976 *DeGraffenreid et al., v. General Motors* case. Emma DeGraffenreid filed suit against General Motors because she believed she was not hired due to being a Black woman. The case was dismissed because the manufacturing plant did hire *Black Americans*, all men usually for industrial/maintenance work, and *women*, all white and for secretarial work, but not *Black women* (Crenshaw). The "court's decision . . . stated that plaintiffs 'should not be allowed to combine statutory remedies to create a new "super-remedy" which would give them relief beyond what the drafters of the relevant statutes intended'" (Gonzalez). This decision suggests that it was unfair to DeGraffenreid to use two forms of discrimination, her Blackness and female sex, in her claims though necessary to tell her story. The court recognized doing so would, therefore, be "preferential" and consequently, she would have "advantages," to Black men and White women with only one claim. "But neither African-American men nor white women needed to combine a race and gender discrimination claim to tell the story of the discrimination they were experiencing" (Crenshaw). Crenshaw coined the term intersectionality to frame issues like the ones DeGraffenreid faced. The simple analogy of an intersection came to Crenshaw when she thought about the complex situations like that of DeGraffenreid's. "The roads to the intersection would be the way that the workforce was structured by race and gender. The traffic would be the hiring policies. Now, because Emma was both black and female, she was positioned precisely where those roads overlapped, experiencing the simultaneous impact of the company's gender and race traffic. The law is the ambulance that shows up and is ready to treat Emma only if . . . she was harmed on the race road or on the gender road, not where those roads intersected" (Crenshaw). Intersectionality highlights the forms of oppression by marginalized people everywhere and influenced the United States legal system to view them appropriately as such.

The movement began as #BlackGirlMagic, responding to negative portrayals of Black women in the media. In 2013, CaShawn Thompson became aware of various outlets releasing misinformation about Black women (Flake). Thompson expressed, "At the time that I put the hashtag online there was this deluge of negative press about black women. An article in *Psychology Today* about [Black women] being the least physically attractive people on the planet . . . on another platform about [Black women] having STDs . . . something about [Black women] not being marriageable; all this negative propaganda" (Flake). This cycle of perpetuated lies was not only furthest from the truth of the real experiences Thompson shared with her contemporaries, but also the opposite sentiments of many in the Black community. CaShawn was raised around Black women and from a young age envisioned the essence of their womanhood as magical. CaShawn took responsibility in transforming the misconstrued perceptions of Black women into the authenticity she witnessed, which seemed only fit to be described as magic. Images of Black girls' celebrations of their lives, beauty, and success flooded social media platforms. A simple hashtag on social media exploded into an international social movement helping to affirm Black beauty and self-worth, concurrently diminishing the continuation of derogatory stereotypes.

Dr. Linda Chavers published an article through *ELLE* magazine in opposition to #BlackGirlMagic on the premise of "Black girls aren't magical. We're human." "Black girls aren't magic. We're human" is factually accurate but contextually degrades the real foundations of the movement. Chavers recognizes that Black women, humans, are merely anatomical twins of one another. She draws from personal experiences to explain that nothing feels magical about being a Black woman; it is just her reality. Chavers goes on to elaborate on new rhetoric that the phrase "Black Girl Magic" reflects the "Strong Black Woman" archetype. Moreover, if Black women are addressed as superhuman they "organically" contrast from other humans. Likewise, Black women then possess the identical essence of being subhuman as well. The effects of the abhorrent nature of slavery which periled Black people superseded by the grueling struggle endured by African Americans during the post-Reconstruction era created a climate of inherent racism and sexism toward African American women. This intense history of treatment has trickled down into today's modern society and still influences prevalent racial fractures. Ashley Ford stated in *There Is Nothing Wrong with Black Girl Magic*, "Magic is about knowing something that others don't know or refuse to see. When a black woman is successful, and the world refuses to see her blood, sweat, and tears behind the win, what does it look like? Magic." This quote by Ford epitomizes the essence of Black Girl Magic.

Contrastingly to Dr. Chavers, Ford conceives the ideology the Black Girl Magic is not about being physically strong but instead grasps the magnitude of the monumental gains women of color have made. Socially and politically Black women brazen societal expectations about themselves to an appropriate degree to describe these strides in excellence as magical. Ford essentializes the movement as "what [CaShawn] Thompson has given us, is something that encapsulates the grand and heartbreaking experience of being a black woman in this world. Thompson knew what she was doing, and she did it well. She helped us name the unique experience of living in this world as black women."

Conventional feminism has failed Black women. Black Girl Magic gives credit to the sacrifices Black women have made despite historical impediments. The suffrage movement in the United States, which bred the first instances of organized feminism, was the result of the prudent successes of its leaders. The most recognized for such progressive strides were Susan B. Anthony and Elizabeth Cady Stanton. Their societal altering accomplishments are justified. However, the accomplishments of Black reformers and the racist undertone of which the suffrage movement was born and raised upon must not go unnoticed. Susan B. Anthony and Elizabeth Cady Stanton are White "classic liberal racists who embraced fairness in the abstract while publicly enunciating bigoted views" (Staples). A logical suffragist mindset would indeed promote the rights for women, but as avid opposers of the 15th Amendment, which granted African American men the right to vote, and as classical liberal racists, Anthony and Stanton too spitefully condemned its consecration. Furthermore, this implicit behavior betrayed the Black woman's sacrifices to the cause. These attitudes created discontinuity between the convictions of the necessity of suffrage. Brent Staples of the *New York Times* categorized the differences in suffrage like so, "It became clear after the Civil War that black and white women had different views of why the right to vote was essential. White women were seeking the vote as a symbol of parity with their husbands and brothers. Black women, most of whom lived in the South, were seeking the ballot for themselves and their men, as a means of empowering black communities besieged by the reign of racial terror that erupted after Emancipation. The two-faced nature of the Suffragists Movement leaders compromised its integrity. After the ratification of the 15th Amendment, racism grew in the time leading up to the 19th Amendment, which sought the voting rights of women. Southern White women used the era of Jim Crow as an excuse for their discriminatory treatment of their black suffragist sisters" (Staples). After the ratification of the 19th Amendment, nicknamed the Anthony Amendment, White suffragists nationwide became apathetic to the women who were left behind from casting their ballots. In 1920, "the former suffragists of the North were celebrating the amendment and were uninterested in fighting discrimination against women who were suffering racial, as opposed to gender, discrimination" (Staples). It was not until nearly half a century later that African American women overcame "fraudulent and intimidating practices" when approaching the ballot box and were granted suffrage (Staples). The hypocritical episodes of White suffragists prompted the discontent many Black reformers, including Ida B. Wells, Frederick Douglass, and Mary Church Terrell, and served as further inspiration for the persistence for Black suffrage. Ida B. Wells is famous for her contributions to the liberation front of African American women. She was a staunch rejector of the accommodationism that was expected of Black activists of the time (Staples). Frederick Douglass summarized the difference between the interests of Black and White suffragists as "When women, because they are women, are hunted down through the cities . . . ; when they are dragged from their houses and hung upon lampposts; when their children are torn from their arms and their brains dashed out upon the pavement; when they are objects of insult and outrage at every turn; when they are in danger of having their homes burnt down over their heads; when their children are not allowed to enter schools; then they will have an urgency to obtain the ballot equal to our own" (Staples). Mary Church Terrell, a prominent patron for the cause, joined Ida B. Wells in an anti-lynching crusade on behalf of African Americans. She championed the "belief that blacks would help end racial discrimination by advancing themselves and other members of the race through education, work, and community activism" (Michals).

Social constructs habitually ostracize Black woman. Black girls are told they are everything except enough. When colloquial verbiage is used outside of proximate communities, accusations of being too ghetto and ratchet present themselves. Vice versa when Black women assimilate through code-switching, they are accused of acting too White. "Code-switching between Standard English and [African-American Vernacular English (AAVE)] is . . . a skill learned out of necessity—not choice. Mainstream America refuses to accept AAVE (and other forms of Vernacular English) as a worthy form of communication" (Lewis). The Angry Black Woman stereotype rose when the legitimacy of Black women's expressed frustrations from racially motivated sexism was questioned. "But what of Harriet [Tubman]'s dream? She dreamed black women might flip, skip, saunter, cry, yell, rage, and have access to the full scope of the human emotional experience that was denied us for so long. She wanted [Black women] to live their lives, not merely survive them" (Ford). The emotional subjugation of Black women raised a false narrative of ill-temperateness. Being suitable to society is nearly synonymous with being disingenuous to being a Black woman. Black Girl Magic advocates for the dynamism of unapologetic auras of Black women. Black Girl Magic reclaims whitewashed

Black culture and simultaneously rejects the subscription to Eurocentric standards of beauty.

Traditional American society represses the appearance of natural Black bodies, while Black Girl Magic commends them. Celebrities stole braids directly from black hair, for trendiness (*ELLE*). Katy Perry, who is known in American popculture to embrace eccentric fashion styles, is an example of this (Virk). By using Black braids, specifically cornrows, in a chic custom to strengthen her image she appropriated Black hair rather than appreciated it. "Cornrow hairstyles . . . cover a wide social terrain: religion, kinship, status, age, ethnicity, and other attributes of identity that can all be expressed in hairstyle" ("Cornrows"). Black Girl Magic endorses the originality of Black hair. The variability of Black hair is openly expressed through the differences in the scalps it relayed onto and the platforms it exhibited with. Black Girl Magic acknowledges the freedom to not assimilate to the standard of beauty set by the West in Eurocentric European beauty standards. Fair-skinned and straight hair women are not the only type of beautiful women. Women with the darkest melanin and prevalent curl patterns in hair are beautiful and of purpose and value. The hashtag has created a plethora of imagery of approbatory media. Furthermore, "digital spaces . . . are part of the glue that is holding [Black women] together, as we collectively maneuver through this moment that seems to desire to punish us as much as possible for simply being Black and woman" (Staff). The internet forced a genuine view of the Black woman and her excellence. Accessible authenticity internationally connects global Black Girl Culture aesthetic and experience (Staff). The movement fosters a sense of interdependence and cultivates palatable reliance. Black women see themselves and are conscious of the diverse beings they are. This sets an example of limitless opportunity.

Once Black women realize their beauty and self-worth, undeterred by social constructs, a new door opens for power and the myriad abilities it contains for political progress, when placed it the hands of those who rightly exemplify the community. Black Girl Magic encourages the face of representation in an underrepresented political sphere. Black Girl Magic nourishes the prerogatives of Black women to pursue their own narratives. "Decisions, policies, and practices continue to obstruct the civic engagement of black women" (Carter). Voter roll purges in addition to the complex history of Black women and suffrage are demonstrations of the obstructions Black women face in politics in the United States as outlined by Carly Carter and Carol Lautier, PhD, in their article "Taking Our Seat at the Table: Black Women Overcoming Social Exclusion in Politics." Additionally, because Black women are a minority, a common school of thought among elected officials is that there is little to nothing to be politically gained by catering to their specific issues. Ninety percent of elected officials are White. These representatives are historically less inclined to respond to the needs of non-White sectors in the community because "deeper relationships that establish trust and reciprocity are necessary to create an inclusive participatory democracy" (Carter). Likewise, Black women were impeded from participating in politics that control their lives. "Women won the right to vote when the 19th Amendment was ratified . . . but most black women could not exercise that right because of Jim Crow laws—buttressed by racist bureaucrats, police, and vigilantes—blocked [them] from full democratic participation until the 1960s. These experiences fostered distrust and diminished confidence in the role of government as a solution to community problems" (Carter). Black Girl Magic offers a solution to overcome these problems, which are not solved by the government, by forcing Black women into leadership roles where they are "responsive" to the needs of a marginalized community (Carter). Due to leadership failing to resonate with community, revelations of the impact of grasps of power have prompted participation in politics by Black women. Black Girl Magic highlights the importance of such participation and creates examples of the lasting effects active political engagement has on the marginalized community. While also serving as a catalyst, Black Girl Magic strengthens the republic by reforming democracy through truly placing the power in *all* of the people, especially those who are often overlooked.

The authentic values of Black Girl Magic aim to maneuver the social and political constraints intersectional society presents to Black women. CaShawn Thompson articulated the emboldened sensation of Black women when she began the movement in 2013 as merely a hashtag on social media. The necessity of Black Girl Magic, from the historically systemic realities of regressive Black feminine perception, is conceivable. The movement has since transcended itself to become a successful mechanism for the empowerment of melanin. Black Girl Magic also illustrates the dynamism of Black femininity, despite social and political deterrents. As CaShawn Thompson herself remarked, "I need everybody to understand that the Black Girl Magic movement was created by a woman who didn't finish college, and had babies young, and grinded in menial jobs for years. This movement is for every black woman—the ratchet girls, the hood girls, the trans[gender] girls, the differently-abled girls. Black Girl Magic is for all of us." To profess the magic of Black women is to celebrate their exceptional essence. ■

The Nelson-Dortch Family Cemetery

POETRY

IMANI SKIPWITH, Grade 12. Mississippi School of the Arts, Brookhaven, MS. Clinnesha Sibley, *Educator*; Eudora Welty Foundation, *Affiliate*; Gold Medal, New York Life Award

Chewing Tobacco
Dedicated to my Great-Grandfather Daddy Percy

They say that you were a mean man,
   Yellowed-skin with a temper matched by none—
   Your can of chewing tobacco sitting at your side.

The wrath of God himself sat in your thin chest—
   Waiting to hurt and to burn in the fireplace of your soul,
   Only activated by what was yours and yours to have.

With your tobacco filled with angst against the bottom of your lip,
   You ruled your own kingdom of eleven plus some.
   There, not even God could beat you.

But your tobacco ran out,
   God finally took it away, sticking snuff in his pocket.
   And your kingdom took to betrayal—all but one.

God had gotten to you—took your being,
   Leaving you to your thoughts and secrets—
   Your hell on Earth.

If you were nothing, there was nothing.
   Or, so you thought.
   You'd prepared for the worst.

The one you hated the most was your greatest alliance,
   She introduced you to Beauty and Love—
   Those you hadn't met before your demise.

You found something that you never knew you could feel.
   Love made its way through your veins and painted your heart.
   It cluttered your mind and blinded you.

Some would say the young takes away the pain;
   Maybe that's why your eyes began to smile as I laid against your brittle chest,
   Pressing my small lips against your cracked face.

I don't remember when you died.
   Mama and my grandmom say I was about two when you left.
   But I remember loving you.

I remember the times I refused to go to sleep unless I kissed you goodnight.
   I hope I taught you love; I hope I brought you joy before you passed.
   Your life was so filled with anger and that toxic chewing tobacco.

My grandmother said you died in her arms.
   I know you waited on her,
   Slowly counting your breaths before she came to you.

She said you tried talking.
   Your last words were "I love you."
   Angst rose from your belly and crawled through the window sill.

And as you shut your eyes,
   You assumed the form of a protector—
   Feeding into the hearts of your now small kingdom.

I know you're still here.
   I can see you tucked into the corner of my room, or sitting on the edge of my bed—
   Sticking the chewing tobacco in your bottom lip making sure I teach love.

Just as we taught you.

Our Moringa Oleifera
Dedicated to my Great-Grandmother Madea

What seems like nearly a century ago
Stood a great Moringa Oleifera—
"The Tree that would Never Die,"
A great, sacred pride to the family.

Your tall stature and beautiful curves
Mesmerized all that passed you by.
The language you whispered into the ears
Of those close by felt like songs of angels.

Despite your beauty, like many pretty things,
Your charming being was taken for granted.
The man with the chewing tobacco began to
Spit his dip on the soil you grew on.

But, you fell in love.
You wrapped your long limbs around his torso,
And he grinned that crooked grin you knew
Meant that he was up to no good.

He uprooted you and planted you into the
Field he prepared for his own bidding.
Maybe you could make him love you
Like you loved him.

However, that was not the case,
For he often came home with the sap of
Magnolia and pine trees tickling his neck
And staining his dirty work collar.

Years upon years he threatened to cut you down,
Chopping your limbs off for firewood.
So you stayed, baring eleven seedlings to satisfy
Him and help with the caretaking.

The seedlings grew and scattered,
And he began to wilt until
It felt as if it were just you.
You reflected on the years that you'd lived.

You were tired,
Angry at the neglect and sadness that
You felt.
Finally, your roots began to give out.

And after a long time you started to
Topple over, breathing out your last bit of oxygen.
Without remorse, the last Moringa Oleifera left—
The beauty of the land chasing behind her.

Did you know the man with the chewing tobacco waited?
He counted his breath waiting for you to return.
And when they told him you'd become the first to topple,
He crumbled in your sapling's bosom in order to find you.

Takotsubo Cardiomyopathy
Dedicated to my Great-Aunt Mildred

The rooms were quiet and the walls barely spoke.
But Her heart kept chattering right before it broke.
Pittering and pattering, waiting for a response.
But, I guess it only found no one.

Loved by the outside but never cared for by the in.
Since when did wanting love from the one you vowed to become sin?
Though Her blood kissed the very ground She danced on,
Her heart wanted to beat for only one.

Her house built for a nation held a one-man town.
The roof tilted and the fire inside died down.
Heart became too tired to dance for him—
And though She wanted to stay for them,

The rooms and walls stayed entirely too silent.
There was so much room—too big to silence the quiet.
She waited for the phone to ring until it fell off the hook—
For her love to be found again and not mistook.

But her love never looked back at the leaning house.
Her heart could bear no more and took its own way out.
Stepping too close to the fire, it turned to ash and withered away.
Takotsubo cardiomyopathy—all she wanted was for her love to return someday. ∎

After the Satellites Came Crashing Down

SCIENCE FICTION & FANTASY

MINNIE ZHANG, Grade 11. J. R. Tucker High School, Richmond, VA. Lee Hall, *Educator*; Visual Arts Center of Richmond, *Affiliate*; Gold Medal, One Earth Award

When I awake, Mischa is praying over me again, lips moving soundlessly as she utters a litany of prayers. I keep my eyes closed. The moment Mischa sees I am awake, she will spring upon me with another tearful petition of the life I have left to live and the joyous virtues of motherhood.

Mischa believes, quite passionately, that the lives of we women are set in stone. We are the tenants of New America, the pride of our subterranean worlds; it is our fruitful wombs that bring forth the brilliant laborers of New America. My uterine linings carry the dwindling destinies of menfolk. For Mischa, my desire to permanently erase my genes from existence is positively catastrophic in nature.

I think Mischa is full of horseshit.

Not that we have either. Horses have been extinct since the first earthquakes, and our pipes system process human waste neatly and quietly, in little satisfied keens that announce, *ah, yes, Suite 301 just shat.* We like to think of ourselves as a neat and quiet society, us New Americans, hiding deep beneath the Appalachian Mountains. We are not the only ones. There is Utopia, in the northern region they used to call Canada. There is the East Republic, thousands of miles away, under the Yellow Sea. The Sub-Confederation and the Grande Résistance share the trenches of the European underground and the secretive Prussia Union operates somewhere close.

But it is *our* region that bursts with fame within our little post-apocalyptic worlds. We deem ourselves the strongest, the fastest, the ones who still keep even as the world savages our broken bodies. Our proof hangs in our Wall of Heroes. Racers of ours almost always place first.

Racing. The thought sends my heartbeat into a frenzy. As soon as I sit up, Mischa launches herself at me, holding onto my hands and brushing my hair.

"Aida, please, change your mind," she pleads as I begin dressing. I am not sure why she is still trying, but I give her credit for sisterly devotion. It is an unspoken rule: once you apply, you cannot back out. My training started as I turned seventeen, but I made my choice far earlier, when Mischa's belly began swelling with the first of her many children. A life like Mischa's, I decided years ago, was not really a life at all. We are opposites.

In another room, Naven cries out, and Mischa shuffles away. I take a final look around our suite. I would not miss the drainage pipes crawling across the stalactite beams, the decaying bulbs peppering our cement ceilings. But there were a few things I *would* miss, like Mischa's aluminum bird clock or even the misshapen plastic drawers I had designed for my middle school graduation project. And most of all—well. Naven, Dal, and Silas have never been the most artistically inclined, but I spend several minutes committing their childish, waxy cinder-block drawings to my memory.

Mischa's footsteps ring out, and she comes back with the traditional final gowning. Leaning down, my sister begins carefully applying my makeup. I have always done my own, and to have Mischa so near my face is strangely intimate. There is not much makeup left down here, not after 13 years away from the surface. But we make do. Mischa smudges ash to darken my eyebrows, taps chalk to brighten my face, smooths juice onto the apples of my cheeks. Her touches are careful, light, and measured; I note, with an acute sense of finality, that this is both a *first* and a *last*. A first because no one has ever done my makeup before and a last because, well, this is the last time I will *ever* have any makeup layering my skin.

I sneak a glance at the mirror. At first glance, Misha and I easily pass as clones. We share the same thin, dark hair and brows, the same gray eyes. The similarities end there. My midriff is flat and pale, unmarked and muscled. In contrast, Mischa's abdomen is scarred and grimaced with little clumps of cellulite. The understanding that my body will never look like Mischa's empties my stomach, but only just a little. This has always been my choice.

"Are you nervous?" Mischa finally asks, as I begin lacing up my boots. My gowning is made specifically for survival—elastic leggings and a camouflage top attached to a helmet heavier than iron. I snap on my racing goggles and peer at Mischa through thick oily lenses. I must look utterly ridiculous and Mischa giggles in a hysterical sort of way, cupping my face and stroking her thumbs across my lips.

"Oh, Aida," She says. "Oh my god. You're really doing this. I can't believe this."

I am not an affectionate person. And yet, Mischa is my sister. I was five when the world ended, when the sea began frothing and the satellites came crashing down. It was Mischa who held my hand and rowed our makeshift raft to safety, even as our parents sunk somewhere in the ocean behind us. In the thirteen years since, it has been just us.

I hold Mischa's hand in silence. She understands.

For a minute, we are one.

* * *

When we arrive at Capitol Hall, the seats are already full. Citizens from the nearby compounds begin to buzz like flies as I walk in. My compound waits in the front, which only makes things harder. I say goodbye to Zio, to the Webnes, to Riva and her ten children. I say goodbye until my throat is hoarse and tears threaten to spill out from my eyes. By the time President Madison's cohort arrives, the tachyscreen is already on and the radios hiss noisily with static.

"Big day, huh, Miss Gray?" Madison says, his smile as plastic as my driving gloves. We pose together for my final portrait. One will be hung on our Wall of Heroes, and the other, Mischa will keep. In my head, I picture my empty smile plastered to Mischa's cinder-block walls, forever eighteen.

My thoughts are interrupted by words crackling on the radio. Utopia's racer is ready. The minutes are counting down. It sinks in that I will never see New America again.

Madison ascends the stage and begins his speech. Nausea lingers under my tongue. I am a wreck. But it is too late to turn back or change my mind; New America would be left without a racer. We all have duties to fulfill. Especially because I volunteered for mine. My country looks down upon cowards, and so do I.

Still. I wonder if I have made the right choice. A life like Mischa's is not inherently *bad*. A life like Mischa's is calm. Predictable.

But then I think of Mischa, eighteen, waiting for her husband to come home. Lying back, thighs open, waiting. Calmly. Predictably. I think of Mischa, eyes twitching, panting, writhing with the force of her contractions. I imagine myself in Mischa's shoes: sealing away my life to a stranger twice my age, my existence defined by a single body part. Anything is better.

Madison pins my ID to my collar. The crowd roars in excitement as we leave, chanting my name gleefully. This, I realize, will be the first and only time they will ever see me alive. I straighten my back and walk with a confidence I do not feel.

* * *

Only immediate family may see racers off, and I am forced to listen to Mischa's snuffling sobs as we head to the garage. Ahead, the path climbs to a steep set of heavy iron doors. Directly before me, I hear Mischa gasp in awe.

"A thing of great beauty, isn't she?" Madison whistles slyly. "It's always their favorite project. Year after year. The engineers are quite proud."

It is my first time seeing my car. She is as sleek and small as a bullet, with thick glass windows on each side, her top rising in a gentle dome. Her coat is a solid, dull black. Thousands of tiny solar panels shield her top, next to two glittering antennas. Three sets of solid white wheels, humming, waiting quietly for my approach.

Indescribably beautiful. The simulators I played while training are nothing compared to this work of art.

"It is an honor to serve New America," I tell Madison, as I climb into the driver's seat.

I strap myself in. "I hope I can bring our country glory. Set a new distance record."

"Certainly. If there's any racer that can do it, it's you. You'll ace that record, Miss Gray. Nothing's out of your reach."

I am sure Madison says the same words to each racer, but it is comforting to hear all the same. Carefully, I place my hands on the wheel. Back in practice, my trainers gave me a plastic disc connected to a tachyscreen. Holding an actual wheel in my hand, with all of its alien bumps and ridges, feels almost unnatural. I glide my fingers over the glossy black command pad is located underneath. This, at least, is familiar; I practiced with the same console in my simulator.

I turn the key, and the car lights up at my command. Mischa, Madison, and his fleet of officials step back. I shift the car and turn. Mischa lifts her hand in farewell, and I have just enough time to smile through the crystalline windows before the iron doors grind open with an awful screech.

I think of my nephews. The sunlight swallows me whole.

And then, I am gone.

* * *

I emerge into scorching desert. Behind me, the iron doors have sealed shut once more. They will never open for me again. My heart aches. For a moment, I feel utterly alone.

But thoughts like these are no way to start a race. Instead of dwelling on what I have left behind, I focus on my mission. I check the oxygen canisters on my command pad. Full for a solid eight hours. If I survive that long, I will have to roll down the windows and take my chances in the alkaline air. From now on, I have only one objective: drive as long as I can. The placements are always compiled later, because signal travels slow from the Eurasia continent. But I certainly won't take last.

I check communications. The radio and cameras are both on. They're set up to be one-way only; I won't hear anything from New America, but they will hear everything from mine—sounds from home are nothing but distractions to a fading racer. For a bit of company, I tune the radio into Utopia's frequency.

It will drain my battery faster.

I am determined not to die alone.

The road beneath me is parched and withered, eroded from years of heat and racing. In the distance, I spy the skeletal corpse of a decaying city skyline. But for now, it is just me and the worn desert. The earthquakes have crumbled the Appalachians into twisted sorrel pillars, dotted with occasional spurts of dull green. I look up at the sky, at the murky gray clouds and the ashen sun. I am driving in a ghost world.

My radio hisses open. "Hello?" Says a dainty foreign voice. "Hello! This is Utopia."

I ignore her. I keep driving, and she stutters out faint greetings before giving up. The Utopia drivers, I know, usually die under blistering hailstorms or crash on the frozen roads.

I wonder how I will go. No one has driven for more than six hours straight. The Earth is not kind to us drivers. Usually it is the heat that gets us, that stalls the car and forces you out into the steaming air. Two years ago, it rained, and our racer literally disintegrated under the acid storm.

An hour in and driving grows monotonous. The landscape shifts from desert to urban wasteland; I drive through fractured highways littered with sun-bleached skulls and automobile husks. Fading billboards from departed worlds slump over makeshift slums, advertising liquor and jewelry and other useless hedonisms. The sun beats down until I am squirming in a puddle of my own sweat; I end up driving with only my right as my left hand swells with cramps. The wind scrapes sand against the car so thick I am forced to squint out of my side windows. There is nothing to do except think.

And so, I do. Racing serves New America well. It gives us a sense of patriotism, that our cars and drivers last far longer than the rest of the remaining world. It weeds out possible rebels and sends them away. Then there are the cameras, I know, tucked somewhere beneath my car, that track the world for a hint of livability. The end result is girls like me, ill-content with the burden of brood-maring, driving out to our deaths in the name of honor and scientific research.

Three hours in, and the heat begins to take its toll on my car. My wheels shift unevenly, wheezing with each turn of the road. The temperature controls have completely died, and my car grows warmer with each passing second. I am not faring well either. My goggles dig into my eyes. The ash in my brows bleeds down my face in rivulets of black. Worst of all, my throat is as parched as the land outside. I picture Mischa reaching into my throat and tearing out my larynx. In my mind, she splits me apart like the broken ground, a spider-web of bloody sinew.

I taste vomit.

I almost consider pulling to a stop and resting, when my radio squawks to life. Someone is sobbing. In the background, I hear high-pitched whirring and odd, dull thumps.

"Please, New America," the Utopian racer cries. "Please answer. I don't want to die alone. I am so scared. I miss my mama. I miss my—"

A blunt roar from the other end. A jeering crash. Mewling whimpers, fading away into the primordial wind. Ten minutes later, there is nothing but silence. The thought occurs that I have just heard her dying words. I wonder what her name was, what she looked like, why she volunteered. I wonder if she was like me, caught in a twisted system, defiant to the point of literal death. Either way, it does not matter, because Utopia is gone.

It is just me on this continent.

Three more hours before I break the record. *If* I break the record. With Utopia's dying sobs in my mind, I resolve to keep going. I envision myself stopping, watching the bony landscape. Sitting there, my thighs, growing wetter and hotter by the passing second, until they melt into the plastic cover of my seat. The skin on my lips, peeling away, my mouth a gaping hole as dry as the air. I blink. The sky is still pallid, as dry as bone.

With a start, I accelerate, chasing my gruesome thoughts away. I veer down another sloping hillside turn and the entire car jolts so sharply I am afraid it will collapse. But the moment passes and fades, and I am left once again with my thoughts. Stopping is a fantasy. Our countries can't exactly send out teams to recover our bodies. We die wherever we fail.

The fifth hour draws near. A dull sense of accomplishment pervades me, but mostly, I feel numb. Time is meaningless. The only thing that remains is the road. Instead of sweating, my body blisters red and crusts over with flaking scales of wrinkled skin. Breathing begins to send painful tremors down my body. I note with a vague, distant interest that I cannot feel my left leg. Every instinct screams at me to roll down my window and allow the wind to sweep me away, but I only accelerate harder.

The car jolts, rattles, and then, seethes to a sudden stop. My mind feels as grimy as the road. It hits me then that my race must be finished. My car is broken; my duty is over. It is time to close my eyes and sleep.

When I wake up, I will be lying in my bed again.

The command pad beeps. I crack my eyes open and note the bloodshot warning symbol blaring across the screen. And then—some ancient instinct pulls me awake again. I lurch forward. The engine is dead. Not enough lubricant.

My head is dizzy with dread, foggy with futility. If I had any liquid, I would be drinking it myself. And then I realize the one thing left to give. I fumble at the car doors, my fingers thick and stupid. Mischa's voice echoes in my head, pleading me to fight.

My helmet is no match for the outside air. I am suffocating under the weight of my own head. Acid stings at my cracked lips. Bitter puffs of sour ozone hammer my lungs. Somehow, I manage to crack the steaming car lid open. *Where—?*

There. I peel back my gloves, until my wrist is exposed. And then I am biting forth into my own flesh, my flaking skin giving way like butter. Blood gushes forth in a fountain of scarlet, fizzling in the atmosphere. Hissing, the engine groans in agony as it begins to toil once more. I can barely keep my eyes open long enough to stumble back into my seat.

The car shudders to life, one last time. A second later and I am driving again, my gloves slick with my blood. My wrists throb. My thoughts are as disjointed as the wind.

In the distance, I think I see Mischa.

I think I see the sun setting. ∎

Caricatures and Citizenship, Intertwined

CRITICAL ESSAY

JEFFERY KEYS, Grade 11. Newark Academy, Livingston, NJ. Rochelle Edwards, *Educator*; Newark Public Library, *Affiliate*; Gold Medal, Civic Expression Award, The Alliance/ACT-SO Journey Award

Due to the nature of the frequent utilization of political cartoons, analysis of American racial caricatures reveals a series of exaggerated characteristics that throughout history were used to suppress or withhold privileges and citizenship from certain groups, with some stereotypes becoming embedded in American society. Tracking trends such as shifts of nativism and nationalism during war and comparing them with the prominence of specific caricatures offers a complex narrative detailing the controversy surrounding stigmatized minorities. Throughout American history, race has been a tool utilized to foster division and discrimination.

From the legislation of the Dawes Severalty Act dividing Native American territory, to the Supreme Court's Dred Scott decision ruling African Americans as property, to even the Immigration Act of 1924 determining varying levels of white privilege, race has served as a blade slicing apart society and citizenship. Stereotypes and caricatures have been sculpted by societal discrimination and refined by racially-charged legislation, reducing minorities to exaggerated traits in order to capitalize on negative sentiments against certain groups. The abundantly common use of such stereotypes in the past continue to display its impact in modern-day American society.

Those who were deemed "unfit" to possess citizenship were dehumanized in order to justify the theft of their human rights. Thus, stereotypes and caricatures sought to portray groups as savage, less than human, and generally unworthy to receive the same respect bestowed upon others. Many factors determine this line of thought, most prominently being limited resources, whether that would be the Native Americans' land or Chinese workers' capitalization of job opportunities, and nationalism, with the need and dependency on free labor shackling the Black slave population and the antagonist Axis Japanese forces giving an excuse to intern Japanese Americans in camps. Racial discrimination has been used to create legislation to exploit and combat these racial discrepancies, with throughout time, different laws and acts stripping away citizenship from American residents. The excuse for these blatant showings of racism were facilitated through years of stereotypes and caricatures being embedded within American society. Therefore, through a thorough analysis of racially charged legislation relating to citizenship, what will become exposed but a culmination of a series of various caricatures that influenced discrimination and dehumanization, coupled with correlations to catalyst events.

The Dawes Severalty Act of 1887 sought to sever Native American tribal relations and eliminate Native culture, working to fully integrate the indigenous peoples into American society. From the fledgling breaths of expansionism, American conflicts with Native Americans were inevitable, seeing as the latter inhabited the land long before Europeans arrived. Neglected treaties and bouts of violence defined American–Native American interactions prior to the late 19th century, with the Dawes Severalty Act attempting a new approach. Allowing President Grover Cleveland to divide communal reservations into land sections to be assigned to individual Native Americans, if the head of a household retained the land for 25 years, the Dawes Act dangled the notion of American citizenship over the heads of Native Americans in exchange for their complete abandonment of their culture and way of life. This, of course, is a result of the European and American belief that Native Americans were savage, primitive beings in need of proper control and civilization. This is further evidenced by the Five Civilized Tribes being absent from the conditions of the original Dawes Severalty Act, with those groups already being heavily assimilated. These five tribes, those being the Cherokee, Chickasaw, Creek, Choctaw, and Seminole, were already subject to European influence, and demonstrated Anglo assimilation through their education, their adoption of written language utilizing the English alphabet, and their widespread use of the printing press in items such as the newspaper. Evidently, as these tribes were already assimilated, there was no need to enforce efforts to integrate them within American culture. However, the chance of obtaining citizenship and becoming a part of "civilized" American society was used as a tool to exploit Native Americans through the Dawes Severalty Act.

The savage, barbaric, primitive caricatures that Native American people were so often reduced to since the beginning of European contact laid the framework for their absence of citizenship impacting them for centuries upon centuries to come. Upon arrival, Europeans regarded the Native people as uncivilized, primitive beings lacking clear structure and in desperate need of religion. European media depicted Native Americans as bloodthirsty savages who relied on barbaric violence, as opposed to the "civilized" methods of war enacted by the Europeans. These early stereotypes seeped into European colonies, adopted by the American public to be further spread to create a negative narrative against their fellow continental residents. These stereotypes and caricatures of primitive beasts even appear in arguably the most important piece of legislation in American history: the Declaration of Independence. Thomas Jefferson writes, "[King George III] has excited domestic insurrections amongst us, and has endeavored to bring on the inhabitants of our frontiers, the merciless Indian Savages whose known rule of warfare, is an undistinguished destruction of all ages, sexes, and conditions." A document so ingrained within American society supports and promotes the caricatures depicting Native Americans as "savages," creating an early onset for conflict between the two groups, the ever-emerging prominence of "primitive Native" stereotypes, and the view that these indigenous "beasts" need to become assimilated and contained. The fight for citizenship for Native American people began with the first steps of foreign feet upon the North American soil, originating from the Europeans' first contact with indigenous peoples, bred within the words that allegedly granted Americans freedom and independence, and fostered for centuries.

With a stereotype so embedded within American history, it should come as no surprise that its impact is still being felt today. The "Indian" stereotype is often used in various forms of merchandise, from the stereotypical tribal savage adorning colonial tobacco packaging to modern sports franchises. Artist Willie Cole expresses the impact of his people being treated as a savage, dehumanized species with his piece *Silex Male, Ritual.* Photographed with ink marks and minimal clothing and captioned with "Fig. 1 & 2. Silex Male, Ritual," Cole compares himself, a Native American male, to a foreign creature being documented within an anthropology, or rather, zoology, textbook. Being treated as uncivilized tribes, devoid of citizenship or respect, the Native American population has endured countless caricaturization depicting them as an entirely separate species. Ultimately, in the fight to take away land from the Native people, America has stripped away their citizenship, humanity, and culture through extensive use of stereotyping.

After slave Dred Scott attempted to sue for his freedom in 1846, the U.S. Supreme Court case *Dred Scott v. Sanford* provided one of the most crucial decisions both in regards to the American division on slavery and the question of citizenship as a whole. In a count of seven to two, the U.S. Supreme Court decided in 1857 that Dred Scott could not sue for his freedom because he was not a citizen of the United States; in fact, no person of African descent was a citizen of the United States and was denied from obtaining any privileges that come with citizenship. The transcript reads, "A free negro of the African race, whose ancestors were brought to this country and sold as slaves, is not a 'citizen' within the meaning of the Constitution of the United States. Consequently, the special rights and immunities guaranteed to citizens do not apply to them." This ruling stripped all Black people of their citizenship and the "unalienable" rights that come with it. With its radical and devastating ruling, both depriving all Black people of their citizenship as well as ruling the Missouri Compromise unconstitutional for breaching the Fifth Amendment's protection of private property, the *Dred Scott v. Sanford* decision inexorably contributed to the fission dividing the country, leading to the Civil War.

When analyzing the decision that allowed Black people to be denied their human rights granted with citizenship, one must consider the plethora of Black caricatures used to dehumanize, parody, and villainize the Black race. These exaggerated stereotypes were used to justify such deprivations of rights and breaches of liberty against Black people. Perhaps an extension of the ash black figures in leaf garments plastered onto colonial Virginia tobacco labels, the "Sambo" caricature describes an unintelligent, primitive Black male. Boston University's Joseph Boskin cites the Sambo stereotype as an instance of American society utilizing humor as a form of oppression. The "Mandingo" caricature depicts a hulking, aggressive Black man, more of a monstrous, beastly animal than a human. Used as a method to better sell laborers and mates during slave auctions, the Mandingo stereotype has plagued culture and society. This caricature was used to justify lynchings, instilling a fear within the American public that Black men have a sexual thirst that cannot be quenched. Rape accusations ran rampant, pairing the Mandingo's sexual desire and strength to frame Black men as delinquents, serving as an excuse to promote the murder and torture of innocent men. Today, the Mandingo stereotype is used to oppress athletes, diminishing or exploiting accomplished Black competitors. Derived from the biblical wife of King Ahab who convinces the king to engage in sin, the "Jezebel" stereotype portrays Black women as sinful and predatory. Twisting the matrilineal nature of African civilizations that allowed polyamorous relationships, the Jezebel caricature was a tempting seductress who lured men into lust and sin. In reality, the Jezebel stereotype was used as an excuse to justify the raping of Black slaves. These stereotypes were used to constantly defend oppression against Black people, with the caricatures being used to sell a false narrative to deny Black people rights, respect, and citizenship.

The prominence of these caricatures aim to emphasize negative aspects of human nature, painting Black people as a helpless race who depended on the Caucasian population to survive. By creating tales of aggression and seduction, excuses were made to rationalize the murder and rape of innocent Black people. These caricatures provided justification for a perpetuated cycle of oppression, keeping citizenship far away from the hands of Black people stereotyped as animalistic, sinful, and helpless.

1882's Chinese Exclusion Act barred Chinese immigrants from arriving on American shores based solely on their race. Regarded as the groundwork for future restrictions on immigration policies, the Chinese Exclusion Act was a blatant act of racism that not only prevented migration from the country for an entire decade, but banned legal residents from becoming citizens. Andrew Gyory, recipient of a PhD in history from the University of Massachusetts, argues that politicians blamed America's industrial crisis on the influx of Chinese immigrant workers, expressing that workers would benefit from the absence of the Chinese. Therefore, the racially based legislation was the product of racist propaganda depicting Chinese immigrants as an evil force intended to destroy America internally.

Drawn with squinted eyes, long queues, buck teeth, and yellow skin, Asian caricatures depicted ratty, primitive, immoral creatures, with this depiction aiming to vindicate the decision to completely ban immigration and deny citizenship to residents based on race. Dominating the East Asian caricature scene is the "Yellow Peril," the belief that primitive beings will flood America from their homeland and invade the country. To American laborers, the increasing competition provided much concern for their job stability, eliminating any leverage in terms of unionization and putting their opportunities in jeopardy. The fear of job stability due to the influx of Chinese laborers manifested itself into a fear of the nation's security against the foreign horde from across the globe. Chinese people were depicted as heavily violent creatures who enjoyed engaging in immoral activities, savages with drug addictions and an affinity for prostitution and gambling. The majority of male Chinese immigrants led to the belief that the creatures from the Eastern world posed a threat to American women, and by extension the male population's relationship to females. Overall, the Yellow Peril stereotype was constructed in a fashion so that the Chinese immigrants posed a threat to all residents of America: the male workers' jobs were jeopardized by the influx of cheap Chinese laborers, while the women of America were at risk in the presence of the violent, immoral yellow savages. This bred a sense of xenophobia against the Chinese which ultimately led to the Chinese Exclusion Act of 1882, but interestingly was applicable to any East Asian threat. During World War II, the Yellow Peril extended to the Japanese and led to the Executive Order 9066, which authorized Japanese internment camps. The Korean War villainized the "gooks," with the subsequent Vietnam War imposing the Yellow Peril upon Vietnam people. The Yellow Peril caricature became relevant multiple times in American society, becoming a blanket stereotype for all East Asian groups. The versatility of this caricature speaks volumes to the xenophobia demonstrated by the American population, conjuring such fear as to oppress multiple countries of people, denying all immigration and prohibiting American residents from obtaining citizenship based solely on their race.

In the Naturalization Act of 1790, a clear distinction was made between all whites and those who were non-white in regards to citizenship with the phrase, "Be it enacted by the Senate and the House of Representatives of the United States of America, in Congress assembled, That any alien, being a free white person, may become a citizen of the United States." This created a clear fission between white people and people of color in America, with only white people having the access to citizenship and rights. Nativists were not content with a line being drawn between only whites and non-whites, however, with the National Origins Act of 1924 introducing subsets to white privilege by limiting the amount of people who could immigrate to America from certain regions. The National Origins Act, also referred to as the Immigration Act of 1924, heavily favored northwestern Europeans and prioritized their immigration, with the newer European immigrants from southern and eastern Europe being discriminated against. Southern and eastern Europeans were practically seen as a separate race, emphasizing the social aspect of race privilege discrepancies.

The concept of "whiteness" and white privilege became more complex with the Immigration Act of 1924, with intentional mistreatment and the denial of citizenship towards certain groups of Europeans being propelled by historical abuse trickling into American culture. By basing the limitations of immigrants from European regions on 2 percent of their area's prevalence in the 1890 U.S. population, immigration from southern and eastern Europe were intentionally restricted by the Immigration Act of 1924. Perhaps the most oppressed and discriminated group from this category is the Jewish people, with stereotypes coming not only from America, but seemingly throughout the Western World. Being a nomadic group two thousand years ago, Jewish people were often always seen as outsiders, and because of the prevalence of Christianity in Europe, religion was often the subject of conflict. America's tendency to be influenced by European values continued with their adoption of European sentiments regarding Jewish people, resulting in a plethora of caricatures and stereotypes against them. As a religion, Judaism was seen as a tribal, backwards way of thought and life for bigoted people that undermined and contradicted the compassionate and kind Christianity, with its strict traditions posing a threat to the progressive American values. The seemingly immoral religion led to the stereotype that Jews were violent and dirty, willing to participate in illegal activity to gain money, another method of drawing stark contrasts between the immigrant Jewish and the American laborers. By popularizing the disparity between the American belief of hard work for honest pay with the stereotype that Jews engage in shady acts to become wealthy illegitimately, the negative zeitgeist against Jewish people became more prevalent in American society, thanks in part to the emergence of such stereotypes in popular culture. These caricatures continued to paint Jewish people as criminals who would do increasingly more sinister acts, such as commit arson, just as a convenient way to obtain wealth. Therefore, the caricatures against Jewish people were utilized as a method to emphasize their contrast to the general American public, highlighting how they would not belong in American society. The stereotypes describing Jews as criminals accumulating assets in ominous, felonious ways seemingly justified limiting their immigration to the United States, as well as created a stigma against them in American society. The different subsections of white superiority became established with the caricatures against Jewish people and other southern and eastern European immigrants, demonstrating the value American citizenship has, and the methods in which it is used to differentiate power discrepancies between classes.

Caricatures were used throughout American history to deny certain groups the benefits of citizenship. As Patrick Wolfe demonstrates in his "Race and Citizenship," "race restored the social inequality that citizenship had theoretically abolished." Stereotypes against races fostered justifications for discriminatory legislations, further embedding racism within American culture. Another method in which caricatures and stereotypes became bolstered within America was through media, with popular culture being a means by which public sentiments against certain minority groups were expressed and enhanced. From early European stereotypes influencing the American view of the savage Natives and the criminal Jews, to the years of dependency upon slave labor creating numerous figures and methods to oppress Black people, to the fear of job security and opportunity creating flexible, versatile stereotype that discriminates against East Asians, caricatures have appeared throughout history to determine who should be treated as human beings. Citizenship has been used as an identifier of sorts, determining which groups should be granted rights and respect. The nature of caricaturization is to emphasize and exaggerate inferior traits and to sell false narratives to promote stigmas, almost determining which groups possess qualities that deem them less than human. Therefore, the study of the relationship between caricatures and citizenship, one researching the legislation denying citizenship to groups that have been heavily caricatured, examines the hypocrisy of America through the constant fluctuations concerning who is gifted the privilege of humanity. ■

Gold and Silver Medals Awards

Students in grades 7–12 may submit works in 11 writing categories. This year, regional programs selected nearly 4,000 writing submissions for Gold Keys, and these works were then adjudicated at the national level by authors, educators, and literary professionals. Gold and Silver Medals were awarded to works of writing that demonstrated originality, technical skill, and the emergence of a personal voice.

Exterminator

SCIENCE FICTION & FANTASY

ZION AMIN COOK, Grade 10. Lusher Charter School, New Orleans, LA.
Allison Campbell, *Educator*; Greater New Orleans Writing Project, *Affiliate*; Silver Medal

I will admit, I might've been a bit disturbed as a child.

Roaches are a natural part of New Orleans. They are drawn in by the moisture of the air, and the prevalence of litterbugs, so to live in New Orleans and not be burdened with a domestic infestation of the creatures is a sign of extreme vigilance, for the slightest drop of grenadine left on the minibar, the smallest crumb left unpicked on the counter, creates a window for a legion of the little devils to enter the home. Even the contents of the family trash can could act as such a portal.

We had plenty of roaches in our house. They thrived on spilled beer and McDonald's leftovers. They established a hidden kingdom within the walls and between them. Like the city of R'lyeh, it was a civilization that were aware of but could not access, and, truth be told, did not wish to access for the horrors that might exist inside. My mother always had a disdain for lizards, but, over time, they became a welcome guest for nothing else but the fact that they ate roaches.

I had my own weapon against them: an unlabeled spray bottle of clear liquid that I had found in the cabinet underneath the sink. It definitely wasn't bug spray. In fact, I'm pretty sure that it was intended for cleaning metal objects, but it worked just as well. Better, I might argue. If you've ever seen a bug spray commercial, it likely had some sort of cartoonish scenario in which the intended target immediately disintegrated after contact. While I have yet to encounter a bug spray that can do this, the liquid in the spray bottle seemed to achieve something quite similar. It seemed to have some sort of chemical reaction with the roaches, some attraction to some substance deep inside them that would be forcefully pulled out of them. The liquid bubbled on their bodies, crackled in the crevices between their legs and between their back and their wings. It was obviously very painful. The roaches would squirm and struggle as if they were being strangled before all movement and reaction, chemical and physical, ceased. I will admit that it was entertaining. It wasn't the pain of my victims that interested me. I held no pleasure in torturing my intruders, nor did I have any sympathy for them. It was the manner of their death that interested me, that all I had done was spray them with liquid, that something so nonviolent and pacifist could undo them, almost mimicking a death by natural causes. It was less like death, and more like transformation. I, of course, felt no impulse to attempt this with human life. I'm no sadist. I simply found my particular manner of exterminating the disgusting little pests that haunted me enchanting.

Once, I sprayed a lone roach of medium size on my wooden floor with the liquid. It bubbled, squirmed, and then stopped all at once, dead. It didn't last long, one of my less pleasurable experiments. I knelt down, focusing on its corpse. Roaches are resilient creatures. They can survive up to a week with their heads chopped off, and even after death, final and true death, one can notice subtle movement in their legs, indicative of their still functioning nervous system. I liked to think of it as their soul slowly leaving their bodies (again, not a sadist). But when I sprayed them with the liquid, it seemed absolute. Not a single trace of them left inside, almost as if a gust of wind could disperse their corpse like dust. My most recent victim was no different. Not the slightest movement. I focused me eyes on it, and poked at it with my pencil. Not the slightest reaction. To make a sure thing of it, I pierced it slowly where I guessed its heart would be.

As the pencil tip sank deeper into its flesh, I felt my hand shake a bit, as if a piece of me were sinking into the void of death that I had implanted in the roach and had consumed its soul. The air in my lungs seemed to be slowly sucked into that of the bug the deeper I got into its flesh, until, suddenly, all of its six legs began to squirm and scurry as if it had been struck by lightning.

Surprised, I jumped back hitting the side of my bed. The roach flipped itself over. I picked one of my shoes up from underneath the bed. The roach turned from me and scurried to the other side of my room, apparently to my closet. I chased it. I don't why, I just wanted the thing to be well and truly dead. It might sound weird, but I often afforded the roaches more intelligence than they actually had. Sometimes I had nightmares that the lot of them would rise against me and take their revenge for my transgressions. The roach slipped underneath my closet door. I opened it. I could see the roach crawling between the several objects on the floor of my closet. I kicked them to the sides until I saw the roach standing alone. I slammed the shoe down on it, killing it once and for all, lifting the shoe to confirm it. As I lifted the shoe, I noticed something that I hadn't noticed before. The entire floor of my room was wooden, as was the floor of the majority of my closet, but the roach's corpse rested on a tile, a clay red tile with a strange symbol drawn on it.

I lifted the tile. Strangely enough, through some optical illusion, the hole that the tile had covered seemed to somehow be larger than the tile itself. It was a gateway, a welcome mat into some humble abode. I don't even really remember jumping inside, even instinctively, but I had to have done so. It was a dark tunnel, I could see and fill the shadows, but I could see through the darkness somehow, as if my vision had adjusted itself. Everything was tinted in red. I still had no idea where I was going or why. I often found myself holding my weight on the walls of the cavern, lost and confused, and then letting my every physical whim and twitch guide me, like the ancient Greeks in their prophetic beliefs. And then there was the voice.

"Queen. Goddess. Powerful. Worshipped."

I was getting tired, but my speed and the strength of my instincts were slowly increasing.

"Others. Traitors. Betrayed. Killed. Broken, mind and soul."

There wasn't a single roach around me and yet I felt their presence everywhere, in the air and on my skin, flowing through me. All going in one direction to one place.

"Pieces. Bugs. Crawl. Crushed. Called unclean. Centuries of suffering."

Closer.

"Death. Death is release. Reformation. You have helped. Much of me freed."

I came to a corner, a curve in the cave.

"Not enough. Too many pieces. Please help."

I turned the corner. Then I saw it . . . Her. She was beautiful. Her skin was dark brown. She had a glowing, willowy, radiant form and long brown hair that seemed petrified in some sort of oval shape around her, framing her entire body. It complimented the two antennae extending from the top of her head. It was the most fulfilling experience any mortal could hope for, but I could also sense that she was incomplete, deprived. That there was supposed to be more.

"Approach."

I came closer to her, face to face. As I looked down, I saw that she levitated off of the ground and had no feet. No complete feet, anyways. Rather than being deformed or disfigured, certain parts of her legs and feet simple were not there, as if wiped from existence. She opened her eyes. Large. Black. No pupils. Only pupils. Only sadness. Only the pain.

Only the plea.

"Please help fix me."

I'm an exterminator now. ■

Wolf Eyes

SCIENCE FICTION & FANTASY

EMMA ROSE GOWANS, Grade 11. Governor's School for the Arts & Humanities, Greenville, SC. Mamie Morgan, *Educator*; Region-at-Large, *Affiliate*; Gold Medal

un

In a tiny house beneath the stars, her heart beats to the wolves crying. With every pounding pulse, she feels the beasts prowling through the outskirts of the village—fangs bleached white with the ethereal glow of virgin moonlight, claws inch-deep into the skin of farmers' watchdogs, red eyes scanning the darkness for another creature to devour. She fears their eyes the most—devoid of any white, only that single bloody hue. Her mother says that their eyes betray their godless natures, but she says that her daughter's eyes are lovely. Adah finds this ironic, because whenever she looks into the mirror, she sees the same beastial red in her own childish eyes as those of the wolves in the wood.

The villagers call her a work of witchcraft. They call her other things, too, but not to her young face. The people see in her eyes the desperate bargain that was made by her mother and father. They bargained to birth a child—born out of the twisted underground magic. The bargain that always brings repercussions, mutilations, horrors.

But Adah doesn't feel like a horror when she's in her family's tiny cabin—in the kitchen, helping her mother pour soup broth into big pots to heat. Cora stands over her, teaching her with the patience of a doting mother, forgetting she ever cried to the witches and warlocks to help her in her barren state. On the earthy wooden table, Adah watches her mother lower a knife on haunches of lamb. She loves her rhythm and her laughter—one smile to drop the cleaver over the blushed red meat, separating muscle and bone.

She hates going out into the market to buy the lamb with her, though. Even with a hood imprisoning her face into hot, sticky, concealed darkness, everyone wonders what she is—Adah more than anyone else. Perhaps it is her mother's ethereal beauty that makes her form so much more sickening to the villagers. She trails behind Cora like a twisted shadow, shaming her with every step.

Her mother is a seamstress known throughout the village—fingerprints woven into the robes and cloaks and winter gloves of nearly everyone. Her hands are lithe but steady, producing flawless stitches through fabric soft and heavy. Cora once tried to show Adah how to sew the complex patterns of her craft. Now, she strenuously tries to teach her daughter the simplest stitching, though there seems little hope for her.

Perhaps it is their whiteless nature, but Adah's eyes never focus on the single plain threads as her mother's beautiful brown ones can. Instead, her sharp vision darts constantly by instinct around the room—pricking her tender hands with needles that draw brilliant red streams from her fingertips. Regardless, the scabs covering her fingers heal far more easily than the wounds inflicted by her former schoolmates. The most organic form of hatred, somewhat hidden and somewhat more easily seen than looking into a mirror and seeing your own bloodied face.

deux

Helv Rue is tall and broad and larger than the forests he chops to the ground. He swings his axe like an executioner, humming symphonies of nothingness to himself as he goes about his daily work. Nearly every day, Adah sneaks out to watch her father and the other men—the tree butchers, she silently declares them to be, always hard at work. Sometimes, even after the butchers have left their craft at the end of their day, she'll remain to pick at the wooden chips and wonder if the trees themselves suffer during their decapitation.

Now that her mother took her out of school, Adah wanders the forests by day. The great trees yet to fall victim never judge her when she pulls off her hood to let her deep brown hair and the light from her gleaming red eyes spill out. In some way, these trees are just like her—all different and twisted and gnarled so that no one specimen ever looks identical. A sharp juxtaposition to the children in Knollsborough, who share the same white sclera. The same pristine, youthful skin. The same joyful laughter.

Whenever Cora allows her to disappear, Adah goes straight to the woods. She does not just go to remove her hood and see the trees. Instead, she goes because it is only here that she feels normal—as though the deep dark magic that brought her into the world flows through the forest streams and hides in the foxholes that she ambles over. The sort of witchcraft that hides in the wood, in tiny societies of warlocks and druids that Adah has always heard are twisted and dark beyond even the stories of fairytale. Perhaps these were the witches her parents connived with to bring about her birth.

"Damn it, Helv!" A man growled at her father one day, clutching his axe less like a huntsman and more a murderer. "Why'd you ever trouble yourself with the dark ways? Didn't you know the cost?"

Helv grunted. "It was Cora's idea, not mine."

Adah doesn't blame her father, though.

Today, she watches her father and his murderous conspirators with as much curiosity as distaste—catching fragments of curses and manly conversations. Her eyes blend into the underbrush like some creature of the night. Her father is bigger than all of the others, tall yet planted firmly on the ground like the trees that he obliterates. She knows that he despises her, but he piques her childish interest. Once when she was younger, she asked him how he kept all of the strength and muscle inside his skin from spilling out like a shrunken old cotton shirt that bursts at the seams when you try to put it on. He furrowed his eyebrows and told her that was the stupidest question he had ever heard. She supposes that any paternal instinct he previously had evaporated when he realized that she was a freak, but Adah still adores him for the simple fact that he is her father.

She loves the underbrush of the forest—the moist leaves wrapping around her feet like some makeshift blanket. She loves the animal tracks that tell the stories of wild journeys taken by night.

"You need help?" A tree butcher grunts at her father, swinging the butt of his axe to rest on his broad shoulders—wider than the horizon.

"No," Helv replies in his usual gruff l tone. "This tree's a formidable trunk but no match for me."

"Suit yourself," The other man replies with a spit.

Helv pauses, returning to his work.

"You still considering it?" The man with spit still gleaming on his lips mutters.

"I don't got the coin to." Helv shakes his heavy head.

"You don't need to give them coin. They have no need for it. She belongs there anyway."

"Nobody wants a child that isn't theirs."

The murderer of the trees shifts his axe off of his broad shoulders. "You don't even want the child that *is* yours."

"She's barely mine." Helv huffs visibly, arching his sweaty back and shifting his weight to lay the fatal blow to the previously indomitable tree. The gargantuan being, now felled at the hands of her father, crashes to the ground with a crack loud enough to rupture the world. Adah lays motionless on the ground—inhaling and exhaling the hatred of her father that rattles in her head louder than the impact of the plummeting giant.

"So take advantage of the opportunity. You'll likely never get the chance to be rid of her ever again."

"I reckon she'd die at their hands."

"You say that like you care." The spit on the man's lips is now mingled with the dust that rose when the beautiful tree fell dying. "No one will blame you for wanting to be rid of her. She's bad fortune—you can see it in those eyes.

Besides, she'll go easy enough. She ain't much of a fighter, is she?"

"She's just a little girl," Helv laughs, as if the whole concept is darkly comical. "*It's* bad omen, you know."

"Why do you think I'm getting rid of her?"

Another bead of spits falls from the executioner's lips. "What does Cora say of all of it?"

Her father sneers—mortal eyes squinting in spite. "She'll have nothing to say of it. She's blinded by the spell of motherhood. She ignores that the child is cursed and a mistake and has no place in our village. She doesn't understand that the little creature has overstayed its welcome."

Adah can hear her heart beating between her ears and behind her glistening red eyes.

Tonight, she does not walk over the bridge and the sky-high hill—through the village gates and back to her parent's cabin. For eleven years the entirety of her existence has been the collection of flickering village lights framed by trees, yet even she acknowledges the truth now—that her home is not where she was raised or born. Not where her father's axe leans up against the side of the tiny cabin, somehow immune to the rust from rainstorms and midwinter frost. Not where the other children have beautiful blue eyes and steady hands to help their mothers sew. Not where for every one kind soul who smiles in pity at her on the street, there are throngs who want to burn her alive or send her away to the warlocks of the wood.

"If they want to be rid of me, then I will find my way on my own."

trois

Adah cannot run from Knollsborough fast enough. She claws at the rich forest soil to pull herself over knotted tree roots slick with deciduous forest mold. Night and day are dark twin sisters under the thick canopy of tree leaves. Her mother once told her stories of the wilderness—mushrooms that would swallow children up, plant specimen with tendrils that could choke you and never let you go—yet even in such a place, the sheer freedom is exhilarating, intoxicating, enough to make darkness and rot unusually beautiful.

She is eleven years old and terrified. She misses stirring soup in the kitchen with her beautiful mother's eyes examining her face with nothing but unabashed kindness. Once upon a time, Cora told her that she would survive Knollsborough and the hatred and go on to make a good life for herself somewhere else, and Adah believed her with all the hopefulness in her young heart.

A jagged root catches Adah's foot, and she falls hard. Her hands scrape against the weathered bark—ripping the skin raw and making breath a slow and agonizing feat to be achieved. Adah lays on the forest floor, allowing her hands to rest on the front of her blouse. The blood stains the powder blue fabric—rough cotton and wool. She listens as a light rain begins to fall, mixing a watery concoction of blood and raindrops and the tears that she wishes she were not crying.

Darkness has long suffocated the wood, but as she looks around her, she sees the eyes. At first, she wonders if there are mirrors hidden by the mysterious sorcerers in the underbrush for some ritual. Or perhaps she is hallucinating a thousand pairs of her own eyes.

But when the first wolf creeps forward, she knows. Its gait is fluid—paws mutilating the rich, dark soil below them. White teeth longer than her fingers are bared with pride through a curiously open maw. It nears her, never striking, but instead staring. Adah stares back—looking into the whiteless eyes so red that if they were not framed by a beastial form she would mistake them for her own. Other creatures emerge from the shadows.

Adah lays motionless, silently daring the beast that is so much like her to act. The pack mother stretches, stepping closer still to her until she begins to wonder if she is preparing to use her godlike jaws.

This creature, instead, leans down in a manner something akin to a horse grazing, and begins to lick at her hands. The sensation is sickeningly kind— almost maternal, not carnal. Adah remembers the way that her mother would clean her hands when she came home with a scratch—the rough cloth lovingly applied that would leave her body feeling cleaner than the day that she was born. Somehow, this feels even better.

The wolf raises her head, only to open her maw and release a howling sound akin to guttural laughter.

"Tell me, pup—did they ever tell you who you really are?" ■

Arming Teachers: A Fatal Solution

CRITICAL ESSAY

CHLOE DUREN, Grade 12. Murphy High School, Mobile, AL. Ashley Cauley, *Educator*; Wiregrass Writing Project, *Affiliate*; Gold Medal

Any American born between 1995 and 2005 is a member of Generation Z— also known as the Mass Shooting Generation. "More children have been killed by guns than U.S. soldiers killed in combat since 9/11" (Sit). In the United States, school shootings in particular have become an epidemic that must not go untreated. It seems as though each day brings a new tragedy with a higher death toll. Students are forced to retain their planned hiding places and escape routes in the back of their minds every day when they go to class. While very few actions have been taken by politicians to remedy this American disease, one solution that has recently been proposed would only further the problem; a few lawmakers across the country have suggested that schoolteachers and administrators be trained and given firearms to carry on school grounds in an attempt to prevent an active shooter. They believe that the only logical resolution to a gunman is another weapon. However, having armed school staff on campuses would risk the safety of students and teachers, be ineffective in stopping school shootings, and cost the United States millions of dollars annually.

To begin, having armed school personnel on campuses compromises the safety of both teachers and students. This is in direct opposition to the argument that more guns equals higher safety. First, the firearm training that educators would be put through would never match the safety standards of a police academy. Even trained officers have difficulty hitting their target, and instructors in stressful situations are likely to wound students in the crossfire. Moreover, about 75 percent of officers that are killed by a gun on duty die within ten feet of the shooter ("Arm"). With this being said, classrooms usually do not exceed 30 by 30 feet, and consequently it would be extremely dangerous for teachers to confront a shooter in such close proximity. Second, considering the fact that some police officers cannot even suppress their internal racism on the job, it is easy to imagine that arming teachers would pose a serious threat to their African American and Latino students. According to Bill Proctor, the Leon County Commissioner in Tallahassee, Florida, "the unarmed children of black taxpayers will become nothing more than target practice . . . [they will] fall victim to potential trigger happy school teachers" (qtd. in Dailey). Proctor goes on to back up his argument by suggesting a potential correlation between suspension rates and teachers' perception of threat. He states that racial minorities have been suspended far more often than their Caucasian classmates in Tallahassee, and he could not expect anything different with how teachers handle misbehavior from their black and Latino students, especially if these educators were to carry weapons (Dailey). Lastly, keeping track of weapons is difficult in and of itself, even for law enforcement. Not only can firearms fall into the hands of students, but in two years alone (2006 to 2008), law enforcement officers in the United States lost 289 firearms simply because they were not properly secured ("Arm"). In larger high schools with a population of 2,000 or more students, the possibility of loose weapons on campus is extremely daunting. Racism, inadequate training, and loose weaponry are severe safety concerns for both students and teachers.

In addition to being a safety risk, it is hard to imagine that arming teachers would prevent or even cut short a shooting, once underway. This thoroughly disproves the idea that teachers with handguns could take down an active shooter. First of all, the more armed persons that are present at the scene during mass murder, the harder it is for law enforcement to locate the gunman. Officers would have to confront more people with guns before being able to track down the actual shooter and arrest him (Givens 213). This would prolong the shooting and cost more innocent people their lives—the exact opposite of what arming school faculty is supposed to achieve. On top of this, it would be close to impossible for a teacher to actually take down a gunman. Even supremely trained officers only hit their target two out of ten times ("Arm"). Therefore, it is highly unlikely an overworked and underpaid teacher could aim any better, and it is even less likely that he or she would wound the shooter in such a way that he would stop firing. Last but not least, the vast majority of school shooters plan their attacks well in advance and would not be deterred by a teacher with a handgun (Givens 217). In general, those planning to open fire on campus do not care whom they hit or if he himself dies in the process. Also, his weapon of choice is most often a military-style assault weapon such as an AR-15, and a simple handgun would prove no match for such a machine. Once one considers the extremely high possibility that arming educators would prove entirely ineffective, it is obvious that better alternatives should be considered.

Regardless of the previous points, the expenditure alone of arming school staff is reason enough to abort this idea. First, the estimated total price for one-fifth of America's teachers to be trained and armed already exceeds one billion dollars (Bump). This price accounts for one weapon per instructor, and training that includes only a single mass-shooting simulation. This number does not even include gun storage, replacement, ammunition, and other expenses. School systems would have to decide whether to have teachers store their firearm in a belt or, the safer and more expensive alternative, a locked safe. They would also need to replace guns that are lost, stolen, broken, or defective and keep a steady supply of ammunition ready at all times. In addition, schools would need policies and procedures written for school life with loaded firearms and systems formulated for choosing which staff members to arm (Givens 215). Most importantly, however, it would be terribly difficult to find an insurance agency to insure the school systems with loaded weapons on campus. Even if one or two could be found, the premiums would be insanely exorbitant (Givens 216). It would cost these schools, who often cannot even afford simple school supplies, ridiculous amounts of money. Moreover, these costs would eventually trickle down to the everyday taxpayer, regardless of their involvement in the schools. Arming school personnel is not only an unsafe and futile solution, but it would also be exceptionally rough on America's economy.

In conclusion, the proposed solution to prevent school shootings by arming teachers is simply not worth the danger, ineffectiveness, and unreasonable cost. First, this approach would make students and teachers even more unsafe at school. People could be injured or killed in the crossfire, teachers could use their weapons at inappropriate times, or the firearm could fall into the wrong hands. Furthermore, this proposed solution would be entirely useless anyway. The lack of training for teachers, distraction for law enforcement, and lack of deterrence for gunmen entirely debunks the reason for implementing the policy in the first place. Lastly, school systems, who often cannot afford the basic education materials such as paper and pencils, would never be able to locate enough funding for training, arming, and insuring their staff. It is just as Emma González, a teenage gun rights activist and school shooting survivor, recently told an interviewer: "Douglas [High School] ran out of paper for, like, two weeks in the school year, and now all a sudden they have $400 million to pay for teachers to get trained to arm themselves? Really?" (qtd. in Alfonsi). It is ridiculous to falsely believe that the solution to America's gun violence problem is more guns. Arming teachers and administrators would only spread the gun violence epidemic that already plagues the Unites States of America. ∎

Essential and Unforgettable: What *Calvin and Hobbes* Teaches Us About Our Daily Lives

CRITICAL ESSAY

ALEX LU, Grade 8. Sycamore School, Indianapolis, IN.
Emilie Molter and Beth Simpson, *Educators*; Clowes Memorial Hall, Butler Arts & Events Center and Hoosier Writing Project at IUPUI, *Affiliate*; Gold Medal

Calvin and Hobbes is a childhood classic filled with hidden meanings and meanders. There is no work more iconic or endearing than this masterpiece. Even though many may dismiss the work as childish and devoid of any real meaning, more exists than meets the eye. From thinly veiled critiques of modern consumerist culture to the issues of environmental protection versus human interests, *Calvin and Hobbes* contains a multitude of revelations that are no less pertinent thirty years later.

To start, *Calvin and Hobbes* often wanders into the realm of gender equality issues. The stereotypes of today are harshly stated in Calvin's earnest and truthful voice: "If I don't play sports, I can't make beer commercials" (Watterson 26 April 1990). Susie coldly responds, "At least you aren't expected to spend your life twenty pounds underweight" (Watterson 26 April 1990). This seemingly naive and unassuming conversation between two children manages to not only reveal facets of gender inequality, but also touches upon the sensitive issues of obesity, health, and anorexia. Those are three issues that will continue to grow in importance as the American consumer culture spreads throughout the world. On top of that, Calvin and Susie manage to explain the issues through two sentences, less than any doctor or expert could do. All the while, the serious issue is juxtaposed with a sense of humor, further impounding the messages revealed in covert sarcasm.

The topic of isolation versus society is deeply explored throughout Calvin's ten-year history. Calvin is divided between solitude and friendship as he engages in rambling excursions with his tiger, Hobbes. One of the issues that often come up in these expeditions is human greed. Throughout the cartoon, Calvin struggles between individuality and his hidden desire for fame. He struggles between "his status as an outsider and free thinker" and "trad[ing] the integrity of his art for riches and fame" (Watterson 2 November 1990). As he discusses his internal struggle with Hobbes, he seems to choose fame. But, in hints dispersed throughout the book, Calvin reveals that this decision is not the truth, only a facade to hide his pain. Calvin desires a reprieve from isolation and torturous school days made worse by unsympathetic classmates. Calvin is not detached and emotionless; he merely wants isolation by gaining an elite status from riches and fame, because his fellow kind has given him little reason to like them. Instead, he prefers the company of nature, as it gives him the peace he desires. In a way, Hobbes represents nature: wild, weird, and profoundly wonderful. In short, Calvin has found a perfect friend in nature. Calvin's willingness to accept Hobbes, make Hobbes his friend, and feed him, albeit somewhat reluctantly, belies his indifference. In reality Calvin can be a caring friend; he only separates himself due to lack of acceptance of his true nature.

Calvin also shows true, unfiltered concern and takes adamant stances on issues important to him, not hesitating to ridicule many things around which today's politicians toe. When Calvin laments about the woods near his house being bulldozed, yet is unable to do anything due to the bulldozer being locked, he is unwittingly posing as an extended metaphor for the conflict between man and nature. Calvin fluctuates between environmental protection and materialism, reflecting mankind's conflict of morals versus living needs. In the end, there is no resolution to the issue, showing how today's issues are too complex to be explained using a single ideology. The arts are also not above Calvin's covert sarcasm, as he creates mockeries of so considered "great art" with his chalk drawings, dinosaur scribbles, and "monochromatic" snow sculptures. He captures a sense of sincerity and honesty not often seen in the modern day world, even though his purpose is not truly to create fine art or to be sarcastic about it, only to have fun with his tiger, Hobbes.

Perhaps the sheer simplicity and ease of conveyance is the most striking part about this cartoon. Without even trying, Calvin manages to explain the complexity of the whole world in four small rectangles on a ratty newspaper. He is a "fierce advocate for the separation of church and state" yet he also "feel[s] the need for spiritual guidance and comfort" (Watterson 11 September 1992). In a way, Calvin struggles with hypocrisy and ambiguity in a very human way, like our minds do every day. When Calvin goes and attempts to burn an effigy of Mrs. Wormwood, he is sent to the principal's office instead. A comic situation is thus turned into a subtle jab at the nearly unrestrained American system of free speech. Like shouting fire in a crowded theater, Calvin is attempting to rebel against the rules his parents and school have set for him, but not without consequences. Bill Watterson perfectly captures the dilemma of freedom versus restraint; Vietnam and civil rights are two pertinent examples that reveal that free speech is not truly free. Calvin reflects the dilemma of unrestrained liberty; what is technically right is not necessarily allowed socially, as Calvin discovers.

He also uncovers some of the rampant hypocrisy in today's world. People say one thing and do another. They slander themselves and pretend to be someone else. But Calvin is not entirely to blame for his situation; his dad sets a hypocritical precedent. One clearly evident example is when Calvin asks his dad to "start buying things that will get the economy going and create profits and employment." In response, his dad says he will "stop leaving the *Wall Street Journal* around" in frustration (Watterson 15 December 1992). The concealed irony here is that Calvin's dad reads the *Wall Street Journal* himself, but doesn't want to let Calvin read it.

Calvin imagines himself as a brave and courageous explorer, but is unwilling to try new foods, tolerate change, or stand up to those who torment him. He shows society's hidden weakness in glaring clarity; it critiques others quite often but almost never sees its own shortcomings. Calvin enjoys raging at the universe, criticizing his friends, and critiquing his mom, yet almost never seeks to improve himself. He is lazy, indifferent, uncaring, and egocentric. Yet he maintains a sense of optimism and hope few of us still have. He manages to laugh at the good and terrible parts of life, and appreciates what little things he can. He gets comfort from Hobbes and comic books, two of the only things on which he can depend. Most of all, he is not yet solid, hardened. He pretends to be cynical, but never is. Underneath, he is everyone as they truly desire to be. He is our best hope, our dreams. He remains perfect and unaltered as time passes. By showing everybody his true self, Calvin implores us to see the silver lining in life. Calvin shows us a clear picture of what is most valuable, hope. He may have been created to represent a juvenile delinquent, but in the end, he is the opposite. He is the example to follow. He helps people everywhere fight back internally against their inner enemies, their Moes and other oppressive tormentors in life.

He shows us that time is fleeting and valuable. He shows us that there are just some fall mornings not worth missing, some moments in the snow that last forever. Most of all, he shows us that childhood is golden. Though he stays static in age throughout the cartoon, things change around him. A dappled forest is replaced by "Shady Acres Condominiums." An evening soon turns into bedtime. Even dreams end, rudely awakened by the shouts of a bedraggled mom. He implores us to go outside, enjoy the rain in your hair the leaves pooling around you. He begs you to build a snowman with him. It's okay if it looks terrible. It's supposed to look that way. It's a space alien. Sometimes, perhaps that paperwork or homework isn't so urgent. There are only so many hours of winter that can be spent speeding down Lookout Hill. Finally, Calvin tells us this: when life bullies you, it's okay to feel defeated. But always start tomorrow with a big smile and your best friend nearby. It's a foolproof solution. ■

Is Space Travel Worth the Cost?

CRITICAL ESSAY

DAVID WANG, Grade 9. Home School, Ripon, CA. Zhijian Wang, *Educator*; Region-at-Large, *Affiliate*; Silver Medal

"We chose to go to the moon." These famous words were spoken by former President John F. Kennedy to the people of the United States in 1962. These words were spoken in a rough time. As the space race commenced, the U.S. appeared to be losing. With the Soviet Union in the lead, America seemed to fall behind on the quest to solidify its spot as the dominant country in space. Because of this, the U.S. gathered all of its might and sent the first astronauts to the moon, proving itself as the top of the race. This is great and all, but it also brings up a rather controversial issue regarding space travel in general. In an era where people are still dying from a lack of food and basic resources, is it justified to waste billions of dollars on space travel? When we still have major issues on earth, is it okay to focus on journeying into space? Despite many reasons to explore the unknown, it is clear that spending tens of billions of dollars on space travel and exploration is utterly immoral when there are still a mountain of problems back on the ground.

The clearest problem surrounding this issue is that there are larger problems on earth. It is an undeniable fact that hundreds of millions of people in the world are still suffering from poverty. "The World Bank says that 10 percent of the world's population lived on less than $1.90 a day in 2015. That means 735.9 million people lived below the poverty threshold in 2015" (Global). This is a problem, and one that should be addressed before anything else. If we believe that humanity should progress forward, then we need to focus on creating a just world for everyone. We cannot waste money enhancing the elite at the expense of the poor. The cost of space exploration since the start of the space race is roughly $900 billion, but the cost of feeding the hungry is only $30 billion according to the Food and Agriculture Organization and NASA. Why should humanity run the risk of reaching for the stars when basic foundational problems are not solved on earth? Many people will reject this claim, saying that global poverty rates have dropped in the last few years. While this may be true to a certain extent, it only focuses on certain parts of the world. According to CNBC, "Poverty dropped everywhere but the Middle East and North Africa, where conflicts in Syria and Yemen actually pushed the poverty rate up to 5 percent in 2015 from 2.6 percent in 2013" (Global). Many point to the chances of saving humanity as a reason to colonize other planets. "But what the droughts, the fires, the hot summers, and the melting glaciers call for is not an escape from Earth, but a redoubling of the efforts to save it" (Etzioni). Instead of investing in the technology to venture into space, humanity should invest in the technology to save the earth because ultimately, our fate resides in the health and prosperity of our planet. It is clear that in an age of ever increasing challenges for humanity, time and money should not be spent on colonizing Mars, but rather on saving the lives of fellow human beings here on earth.

The second most important issue to consider is that space exploration comes at a great expense with little return. A great example of this is sending satellites into space. Satellites in orbit help us by providing GPS communications, the internet, and most importantly, measurements and analysis of the earth's surface. These could help solve the earth's problems, and while these are beneficial in some ways, it is undeniable that the cost of sending these satellites into space and the little benefits that they provide are utterly incompatible. Such a high cost for the leisure of the internet is not worth paying billions of dollars. For every dollar that we spend sending rockets into space, we would be wasting a dollar that could go to help make more cost effective improvements and advancements in science and technology here on earth.

The last and perhaps most intriguing of all is that space travel is polluting in a devastating way. Every satellite or space debris in space will stay there for a long time. "In 2007, the Chinese government tested a missile by smashing an old weather satellite, and those 150,000 chunks of debris are floating around space. Two years later, in 2009, two satellites crashed into one another, and those shards, too, are somewhere in the universe" (Weindling). This pollution is potentially deadly in the sense that the more pollution there is in space, the harder it is to get rockets out of the earth into space. This would make space travel impossible, and as more satellites and rockets smash into each other, the problem would only get worse. And, as satellites smash into each other, it would waste even more of our money and time. As noted by the author of the article, this could also result in something very similar to what happened during the Industrial Revolution. "And we probably won't know until it's too late to correct it" (Weindling).

In the end, it is hard to justify space exploration. On one hand, it creates an opportunity to explore the unknown, while also helping to improve the lives back on earth. Unfortunately, the negative impacts of what seems like a great journey into the unknown are too great to be set aside. When there are still diseases like cancer to be cured, wars to be pacified, and poverty to be ended, it is utterly unacceptable to spend time and resources to risk space exploration. There is too much to be sacrificed in order to satisfy our curiosity. It is a great expense with very little return. But perhaps most concerning is the possibility that by exploring space, we may bring about consequences that are irreversible. When there is so much at stake, why risk so much for so little? ∎

Tailspin

DRAMATIC SCRIPT

SARAH FAUCETTE, Grade 11. Ardrey Kell High School, Charlotte, NC.
Terry Gabbard, *Educator*; Charlotte-Mecklenburg Schools, *Affiliate*; Gold Medal

For Mom, who never did get to be a pilot, but taught me to fly all the same.

Lights up on a warehouse setting, mid-1960s Atlanta, Georgia. The US, SL, and SR walls are sheets of corrugated metal paneling that stretch up and up beyond the audience's view. A large sign with chipping gray paint reading "WHIT-LOCK" in thick black block letters is mounted to the upper part of the US wall. A desk with a low backed office chair sits SR, facing the SL wall. It's meticulously organized, with stacks of paper sorted neatly, and nothing extra except for one photograph of a smiling mother and daughter. Farther SL is a larger, grander desk facing directly toward the audience. This desk is clear of papers and is more personalized, lined with model airplanes and a sleek black rotary telephone. After a moment, the mother and daughter from the photograph on the first desk enter stage left. The mother, JOAN, is dressed in a white button-up blouse and a black pencil skirt. She looks stressed but she smiles at her daughter, CARRIE, and holds her hand. CARRIE is the image of a young schoolgirl; pigtails and a pristine white headband with a blue-and-white checkered dress. CARRIE deposits her backpack on the floor next to her mother's desk on the DS end and lays on the floor, bracing herself on her elbows as she takes a coloring book from her bag. JOAN sits and begins shuffling papers around. A man enters from SL in a beige suit and glasses, his arms crossed. This is HOWARD, JOAN's father and employer. When she sees him, JOAN stops moving abruptly. CARRIE begins to color, oblivious.

HOWARD: *(Emotionless)* You're late.
JOAN: Carolyn's bus was running behind. I can stay late tonight to make up for it.
HOWARD: If you stay late, someone else has to stay and be here to lock up when you're done.
JOAN: I could lock up.
HOWARD: *(Sighing)* You know that won't work.
CARRIE: *(Looking up from the floor)* It's not Mom's fault, Granddaddy. Steven Winthrop got sick in the parking lot and they had to clean it up before

we could leave. It took forever, and Steven couldn't even go home on the bus! The nurse said—

(*JOAN leans over to shush CARRIE gently, but HOWARD smiles indulgently.*)

HOWARD: Hey there peanut. How was school?

CARRIE: It was fine.

HOWARD: Did you learn anything?

(*CARRIE gives a noncommittal shrug.*)

HOWARD: Well that won't do. Come on now, give me one good thing about today.

(*CARRIE'S eyes light up when she remembers.*)

CARRIE: A plane flew over our school while we were outside at recess! It was so low that Georgie said it was going to crash, but I told him it was only the pilot beginning his descent, because our school is close to the airport and a pilot begins their descent at a hundred miles from their designated airfield.

HOWARD: Right you are. What did Georgie say to that?

(*CARRIE scrunches her nose.*)

CARRIE: He said I was being a bratty know-it-all and I've probably never even seen a plane in real life before.

HOWARD: (*Scoffing*) That shows how much he knows. What kind of plane was she?

(*CARRIE thinks for a second.*)

CARRIE: I couldn't tell. It was a passenger for sure. Boeing, probably.

HOWARD: How many engines did she have?

CARRIE: Four.

HOWARD: Were they housed or were the propellers visible?

CARRIE: Housed.

HOWARD: (*Gesturing patiently*) And that makes it . . .

CARRIE: A 727?!

HOWARD: That's my girl.

(*HOWARD gives CARRIE an approving smile before turning back to JOAN, who still looks apprehensive.*)

HOWARD: (*Speaking to CARRIE, looking at JOAN*) Would you mind giving your mom and me a minute, peanut?

(*CARRIE puts on a pouty face.*)

HOWARD: I think Mr. Carl had some things to show you in the warehouse. Tell him I sent you down, he might let you help out with a repair or two. There's a shiny Skyhawk with some busted landing gear that needs fixin'.

(*CARRIE'S eyes light up, and she nearly trips over her own feet running across the stage and off SL.*)

JOAN: *(Voice raised)* Be careful!

(Once CARRIE'S footsteps fade, HOWARD turns to JOAN, his smile from earlier pressing into a line.)

HOWARD: I've reviewed your request.

JOAN: For my raise?

HOWARD: Yes.

(JOAN stays still waiting for HOWARD to speak.)

HOWARD: *(Sigh)* I just don't think it's possible at this time.

JOAN: Dad—

HOWARD: —Now look, you have to understand, we don't have the money.

JOAN: All of your mechanics got raises this past month.

HOWARD: I've run the numbers, and it's not going to work.

JOAN: What numbers did you run? I do "the numbers" for this whole business, Dad. I've run those same numbers myself, and the fact is we do have the money. It's just not going to me.

HOWARD: The boys all have families to take care of.

JOAN: And what about your own family?

(HOWARD sighs and runs his hand over his face.)

HOWARD: Haven't you been getting money from Charlie?

JOAN: I wouldn't exactly call that a considerable asset. Without his army benefits, Carolyn and I would be on food stamps.

HOWARD: Money is money.

JOAN: I suppose I should be thankful, then, that he left us for Vietnam? *(To herself)* I hope it's worth it for him.

HOWARD: *(Stiffly)* The military is an honorable calling. You should be proud.

JOAN: *(Sighing)* I'll be proud if we make it through this deployment without me getting any divorce papers in the mail. Or sending them to Saigon myself, for that matter. *(Pointedly)* That is if I even have the money to send them.

HOWARD: Joan, these boys rely on me. I'm just trying to give them their dues.

JOAN: What about my dues? If I were your son, my title would be "Accountant" or "Financial Manager" instead of "Secretary," and I'd be making the same as any of the boys here.

(Beat.)

HOWARD: That's quite a thing to say.

JOAN: *(Sharply)* Then deny it.

HOWARD: The fact of the matter, darling, is the knowledge needed to work on these planes just isn't the same as—

JOAN: *(Interrupting)* It isn't the same as what I do? Even if I work the same hours, keep this whole business afloat making sure we pay our taxes on time.

Even if I spend my lunch break picking Carolyn up from the bus, because she has nowhere else to go after school. Even if I am your flesh-and-blood daughter, I don't do enough to earn a living wage as a single mother providing for myself and your granddaughter?

(*HOWARD blinks, but he squares his shoulders, and his face remains impassive. As JOAN is speaking, CARRIE reenters from SL, but she hears her mother's voice and stops, crouching next to HOWARD'S desk to eavesdrop. She twitches when she hears her name and her eyebrows pinch together.*)

HOWARD: If you're worried about Carrie, I can always pitch in a bit, anything she needs.

JOAN: You don't get it.

(*HOWARD picks up the photo of JOAN and CARRIE on the desk and looks down at it.*)

HOWARD: Please, educate me.

JOAN: If I take handouts from you, you're providing for us.

(*HOWARD places the photograph rather abruptly back on the desk.*)

HOWARD: And what's wrong with a working man providing for his daughter and granddaughter?

JOAN: Because you refuse to let me be the one to do it! *I* should be able to buy Carolyn's Christmas presents. *I* should be the one to pay for new pencils, or stuffed animals, or tickets to see a picture at the multiplex. I have earned that much. But your pride won't let you. You're denying me the ability to fulfill the basic responsibilities of a parent! You—

HOWARD: (*Interrupting*) Then why don't you leave!

(*A moment of silence. HOWARD is stranding rigidly, and JOAN's hands are clenched into fists, her eyes wide. Still crouched by the desk, CARRIE furrows her eyebrows; she's not used to her grandfather raising his voice.*)

HOWARD: (*Deep breath*) I'll tell you why. You don't leave because you can't. You know that I'm giving you a square deal here, and you can't find better anywhere else out there.

JOAN: I can, actually.

HOWARD: What is that supposed to mean?

JOAN: Times are changing, Dad. People are starting to look more closely at the credentials on the application than the face that's attached to them. So with enough looking, I could find something better. I can. You want to know the real reason why I don't leave?

(*HOWARD says nothing. JOAN takes this as permission to continue.*)

JOAN: The same reason I do anything else. For Carolyn. She adores you, and if I left we wouldn't see you anymore. That would devastate her. She looks up to you like no one else. I can't take that away. All her happiness is stored in this warehouse, with these planes, with you.

(HOWARD looks guilty, but only for a moment.)

HOWARD: We don't have the money to give you a raise. If Carrie needs anything, and I mean anything, you ask me.

(JOAN nods, her eyes empty, and looks over at the stacks of paper on her desk.)

JOAN: You should go find Carolyn. I have work to do.

(HOWARD turns stiffly and crosses to his desk, where CARRIE is still crouched. She hears his footsteps coming and stands upright, innocently picks up one of the model plans on the desk and starts examining it. HOWARD is surprised to see her in his office.)

HOWARD: Carrie, how long have you been in here?

CARRIE: I just got here. *(Changing the subject)* Mr. Carl let me help replace the landing gear on the Skyhawk!

HOWARD: Ahh, the Cessna. What'd you think of her?

CARRIE: I like it! It's pretty, but your Bonanza is better.

(CARRIE holds up the model plane she picked up, a Beechcraft Bonanza, extremely detailed and polished to perfection.)

HOWARD: I'll tell you what, let's find a weekend we can take her up, and I'll teach you a thing or two about flying. I'd say you're old enough now.

CARRIE: Really?! That would be amazing. Thank you so, so, so much!

(CARRIE gives HOWARD a hug around his waist and then flops on the ground, examining the Bonanza model. HOWARD smiles and joins her, sitting on the floor, mildly undignified for a serious business owner, and leans up against his desk. He points to the miniscule series of numbers and letters on the side.)

HOWARD: See that? That's the same registration number I have on my Bonanza. Your grandmother gave me this for our anniversary one year.

CARRIE: *(Reading the numbers and letters)* November, one, niner, two, two, delta.

HOWARD: Exactly.

(CARRIE waves the plane around in a "flight pattern." HOWARD chuckles.)

CARRIE: Have you ever flown a helicopter before, Grandaddy?

HOWARD: I wish, sweetie, but no.

CARRIE: Mommy said that's what Daddy flies in the army.

HOWARD: Oh. Well yes, he does.

CARRIE: You're a pilot, Daddy is a pilot, and one day I'm going to be a pilot too!

HOWARD: Is that right?

CARRIE: Yeah! I'm going to fly planes like you but be in the army like Daddy.

HOWARD: *(Chuckling)* Really now?

CARRIE: Positively. *(She sits up and looks at HOWARD)*

HOWARD: I think the army might be a ways away from having their first female pilot.

(CARRIE lifts her chin defiantly.)

CARRIE: Then I'll be the first!

HOWARD: *(Without hesitation)* I don't doubt that.

(A brief look of confusion flickers across CARRIE'S face. HOWARD is oblivious to it. He looks at his watch and starts to stand, brushing invisible dust off his pants and reaching out a hand to help CARRIE up.)

HOWARD: Why don't we head back to your mom's office?

(HOWARD and CARRIE cross to JOAN'S desk, where she still sits hard at work. HOWARD clears his throat when they get close, and JOAN flinches before looking up at her father and daughter.)

HOWARD: I'm going to send you off early, Joan.

JOAN: *(Suspicious)* It's still two hours from closing.

HOWARD: I think you could use a free afternoon. Just the two of you. Go see a picture at the multiplex or something. My treat.

(JOAN gives HOWARD a slightly incredulous eyebrow raise, before shaking her head.)

JOAN: I think I should stay. I've got a lot on my plate.

(CARRIE gives her best puppy-dog eyes, and HOWARD gives her a meaningful look over CARRIE'S head.)

CARRIE: Please, Mom, please?

HOWARD: Take some time to calm down and think things over.

(JOAN meets HOWARD'S eyes and doesn't look away for several moments of silence.)

JOAN: Alright. *(Smiling gently at CARRIE.)* Give me ten minutes, sweetie.

(CARRIE squeals and dashes to pick up her backpack as JOAN squares away a last stack of paper. HOWARD turns to exit stage left, but only makes it a few steps before he returns to JOAN'S desk. He attempts to discreetly pass JOAN a handful of money. JOAN looks at the money, looks at HOWARD, and then looks away, refusing him. HOWARD puts the money in his pocket and turns to leave. CARRIE watches the whole exchange silently. HOWARD looks over his shoulder one last time to address CARRIE.)

HOWARD: Next weekend, we'll take the Bonanza up, sound good? Start getting you ready to be in the army.

(At the mention of the army, JOAN'S attention turns sharply to her father, eyebrows pinched together, but CARRIE is glowing. She nods eagerly and gives

HOWARD *a mock salute, which he returns before exiting.)*

JOAN: I'll just finish up here, and then we can go do something fun, alright? *(CARRIE nods and sits on the ground, leaning up against the end of JOAN'S desk patiently. She bounces her leg absently.)*

CARRIE: Mom, why were you and Granddaddy fighting?

(JOAN stops moving.)

JOAN: You heard that?

CARRIE: Some of it.

JOAN: It's nothing sweetie, your grandfather and I just had a disagreement.

CARRIE: Grown-up stuff?

JOAN: Exactly. You wouldn't understand.

CARRIE: It sounded like it was about money.

JOAN: It was, a little bit. Nothing you need to worry about.

CARRIE: *(Quiet)* It sounded like it was about me too.

(CARRIE curls her legs up into her chest and wraps her arms around her knees.)

JOAN: Oh, honey.

(JOAN sits next to CARRIE on the ground, legs crossed off to the side so both of them are facing out towards the audience.)

JOAN: It wasn't about you.

CARRIE: I heard my name. You said you only worked with Granddaddy so I wouldn't be sad. And you sounded mad when you said it.

JOAN: It's more than that.

CARRIE: It's because he doesn't share the money from work?

JOAN: Yes.

CARRIE: Why not?

JOAN: Granddaddy grew up when a lot of things were different. More . . . traditional. Old-fashioned.

CARRIE: So he doesn't think that a girl can do the same things a boy can?

JOAN: That's how he was raised.

CARRIE: Oh. *(Beat)* But he's your dad! Shouldn't he want me and you to have a lot of money and be happy?

(JOAN puts her arm around CARRIE and pulls her close.)

JOAN: I don't need a whole lot of money. Money would sure make things easier, but as much as I get wrapped up in numbers sometimes, I want you to know that you can be plenty happy without all the money in the world.

(A few moments of silence.)

CARRIE: Mom, is being in the army a boy's job?

JOAN: I think it is right now, at least in the way you're thinking, but I hope it won't always be that way. Why?

CARRIE: Because Granddaddy thinks I can be the first girl pilot in the army someday.

JOAN: He told you that?

CARRIE: But why does he think that you can't get paid for your job, but I can do something that people think girls shouldn't do?

JOAN: That's a very hard question to answer.

(CARRIE waits patiently as JOAN forms a response.)

JOAN: *(Beginning slowly)* When he was a kid, girls weren't supposed to do anything but get married and cook dinner. That's what happened with him and your grandmother, and he thought it would work the same way for me and your daddy when we got married.

CARRIE: He didn't want you to have a job?

JOAN: He thought that your daddy could earn the money, and I wouldn't have to worry about anything. I could spend all my time at home with you. I still wish I could have that, sometimes.

CARRIE: But Daddy isn't making enough money for us anymore. So you need a job. Why doesn't Granddaddy understand that?

JOAN: Things were different then, he hasn't quite caught up yet.

CARRIE: That's not fair for you.

JOAN: No, it doesn't feel like it is does it, but that's the way things are.

CARRIE: When will Grandaddy change?

JOAN: He is changing. *(Beat)* He's trying to change, I think. A lot of men are right now. My biggest hope for you is that when you're big and grown up all those men will have finished changing.

CARRIE: Is Granddaddy a bad person because he hasn't changed yet?

JOAN: I think you have to decide that for yourself.

(CARRIE sits silently again before looking up at her mother.)

CARRIE: Do *you* think I could be a pilot, Mom?

JOAN: I think you could be the best pilot who ever lived. I just wish all those men could hurry up and see what they're missing.

(JOAN stands up and pulls CARRIE to her feet. CARRIE picks up her backpack and takes her mother's hand as the pair exit stage left. Blackout.) ∎

As Nation Mourns "Death of Journalism," Yang, a Presidential Candidate, Offers Solutions

JOURNALISM

RAINIER HARRIS, Grade 11. Regis High School, New York, NY. Allison Tyndall, *Educator*; NYC Scholastic Awards, *Affiliate*; Silver Medal

Everyone reads the news and depends on the journalists in their areas and nationwide to report accurately, efficiently, and frequently on topics ranging from music, to arts, to entertainment, and to politics. In the United States, 93 percent of adults receive at least some news online (via mobile or desktop). Yet, journalism, particularly local print newspaper, employment is taking a nosedive.

According to the Pew Research Center, newsroom employment dropped 23 percent between 2008 and 2017 with the number of newspaper newsroom employees having the steepest decline, plunging from 71,000 in 2008 to 39,000 in 2018, a 45 percent decrease. In addition, 36 percent of the nation's largest newspapers and 23 percent of the highest-trafficked digital native-news outlets have experienced layoffs between January 2017 and April 2018. In 2018, 171 counties lacked a local newspaper, and 1,449, nearly 50 percent of all counties in the US, had only one newspaper, typically a weekly.

As AP News reports, steep declines in readership and lack of advertising is the main cause of these newspapers closing down. People are becoming less and less engaged in their local communities and are shifting their attention away from their local officials. Local journalists are critical to making sure these officials are held accountable for their actions. Some veterans believe rumors that journalism is dying are ill-founded.

Dr. Jock Lauterer, adjunct professor at UNC-Chapel Hill School of Media and Journalism and the former director of the Carolina Community Media Project told me in a phone interview that he objects "strongly to the notion that newspapers are 'dying.'" He believes the profession is "morphing, [and] adapting."

"The tragedy is that the stories we don't know and never know because we don't have enough bodies to cover it," said Steve Cavendish, editor of the *Nashville Banner* in a phone interview.

A daily newspaper is an apt place to send out messages such as where a string of crimes occur in a certain place in your locale and for close-knit communities to catalog each other's experiences in news clippings. The problem is beginning to be confronted and remedied, particularly in the local arena.

The business of local journalism must fundamentally change in order to adapt for the future and be sustainable in the long term. As Cavendish said, "local media doesn't change until the business behind local media changes. The revenue model for traditional for-profit media is broken," since print advertising is on its deathbed.

The whole industry necessitates rejuvenation, but the key to energizing journalism on a broader scale is by engaging the local communities first and foremost. Andrew Yang, one of the 2020 Democratic presidential candidates, says if elected, he plans to implement two programs to combat the downward trend in local journalism: establishing a Local Journalism Fund and selecting American Journalism Fellows.

The Local Journalism Fund would be a "dedicated $1 billion Fund operated out of the FCC [Federal Communications Commission] that will make grants to companies, nonprofits and local governments and libraries to help local newspapers, periodicals and websites transition to sustainability in a new era." Contrast this stance with our current president who, as of January 30, 2019, has sent "1,339 tweets about the media that were critical, insinuating, condemning, or threatening." Yang says he holds journalism in the highest regard and respect noting it as an "important safeguard to democracy."

He knows it is imperative we halt and reverse this downward spiral in local journalism quickly and efficiently. The American Journalism Fellowship program would have reporters, "nominated by a body of industry professionals from each state and selected by a nonpartisan commission . . . be given a 4-year grant of $400,000 ($100,000 per year)" and station these reporters at local news organizations, presumably ones with either a scarcity of local news reporting or a complete absence of one, "with the condition that they report on issues relevant to the district during the period of their Fellowship."

The ramifications of this rapid decline in local journalism are much more extensive than you would think. When fewer reporters give coverage to an area, fewer people run for mayor, and voter turnout diminishes. In other words, reporting has a direct correlation to overall political participation both with the constituency and their elected officials. It is critical reporters remain the binding factor holding the people and the elected together. In addition, when local newspapers close, local governments are forced to pay higher interest rates for public works projects such as schools, hospitals, and roadways. While the decline in local journalism may seem negligible on the county or city level, it has greater implications once it becomes a nationwide trend.

Organizations such as Report for America (RFA) and the American Journalism Project (AJP) are helping to salvage local journalism. The AJP's mission mimics the intentions of Yang with the Local Journalism Fund: "to catalyze an incremental $1 billion in annual financial support for independent local news." RFA is akin to the Peace Corps applied to the field of journalism. Each year, they select a group from an extremely competitive pool of applicants to go into local communities and report, making themselves available to residents and covering issues in the local areas.

Yang, so far, is the only 2020 candidate who's offered practical policies to combat the crisis in the journalism profession. ∎

Shining a Light on the Dark Side of K-Pop

JOURNALISM

GIA SHIN, Grade 9. Tenafly High School, Tenafly, NJ. Rosanne Rabinowitz, *Educator*; Newark Public Library, *Affiliate*; Gold Medal

You pass rows of brightly colored tents in the Citi Field stadium parking lot in New York where fans have been camping out for the past three days. You enter the stadium after purchasing a $211 resale ticket and find your seat so far back the stage is the size of a textbook. You're surrounded by a thunderous roar of 40,000 people as seven boys rise up from the middle of the stage. Their ascendence first reveals their variegated hair, then their doll-like features, and lastly their tall, slender bodies dressed in clothes worth the price of a new car. The current Guinness World Record holders for the most viewed music video in 24 hours and most Twitter engagements, the seven-member boy band BTS is the first Korean popular music (or K-Pop) group to top the US charts and score a Grammy nomination.

The band members—RM, Jin, Suga, J-Hope, Jimin, V, and Jungkook—open the concert with "Idol," a traditionally themed, hip-hop-style track with thumping drums and a pulsing bass. You twirl your $57 lightstick and watch it blend in with a sea of vibrant colors radiating off everyone else's. Waving the lightsticks in sync with the music, the colors are triggered via Bluetooth, painting rainbows and the words 사랑해—"I Love You"—in the crowd.

Twelve days before BTS performed at Citi Field for their *Love Yourself* 結 *'Answer'* world tour, leader RM spoke at the UN about self-love and chasing his dreams, declaring that "true love first begins with loving myself." However, while their long list of achievements and colorful, carefully scripted stage performances are impressive, a look behind the scenes reveals that, in the K-Pop world, "loving oneself" isn't on the record studios' agenda. For those who are unfamiliar with the world of K-Pop, here's some background: K-Pop is most commonly organized into boy groups, girl groups, and solo artists. These successful artists—called "idols"—are often cast as pure, innocent, and youthful, with their upbeat rhythms and positive lyrics appealing to a younger audience of teens and 20-somethings. The genre originated in South Korea but has exploded beyond the country's radio stations, reaching an international audience. According to Tamar Herman, "[2018] saw BTS . . . land atop iTunes charts in over 60 countries." Collaborations between K-Pop groups and Western artists like John Legend, Kanye West, and Missy Elliott have become increasingly common as well. We call it *Hallyu,* the Korean Wave, and BTS has been at its forefront.

Public Image Pressure

But all this "success" seems tempered by enormous sacrifice, both physical and psychological. K-Pop members are expected to be "perfect," and to that end, unsafe weight loss and extensive plastic surgery appear to be the norm. In 2017, the four-member girl group Six Bomb spent $90,000 on "almost every kind of surgery that could be done on a face" for a single music video. "I wanted to see my image on the screen and not feel insecure," explained Soa, the group's petite 101-pound leader. Men in K-Pop commonly get procedures done as well: according to Joy Kang, CEO of Eunogo, a Singapore-based Korean plastic surgery concierge service, "When you see [male] K-Pop stars, they all have sharp V-line jaws with perfect flawless skin, and masculine bodies."

Drastic weight loss is also prevalent. Jimin, the 134-pound vocalist and main dancer of BTS, has struggled to appeal to K-Pop's beauty standards. "I came to Seoul from Busan. I left everything behind and . . . was scared because I didn't know how it would all end up." He was called chubby and started to starve himself on extreme diets to the point of losing consciousness. In the TV show *Please Take Care of My Refrigerator,* he reveals, "I went on a diet where I survived off of one meal for 10 days."

IU, a thriving solo singer who has dominated the Korean chart more than any other artist since 2010, "went on a diet that consisted of an apple for breakfast, one sweet potato for lunch, and [a] protein shake for dinner"—all while stretching and exercising strenuously. The struggles Jimin and IU went through to maintain a certain weight and shape is representative of the pressure most K-Pop idols face.

This pressure does not come solely from the Korean public; management companies set rules for each trainee's weight loss. According to Kathy Benjamin, a writer for *Grunge,* "being skinny is so important that no less than the CEOs of record companies supervise weigh-ins. If the number is too high, stars are told to lose weight immediately. And they do." In an interview on the talk show *Follow Me 8,* Chaeyeon from the girl group DIA revealed, "There is a general guideline for my weight, but if I go over that guideline, I get punished . . . When my boss tells me to lose weight, I have to comply." She added that she checks her weight daily and scrupulously measures the size of her thighs with a tape measure. In 2015, the entertainment company JYP forced TWICE's

Momo to lose seven kilograms the week before her debut. If she didn't shed the weight, she would not be able to perform on stage with the rest of her group. Momo shared this experience on a live broadcast, saying "I didn't eat anything for the whole week and went to the gym. . . . I spat all the time so there was no water left in my body. When I laid down on my bed and tried to sleep, I was scared that I wouldn't wake up again." Her fellow group members feared for her, too.

The idols who go on extreme diets still have to perform in their tired, sick, and weakened state. They train for at least six hours a day; some, like BTS, train up to fifteen hours a day. The youngest member of BTS, Jungkook, exhausted and overworked, passed out backstage at one of their performances in Chile. Medics rushed in to administer an oxygen mask, but he returned to the stage afterwards to finish the performance because, he says, "We only had two days of shows [in Chile], so I worked myself until my body couldn't take it anymore."

Slave Contracts

Even if an idol wants to get off this unhealthy train of perfection, it's not always an option thanks to "slave contracts," which are what aspiring K-Pop idols—often as young as twelve or thirteen—must sign with an agency as "trainees." These trainees practice and train until they are deemed fit to debut. During their trainee period, their agency has near total control over them; most agencies restrict them from dating, having social media, and driving. Former K-Pop idol Henry Prince Mak claims on his radio show *The Prince Mak Hour*, "Typical contracts are about seven to 15 years. Seven years is the least I've heard of . . . I was seven years myself and I considered myself lucky." To intensify matters, the clock only starts ticking after the trainee's debut and not when they initially join an agency. Choi Junghan, former head of the Korea Entertainment Law Society, justifies this practice by saying that "top stars [are] 'made' into stars by their agencies. These young artists need to be 'invested in' for at least 10 years." As the agencies make millions off of the most successful trainees-turned-idols, their investment pays off; however, the trainees' investments in K-Pop do not always turn a profit. Most trainees are still in school, juggling their academic life and trainee life; their daily schedules may begin as early as 5 a.m. and end at 1 a.m. Non-Koreans spend additional time mastering the Korean language and assimilating into Korean culture. Companies also hold monthly evaluations where height, weight, and performance skills are all meticulously graded and recorded. If the trainers feel that there hasn't been enough "improvement," the trainee will be kicked out of the agency. To make matters worse, the agency requires the trainees to repay the costs of their wardrobe, vocal, dancing, and acting lessons, not to mention their living costs—regardless of whether or not they debut. The more time spent as a trainee, the more debt has to be paid off.

In fact, in 2017, the country's Fair Trade Commission ordered eight large entertainment agencies to end their unfair contracts. According to Sonia Kil, a Seoul-based writer at *Variety*, "Penalties imposed by the agencies on early stage trainees, typically teenagers who breached their contracts . . . were found to have been excessive—ranging from $86,200 to $129,000." Critics argue that these trainees are signing away their lives—and their bank accounts—on a path of uncertainty, because achieving the debut milestone only happens to a rare few.

It's difficult to determine precisely the amount of trainees that debut, but several sources claim that less than 0.1 percent of K-Pop trainees make it to their debut stage. Once they debut either as a group or solo, most don't start making money right away. When the artists debut and make money, it goes towards paying off the "debt" accumulated during their time as trainees and the costs formed after their debut, including money for song production, music videos, and choreography teachers, just to list a few. According to BBC News, "The bill can add up to several hundred thousand dollars. Depending on the group, some estimates say it is more like a million." The average K-Pop "rookie" group that has just debuted generates about $4,000 per show, and most of the proceeds go to the entertainment agency. In his YouTube video discussing the amount of money he made as part of the boy group JJCC, Prince Mak reveals that the company took 80 percent of the group's profit, leaving them with only 20 percent. There were seven members in his group, meaning he had to split 20 percent of the $4,000 among his bandmates, resulting in a mere $114 per person, used to pay off a massive debt.

Prince Mak's case is not an anomaly. In most situations, the company usually takes around 80 to 90 percent of the money an idol makes, leaving 10 to 20 percent to slowly pay off the idol's debt; the idols won't see any money in their hands until all of the debt is paid off. In 2009, former members of the K-Pop group TVXQ sued SM Entertainment, claiming that their income was distributed unfairly even after working to their physical limits, operating on less than four hours of sleep every night. The case ended in a settlement that highly favored SM Entertainment.

Shin Hyung Kwan, the general manager of Mnet (Korea's version of MTV), justifies keeping artists under slave contracts in order to discipline and instill proper manners in rising stars and minimize the appearance of scandals that may cause the downfall of a career. "If you are not careful, the whole thing can be spoiled. Westerners do not understand. The performers could get into some kind of trouble," causing their investments to tank. Despite—or perhaps in part *because of*—the restrictive contracts, the K-Pop world is full of scandals, ranging from drug abuse to sex scandals to suicide.

Scandals

As K-Pop increases in global popularity, so too does the significance of its scandals. When a scandal occurs, not only is the image of the artist tainted, but the image of the group and of K-Pop in general is affected as well. In 2014, 2NE1's Park Bom made international headlines when she was found to "smuggle" drugs from the United States to South Korea. Although an investigation found that these "drugs" were prescribed medicine, K-Pop followers continued to attack Bom on social media. The K-Pop idol was removed and edited out of the variety show *Roommates* and ended up suffering from depression. Soon enough, she was no longer active in the K-Pop entertainment industry, and her girl group 2NE1 disbanded the following year. Unlike in the United States where drug use is fairly common—and sometimes praised—among musicians, even just an association with drugs in South Korea can bring the downfall of an idol's career. This year, iKon's B.I was forced to drop out of the group because he admitted that—three years earlier—he had *considered* taking marijuana and LSD to deal with the stress of being an idol.

Sexual exploitation has also recently emerged from the underside of the K-Pop industry. YG Entertainment, one of the biggest entertainment labels in the country, has seen its star idols involved in several major scandals. Seungri from Big Bang, a band of five members who soon became known as the "kings of K-pop" after their debut in 2006, was arrested in March of 2019 for sex bribery and offering sex workers to clients in his famous nightclub, *The Burning Sun*. This scandal made the front page of top news sources and first opened the public's eyes to a dark side of K-Pop. This "news," while new to the public, is not so new to those in the industry. Actress Jang Jayeon left a seven-page suicide note in 2009, claiming that present-day sex slavery was widespread across Korean entertainment. Sexual exploitation, however, is not the only cause of suicide among artists. The stars in the entertainment industry are no exception to the competitive, cutthroat culture of South Korea that places the nation first among the highest suicide rates in developed nations. In 2017, the positive, colorful facade of K-Pop collided with the shocking news that Kim Jonghyun—one of the nation's most famous idols—had poisoned himself with carbon monoxide. The suicide of the 27-year-old lead singer from SHINee, one of the most popular boy groups in K-Pop history, flooded headlines. "Jonghyun

Suicide Note Points to Brutal Pressure of Korean Spotlight," anounced *Variety*. The *Guardian* reported, "K-Pop Singer Jonghyun's Death Turns Spotlight on Pressures of Stardom." Even the *New York Times* weighed in: "Fans Mourn Kim Jong-hyun, a K-Pop Singer Whose Style Was Instantly Recognizable."

Even with all of the support Jonghyun garnered from fans and other idols while he was alive, his publicly released note allowed fans a rare glimpse into the struggles hidden behind his innocent smile: "The depression that gnawed on me slowly has finally engulfed me entirely," he wrote, adding that he "couldn't defeat it anymore." What surprised his fans the most was that Jonghyun seemed perfectly happy in public appearances on the days leading up to his death.

Although Jonghyun's suicide is arguably the most well-known in the K-Pop world, the plague of suicide permeates all levels of K-Pop artists; bogged down by the pressures of crafting thier perfect public image and obeying "slave contracts," several lesser-known K-Pop entertainers have also succumbed.

Twenty-two-year-old Ahn Sojin entered a survival reality show known as the "Baby Kara" series. She made it to the top four contestants, but was ultimately eliminated and failed to debut with the girl group Kara. Later, when she missed the chance to debut once again with a new girl group called April, Sojin, devastated, sunk into depression. The contract with her agency DSP Media soon ended, and she threw herself from the tenth floor of an apartment. K-Pop singer U;Nee hanged herself at the age of 25 after posting on her website, "I feel everything is empty. I am again walking down a path to reach a destination that I don't know." Boy group M.Street's lead singer, Lee Seohyun, also hanged himself after writing a letter apologizing in advance to his loved ones. Suicide among K-Pop artists is not a new phenomenon. Twenty-three years ago, Charles Park was one of the first K-Pop idols to commit suicide at the age of 19, revealing in his note that the burdens of his second album succeeding were far too great, after the major acclaim of his first one. More than two decades later, the dark side of K-Pop is too often glossed over.

Rewind

You pass rows of brightly colored tents in the Citi Field stadium parking lot in New York where fans have been camping out for the past three days. You enter the stadium after purchasing a $211 resale ticket and find your seat so far back the stage is the size of a textbook. You're surrounded by a thunderous roar of 40,000 people as seven boys rise up from the middle of the stage. Their ascendence first reveals their variegated hair, then their doll-like features, and lastly their tall, slender bodies dressed in clothes worth the price of a new car.

You're focusing on their song lyrics telling you to love yourself; you're not thinking of the eating disorders, you're not thinking of the slave contracts, you're not thinking of the suicides plaguing the K-Pop world. Instead, you only feel a sense of unity among fellow K-Pop fans you have never met.

Eleven months later, the news of BTS taking a break pops up in your newsfeed, and you're reminded of who these idols really are when you strip away the facade of perfection. After six years of nonstop music production and tours, they are, for the first time, stepping away from the exhausting K-Pop scene and experiencing the life of average twenty-year-olds. Just as BTS' members have taken it upon themselves to encourage us to love ourselves, it is time we take it upon ourselves to shed light on the darker side of K-Pop—and to remind these K-Pop artists to love and take care of themselves, too. ∎

The Unraveling of the Narrative

JOURNALISM

JOSHUA YANG, Grade 11. Henry M. Gunn High School, Palo Alto, CA.
Kate Zavack, *Educator*; Writopia Lab, *Affiliate*; Gold Medal

All private individuals have had their names changed for the purpose of this submission.

The sprawling white canvas tents propped up along the broad red brick plazas of Atlanta's Centennial Olympic Park looked like structures out of a busy fairground or festival, but on the morning of July 29, they stood vacant, devoid of movement except for the gentle rustling of fabric in the wind. The tents were fenced off by metal gates and security guards wearing fluorescent yellow vests, blocking public access to the entire north end of the park.

It was here, among soaring stone sculptures and the distant sounds of downtown Atlanta traffic, that I started looking for the traces of something that had happened two decades ago.

These traces were, admittedly, quite easy to find: the white tents all surrounded an elaborate, orange-purple concert stage embossed with the logo of the 1996 Olympic games. Other anachronisms were just as commonplace, as evidenced by the '90s police cars and television production trucks lining the open avenues.

Only the filming towers accompanying the white tents and prop vehicles distinguished the tents' true nature: the film set of Clint Eastwood's *Richard Jewell*.

I wasn't here to cover the filming, though; instead, I was here to relive the real-life subject of the film: Richard Jewell, an ordinary man suddenly thrust into the national spotlight as a hero figure, and whose narrative had begun in this park. It was a narrative that took a dark turn, for just days after Jewell was minted a hero, his fame became infamy as the press portrayed Jewell to be the murderer of the people he had tried to save.

I use the word "relive" because this happened 23 years ago; Jewell himself died in 2007. As a journalist, the reason I was interested in a long-closed case and Jewell's downfall in the media was for one simple reason: Jewell wasn't actually the villain. He had been a hero all along.

As an institution, journalism has been subjected to more and more scrutiny in recent years. Cries and accusations of "fake news" and bias in the media have frequently plagued the fourth estate, but the vilification of Richard Jewell was a shortcoming of journalism two decades before "fake news" was first coined by President Trump as a moniker for the critical coverage he faced.

I was in Atlanta to understand the impact the Richard Jewell story had upon an ordinary face in the crowd, as well as to see what has changed about journalism since—or if nothing has changed.

The Bombing

The story starts with the bombing.

Shortly after midnight in Atlanta's Centennial Olympic Park on July 27, 1996, in the midst of the 1996 Olympic Games, a homemade pipe bomb placed in the north corner of the downtown green space exploded, sending shrapnel into thousands of revelers attending a concert. In the end, two fatalities and more than 100 casualties were reported in what is known today as the Centennial Park bombing.

Richard Jewell had been a security guard that night; Jewell discovered the bomb in a suspicious backpack shortly before the explosion and led an evacuation away from the bomb site, clearing the area and saving dozens of lives.

Jewell was initially hailed as a national hero, but on July 30, three days after the attack, the *Atlanta Journal-Constitution* reported Jewell was being investigated as a suspect by the Federal Bureau of Investigation (FBI) for perpetrating the bombing. In the course of just a few days, Jewell came to be regarded as a terrorist by the public.

The press—not to mention investigators—encircled Jewell, eager to receive any scrap of new information. According to a 1997 *Vanity Fair* article, sound trucks and boom microphones constantly surrounded Jewell's apartment and unmarked cars followed his every move. In the papers, Jewell's name was repeatedly dragged through the mud; he was compared to Wayne Williams, a known serial killer, and was called a "fat, failed former sheriff's deputy" by the *New York Post*.

Jewell was eventually exonerated two months later, when the FBI officially deemed him no longer a suspect, but by then, the press had tarnished his reputation irreparably.

The Eyewitness

I was in Centennial Park that morning because I had hoped to encounter a survivor or witness of the bombing. Even better, I was looking for someone who remembered Richard Jewell. At first, I had little luck: nobody seemed to have lived in Atlanta so long ago; some had no idea what the bombing was, let alone who Jewell was.

That all changed when I met Victor Major, a tattooed, bearded fifty-some-thing security officer with a gruff Southern drawl overseeing the film set behind from his makeshift command post of a folding chair.

He was gazing into the distance when I introduced myself and knelt in the gravel next to him. Just as I had been doing all morning, I asked him if he had been there at the bombing two decades ago. I couldn't see Major's eyes behind his sunglasses, but there was a brief pause before he replied. Yes, he told me. I was there.

Would he be willing to be interviewed about it? Sure, he said.

I pulled out my notebook and started writing.

Reliving the Past

Out of everyone in Centennial Park I talked to that morning, only five people clearly remembered the bombing, and only Major correctly remembered the subsequent events and Richard Jewell's story.

Major can clearly recall the portrayal of Jewell at the time. "Everybody was convinced that's who [the bomber] was," he said. "That's what they kept coming on the news and saying. It was pretty much projecting it to everybody."

Unsurprisingly, people still misremember the details of what happened to this day, especially regarding Jewell; this is often attributed to the media's portrayal of Jewell. "When a lot of people are paying attention to the news, you think you're looking at facts," Major said.

As a result, the media storm Jewell faced has had far-reaching consequences.

Ron Martz should know; after all, he's one of two reporters that wrote the original article in the *Atlanta Journal-Constitution* revealing the FBI considered Jewell a suspect.

According to Martz, who has since retired from journalism and works as a ghostwriter, co-writer Kathy Scruggs obtained a tip from a law enforcement source that Jewell was under investigation, but the newspaper deliberated over whether to publish the story. "The consensus was that we needed to get a lot more than what we had," Martz said. "Kathy basically had one source, to my knowledge, at that point."

The staff at the *Atlanta Journal-Constitution* spent a day corroborating their source, according to Martz. As part of their efforts, the two reporters reached out to interview Jewell, but he did not return their calls.

After finishing their draft, Martz attempted to verify the information through an FBI source. "I called my source at the FBI, and read the story to him over the telephone," he said. "I said, 'Are we going to hinder the investigation in any way if we publish the story?', and he said, 'Everybody knows about it already. It's going to get out sooner or later.' So we decided to go ahead with it that afternoon."

To Martz, the FBI confirmation drove the decision to publish. "My boss at the time came to me and said, 'Call the FBI. If they'll verify this we'll go with the story,'" he said.

I asked Martz if he would have published if the FBI did not verify the story. "No, we would not have," he told me.

Twenty-three years after the bombing, Martz still argues there was nothing factually wrong with his story. "I continue to insist that we had the story correct," he said. "The implication initially was that Kathy and I made this whole thing about Jewell up, when in fact we had law enforcement sources from at least two different law enforcement agencies."

The article had long-lasting ramifications: after Jewell was declared innocent, Lin Wood, Jewell's lawyer, personally attacked Kathy Scruggs in the resulting libel lawsuits. "Wood tried anything he could do to drag her down," Martz said. "This whole story had a severe health impact on her."

Scruggs's colleagues watched her slip deeper into poor health and reckless behavior. On Sept. 2, 2001, Scruggs was found dead from a drug overdose.

Joie Chen, who worked as an anchor at CNN during the 1996 Olympics, broke the news of the bombing on air. Chen echoed Martz's argument that the press coverage was a logical decision at the time. "I don't think that the press was unfair to Jewell," she said. "I think the press was doing its job the best way it knew how to at the time given the circumstances and given our understanding of the relationship with investigators. I think that reporters at the time really were doing their best to get the story right."

Despite this, Martz knows there were still problems in the way he reported the story. According to Martz, the main issue lay in what he called "voice-of-god" style: *Atlanta Journal-Constitution* management did not allow citing anonymous sources and instead instructed reporters to state everything authoritatively. "If we had been allowed to add five words to that first paragraph—'according to law enforcement sources'—none of this would have hit us as hard as it did," Martz said.

At the time, Martz did not have the foresight to insist upon including the five words, but he has since realized what he could have done.

Martz said he was aware of the consequences Jewell would suffer. "I said [at the time] this guy's life is never going to be the same," he said. "And I knew that there was going to be an undue amount of attention on him from the media."

Members of Jewell's immediate family did not respond to requests for comment.

Assigning Responsibility

Both Chen and Martz reflected on the broader view of the events, citing multiple factors that led to Jewell's trial by media. "It was a perfect storm of circumstances that allowed the story to snowball so quickly," Chen said.

It was easy for the public to target Jewell. He was overweight. He lived with his mother. He was, as Martz called him, a "Southern redneck, the kind of guy that people are willing to look at and say, 'Here's a guy that's a real loser.'"

So which party—the press, the police, or even the public—should bear responsibility for Richard Jewell's vilification?

Chen's answer was exactly what I had expected. "Either nobody was guilty, or everybody played a role," she said.

Martz was reluctant to cast blame on a single party.

"It was a combination of the FBI's overeagerness to find a suspect and the media's overeagerness to portray Jewell as, you know—"

Here Martz stopped, refraining from saying the words he had said earlier. According to Martz, that's just the way things happened.

What Has Changed?

Jon Shirek, a local Atlanta news anchor at the time of the bombing, said that situations like Jewell's have only become more commonplace; indeed, similar events have occurred in the Boston Marathon bombing and the Navy Yard shooting. "With social media, everybody is a journalist," he said. "Not everybody is as careful as maybe journalists hope that they are in conveying that information. We have situations where people's lives are impacted in the way that Richard Jewell's was."

Chen agreed, warning journalists to take heed in the future. "I think that it's a caution to all of us," Chen said. "We owe it to the people we cover and the stories that we cover to be more skeptical, to be more careful and to ask harder questions."

Martz took a more pessimistic view; pressure from social media forces journalists to move quickly, sometimes at the cost of fact-checking. "I don't think [journalism] has changed," Martz said. "I think it may—to a certain extent—have gotten worse."

Shirek thinks journalists can learn from Richard Jewell. "This is a textbook case of how one man's life was impacted, even ruined, by this perfect storm," he said.

Rewriting the Narrative

When I visited the film set of Clint Eastwood's *Richard Jewell* in August, the tents were silent and the replica concert stage was empty; filming was due to begin that night. But even while standing vacant, the set has understandably drawn visitors and their questions. While sitting outside, Major told me about how he has to educate curious passersby on who exactly Richard Jewell was.

To Major, the most tragic aspect of Richard Jewell wasn't his public downfall, but the oft-overlooked fact that Jewell was a hero. "Half the people don't even know who [Richard Jewell] is when they ask me coming through here," he said. "He has nothing here. He's got no plaque. There would have been 50 or more people [killed] had it not been for Richard Jewell. Nobody even knows that." ∎

The Morning

NOVEL WRITING

SERENE ALMEHMI, Grade 10. Vestavia Hills High School, Vestavia, AL.
Ben Davis, *Educator*; Wiregrass Writing Project, *Affiliate*; Gold Medal

Chapter One: In the Middle of Things

My parents were sitting in the kitchen, right by the window. They were perched on the kitchen table. This was back when it was new. My mother had her hands on her temples and she looked all stressed and it was because I made her all stressed. My dad was talking all hushed and I know that cause his lips barely moved. I bet he was hissing his words. I'm always hissing my words because you can pass down hostility to your kids just like you can pass down your blue eyes.

My dad stacked up bricks in our garage. I guess they thought nothing of me going outside. I thought nothing of it either. They'd yelled at me till my ears rang. I needed a walk. I said, "I'm just gonna go get some fresh air." Fresh air does me no good and brings me no calm because I stared at the bricks and then grabbed one and then I hurled it right through the windshield of my father's red car. I hurled it like I hurled baseballs when I played pitcher in the second grade.

It made a big, awful sound. It was so loud it cut right into the noise of outside, silenced the crickets and froze the birds. Glass, in horrible little triangles, ones that would take forever to clean, crashed onto the ground and poured into the car. All the shards just sat there on the driveway, glimmering blue in the light. I just looked at them.

And then my dumbass screamed like I wasn't the one who threw the brick. I looked at the kitchen window, saw my mom standing with her eyes wide enough to pop out of their sockets. I was just thinking, *I am going to get killed. I am really going to get killed.* My dad came bolting out the garage door and I knew it was going to happen because he's never been a man to ponder things. Neither have I. I grabbed a brick and before I even really realized I picked up a brick, my windshield of my dad's red car fell into shards. That's how level-headed I am. That's how well I think things through.

He came out storming, with his tie blowing behind him, looking too angry to fit his malice in a button-down shirt. I looked at him and then I looked at the pieces of glass on the driveway and they started to look sort of blue in the light. Caroline was in the kitchen now, with her hand over her mouth. I bet she was praying for me.

"Baxter!" He was standing right in front of me now.

I wanted to laugh. I clenched my jaw so I couldn't. I clenched my fist, didn't even think to. It does it by instinct, completely on its own.

"Why do you do shit like this? When are you going to understand things have consequences?" He shoved me, pushing my shoulder. "Why isn't that clicking, Baxter? Why isn't that clicking?" He shoved me again. He dragged me by my arm, through the garage, past his neat pile of bricks, into the kitchen. Caroline was standing at the edge of the table, opening her mouth to speak.

He pushed me again and my body rammed into the counter, stomach first.

"Dad," Caroline began.

My father just kept on screaming, but I wasn't listening.

He shoved me forward, let me jolt my forehead right into the wood, probably reveled in the thud. He yanked me by my shirt, pulled me back, then pushed me forward. The back of my head just kept on slamming into the cabinet, and I prayed not to hit the knob. It felt like my brain was rocking inside my skull, like I could hear it swish.

"Paul." My mom choked out her words, kind of whiny. He pushed me harder. He grabbed my wrists, began twisting them, holding on so tight I would have fingerprint bruises. I knew how bruises bloomed. I would turn black then blue then gray then green. I'd feel like a mood ring.

"Paul, stop it!" She sounded almost intimidating, nearly there. He kept on slamming my head. He grabbed fistfuls of my shirts and shook me, the way they tell you not to shake a baby. My head throbbed.

He paused. He took a moment to look at me. He just looked at me. My father looks just like me. My father has my same eyes and it's not the color or anything. He has beady, angry eyes. Eyes are the window to the soul and all that. We had angry eyes.

He pulled his fist back and shot it right at my cheek. My mother began to cry, and she put her hand over her mouth to muffle herself. That made a bigger show of it. My mother cried rivers then, I remember. And there's no sound I hated more than my mother's cry. My father heard it and began to back away.

My mother went to the guest room or something. My father left, drove my mother's car somewhere. They disappeared so fast. I didn't care. Caroline lingered and stared at my face. Her eyes welled up, big and babyish. She had eyes that were meant to sympathize. She looked most like my mother when she cried. I sat down at the kitchen table and she just studied me.

"I hope it doesn't bruise." She spoke gently like a mother.

"It won't." She wiped her face.

"Quit." I whined.

"I can't." People talk about a maternal instinct and whatever. Caroline had it. Caroline could make you really believe in it. She was born motherly, born to cradle baby dolls and little boys when they cried. She cradled my mom sometimes when she cried. Caroline tears up fast. She tears up when she's happy too, and that's something you do when you're old. Caroline just felt old.

"No one's gonna tell me sorry or anything?" I smiled a toothy smile.

"You broke a windshield, Baxter." She scoffed that.

"I got hit right in my face."

"It's part your fault."

"I know. I know."

I dragged myself up the stairs and into my room, rested with an Incredibles ice pack sitting right on my cheek. I hated my father and I would change my mind within an hour but I hated him so much in that moment. I heard his voice every morning, every night. I heard his voice in mine. I saw him in me. I saw him in mirrors because I mirrored him. And if there was a single thing I could change about me, it would be that I am more like him than anyone in the world. Thinking of it made my hands shake. I wanted to shatter everything.

The sound of my phone ringing interrupted me. I was sitting, fists clenched, staring so hard at my ceiling I could put a hole in it. But I didn't. My phone chimed and it broke my stare. I let it ring. The ice was starting to melt on my face. It rang again. And I knew it was going to ring a third time so I snatched it off my bedside table. It was Will.

"Me and Mohammad are coming over." He opened with that, without a hello or a how are you or anything.

"You can't."

"Well I told Mohammad we are."

"I'm in trouble with my parents."

"Oh," He paused. "You need out then."

"I'm betting I'm not allowed out."

"We'll sneak you out tonight then, Bax. It's Saturday. Don't be in on a Saturday."

"You've got to come late. I'll be grounded. I'll be grounded till I die." I didn't even feel like I was exaggerating.

"What'd you do?"

"I threw a brick at my dad's windshield. Right through it."

"Oh my God," I could hear Mohammad yell in the background, his voice a little muffled. Will laughed a little, then stopped all of a sudden.

"We'll see you around one, Bax. I'll be driving the truck." Will only had his permit, but he didn't care. Will didn't care about most things.

My mother burst through my door maybe an hour later. She made her voice stern. She was trying to scare me, so I pretended to be scared. I sat up straight in my bed. She stood as tall as Caroline, barely 5′2″. I already towered almost a foot over them. She was not intimidating. She was meager and frail-boned. And she crippled so easily, fell into tears so fast. But I listened to her. I thought I owed her that.

"You're grounded for two weeks. No going out." My eyes didn't even widen. I expected that. "And you're paying for half of the windshield." She did not break eye contact with me. She put out her hand. "Give me your phone." I nearly gasped.

"Please, Mama, I just want my phone. I'll be good. I'll do everything else."

"No. Give me your phone." I handed it to her.

She shut the door and I threw a water bottle at it as soon as it closed.

I texted Will off of Caroline's phone. I peered out the window and he sat smiling wide with straight white teeth because we all boasted braces for a good two years during middle school. He liked to hang his head out of the window of his silver Toyota Tacoma that wasn't his at all. People always mistook us for brothers because we had the same blue eyes and not-really-blonde, sitting-right-on-the-line-of-brown hair, and he was only an inch taller than me. I called him fast, and Caroline sat pouting on her bed because she was sick and tired of me using her phone.

"Will, I can't go downstairs."

"Just be quiet about it. Tiptoe."

"I might climb out of the window."

"On the second floor?" He huffed. "Gonna crack your head like that windshield."

I tried to keep quiet going down the stairs, but they squeaked. I'm heavy-footed. Caroline snuck out often and she walked gently, swiftly. Caroline walked like she had secrets. I kept thinking, *God, God, please, God, leave them sleeping. Leave them sleeping till I get back.* I slipped out of the front door and flinched when I shut it. I scrunched up my whole face, waiting for my father to come screaming down the stairs, flailing his arms all around, and threatening me. He didn't.

I threw the truck door open and jumped in.

"Hey, Bax." Mohammad and Will sang like a choir. I nodded and grinned my big, stupid grin.

"Fucking idiot." Will muttered and I just laughed, letting my shoulders fall for the first time in hours. I was dumb. God, I was really dumb.

We rode to a gas station that was barely a mile away. Will liked the feeling of stealing his father's truck. He liked being all nervous when he pulled out of the garage and he liked feeling all proud when he sat the keys safe on the counter. That's why Will did half the things he did: for no good reason.

It was that weird time in the middle of the night. It was Sunday, but it didn't feel like Saturday had ended yet. The roads were empty, most houses dim, and everything felt all hushed. We went to a gas station, the only place open. I just bought a slushie, shoved a pack of gummies in my hoodie because I didn't have the money to pay. Mohammad shook his head at me when I did. He got these stupid energy drinks that tasted awful but he drank them like spring water.

"You wanna go up on the parking garage? Like middle school." Will asked in the truck. I loved that parking garage, the one by Dawson Church. It was always kept unlocked. All through the 7th grade, we sat on the very top and ate. Once, Will hung off the edge, and somebody below had called the police. That was the most exciting day of my 13-year-old life, and I had to force my jaw to clamp so I couldn't smile when the policeman scolded us. But Will just wore his big, sugary smile, didn't bother to hide it. That was the first drug a kid ever tried, before everything. Will was giddy off defiance. Hanging off of buildings and stealing trucks and breaking windshields, that's all one in the same. And Will and I were so often mistook for brothers. Will and I, we were one in the same.

We had to walk up this spiraling staircase to get up to the top. It was eerie, made of all concrete, and once you escaped the stairs, you were let out to the top and it felt like real freedom. It was a good place to bring girls, and they'd always say something about the view even though all they were seeing was a Baptist church and a few restaurants and a neighborhood behind that. It was where I had my first kiss.

"Yeah," Mohammad nodded with a smile. His eyes flickered with nostalgia. "I haven't been in forever."

We hopped out of his truck, passed the metal gates of the entrance. Will began running up the stairs, spinning round and round till he reached the top. Mohammad and I started after him. It felt like diving into a pool once I reached the top. The air was cold and quiet. I set my slushie down and ran to the edge to look out at all that was below even though I couldn't see much in the dead of the night, just the gas station under streetlights. I beamed looking at it. I heard tennis shoes pattering behind me, and Will laughing. I felt his hand creep on the back of neck and he pushed me forward so that my whole upper body hung off of the garage. I stared five stories down into darkness that led into bushes. I grabbed onto the wall and the breath was snatched out of my lungs.

"You scared, Bax?" Will giggled. He had fun with all these things and I thought about how quickly his fun would cripple if I toppled down the side of the building and slammed onto the sidewalk. My heart raced, speeding all the way up to my throat. He paused and then pushed me a little bit harder, hand only on the back of my neck.

"Will, Will. Will!" I yelled it and it felt like an eruption. I was so panicked. He took fast steps backwards and I sprung up and ran away from the edge.

"I was just playing. I'm sorry. I'm sorry." He put his arms up, palms forward.

"Are you okay?" Mohammad yelled. I staggered towards my slushie and brought the straw to my mouth.

"Yeah, I'm good."

I saw death down in the bushes but that was only for half a second. I didn't want to sit against the brick edge after that. Mohammad started talking about car shopping like nothing was ever wrong. It all became fine in five minutes. I opened my gummies. Will bought too many Little Debbie Snow Cakes, enough that we could share. In the midst of calm conversation, Mohammad squinted at my face, and said, "Is that a bruise?"

My father hit me hard, enough for me to turn dark purple within a few hours. Skin on the face is delicate, especially right on bone. It still hurt to touch, and I knew it was going to be bad and big, so deep in color that Caroline's thickest concealer couldn't cover it.

"I got hit playing baseball," I said.

Mohammad shined his phone flashlight on my face.

"It's not baseball season."

"I was just practicing."

Mohammad shifted uncomfortably, planning his words. Mohammad always planned his words. He was better friends with Will than me, served as his reason. Maybe I needed somebody to be my reason.

"If something's wrong, you can say, you know." He said it gently because Mohammad knew to be careful with me. Heat crept up my face. I bet it got red. I bet it got so red it drowned out the bruise.

"What do you mean if something's wrong?"

"If someone hit you,"

"No one's hit me."

"Like your dad," he continued.

"My dad isn't doing anything."

"Alright." He nearly stopped.

"Don't say shit about my dad."

"You say shit about your dad, Bax." He wasn't wrong. "Always say you hate him."

"Everybody says that."

"Not like you." He leaned forward to look at me. "You've always got bruises and I'm not going to say anything to anybody. You can tell the truth though.

I'm not sayin' it to pry. You broke a windshield and then you come around with a bruise. You could just say—" I shoved his shoulders so that his chest flew back, head almost hitting the concrete. My voice grew mean and ugly. I stood.

"Shut up," I spat at him.

"I'm sorry."

"Shut up." I screamed. He put more space between us. Will winced. My own friends winced when I was angry, flinched when I lifted my arm. "Stop saying I'm lying. If I said it, it's true. Were you accusing me?" I was roaring at him. He jumped to his feet.

"I wasn't accusing anybody."

"You were accusing my dad."

"I was just asking."

"Don't ask!"

"You know what, I think I'm right, Bax. I think I'm right." I swayed him. He was so patient, always, and I made him a little angry. I walked towards him and he stumbled back.

"You're fucking insane," he mumbled.

"What? What'd you say?" My hands became fists like they so often did.

"I said you're fucking insane."

I swung. I swung right into his cheek, right where my father hit me. ∎

Slip Knot

NOVEL WRITING

ADDISON WRIGHT, Grade 8. Walter Reed Middle School, North Hollywood, CA.
Michele Szymanski, *Educator*; Region-at-Large, *Affiliate*; Gold Medal

I woke up the next morning at 7:00. Joey and Ben had just awakened too. I stood up, feeling a bit strange, and walked into the bathroom.

Joey screamed.

What a nice way to start the morning. I ran back into the bedroom to see Joey standing by my bed—petrified—staring down at the sheets. There, right smack dab in the center of my fucking white sheets, was a huge-ass puddle of period blood. *Shit.* I looked down and sure enough, all over my underwear was red.

"You *bleeded*!" Joey shrieked, looking completely mortified. I grabbed a pair of clean underwear and peeled off my sheets. Ben was attempting to explain to Joey that I wasn't dying.

It's a somewhat unspoken rule in the house that when I'm on my period, nobody can bug me. If I start crying, it's probably mood swings, and NO ONE TELL JOEY OR HE WILL FREAK OUT. Sometimes, however, my body doesn't follow the unspoken rules.

I frantically threw the sheets in the washing machine and changed my underwear, throwing the bloody ones in the trash and a pad in the new ones.

Well the first morning of the first day of school was already not going as planned. I ran back into the bedroom where Ben had pulled on a pair of navy shorts and had his arms wrapped around Joey's torso/upper arms. Joey was still freaking out.

I grabbed a skirt that was a bit too short and a polo, hooking my bra and pulling a Rudson sweatshirt on and brushing my hair.

"Joey, she's not dying, see?" He nodded towards me and Joey looked over. He squatted down and escaped Ben's grasp, running over to me and squeezing my waist.

"Joey, I'm fine!" I said, almost out of breath.

"Oh good, oh good, oh goooood!" he squeezed tighter, practically crushing my ribs and lungs.

"Joey, I—have to go—" I pulled away from his embrace and grabbed a pair of socks and put them on as I ran downstairs.

Dad had put some toast in the toaster for Ben and me. I popped a slice out and grabbed an apple. I could finally sit down and relax. I had a feeling that

I wasn't looking too great, so I was planning on going back upstairs to put on mascara and fix my hair.

The toast was dry and the apple tasted weird. I walked back upstairs and Joey was bouncing up and down on the bed.

"Joey, get down please." Ben left the room and walked downstairs to eat the other piece of toast.

Joey hopped down and sat on the floor, "When do you leave?" His legs were in butterfly position and he was bouncing his legs up and down. I checked the watch that was on my nightstand and strapped it to my wrist.

"Ummm about 15 minutes." It was 7:20 now. Just enough time to fix my hair. I walked into the bathroom. Joey followed.

In the bathroom, I opened a drawer in the vanity, and pulled out my mascara in a black bottle. I rolled it over my eyelashes and it made them sticky and long.

"What's that?" He asked, sitting down on the closed toilet seat lid.

"Mascara." I rolled on one more layer.

"Macara?"

"Ma*scara*," I corrected him.

"That's what I said," he mumbled to himself.

I brushed my hair and Joey fiddled with his hands. I wasted 10 minutes concerning myself with my appearance when no one really gave a shit. My phone rang. Joey grabbed it and ran down the hallway and I chased after him. He ran into the bedroom but I grabbed my phone before he could. It was a number I didn't know, but considering that it was 7:30 and the first day of school, I figured I should open it.

"Hello?" Joey began acting spazzy and jumping up and down and poking me.

"Hey, is this Harper?" I heard Leo's voice ask.

"Oh, Leo," I smiled. Joey was getting impatient. I grabbed his skinny wrists in a fist and held them there.

"You're coming to school, right?" He sounded nervous, and I could hear the people at school behind him.

"Sadly," I chuckled.

*"Harper Harper Harper Harper—"*Joey was repeating my name over and over again, trying to get my attention. I let go of his wrists and covered the microphone.

"What do you want!" I shot at him.

"Who is that?" he responded urgently.

"My friend." I turned back to the phone.

"Sorry about that." I tried to shrug it off.

"Who was that?" he asked. I inhaled sharply.

"My brother," I said quietly.

"Oh, ok. What's your schedule?" he asked. I pulled up my schedule and screenshotted it. I then texted him the picture. It was quiet as he read it over.

"Oh cool, we have 2, 3, 5, and 6 together." Leo sounded very happy about this.

"Yay, now I won't be alone." Joey was still poking at me but I was trying to ignore him.

"Yaaay. Well I gotta go. See ya soon!" He hung up before I could say bye.

"Joey!" I glared at him; he had a face of someone who didn't do anything wrong. Ben came back up, combed his fingers through his hair, and looked at us.

"What's up?"

"Joey was being an as—annoying while I was on the phone," I said simply.

"Oh, Joey?" Ben crossed his arms across his chest and looked over at Joey.

"I didn't do nothin'!" He flapped his arms and they landed at his sides.

"Just be careful, 'kay?" Ben uncrossed his arms and pulled on pair of socks. Joey nodded.

I put all of my notebooks into my blue backpack that I've had forever and tossed in my earbuds, my phone, some pads, and a pack of gum. My bag was surprisingly light. I walked downstairs and Joey followed. Ben was putting things in his black backpack. Ben's colorblind (deuteranopia) and his wardrobe doesn't consist of a lot of vibrant colors. Mainly grays and blacks and navy blues.

I slipped on my checkered Vans and stood by the door. Dad and Ben came down, too. Dad ruffled Joey's hair and tried to do the same to me but I ducked out of the way. Joey laughed.

"Ready for school?" Dad asked, slipping on a pair of sneakers.

"You driving us?" Ben asked, countering his question.

"Sure, why not?" Dad chuckled. Ben and I gave each other a knowing look.

"We can walk," I checked my watch; it was 7:38 now. We were going to be late if we walked but we'd make a scene if we drove. Correction; Joey would make a scene if we drove.

"It's fine, I'll drive you guys," Dad grabbed his keys and opened the door, "Joey put on your shoes." Joey giggled excitedly and shoved his feet into his Natives. We all walked outside and Ben sat in front while I sat in back with Joey. Dad drove us the 6 blocks it took to get to go school. We could have walked. We would've been hella late but at least we wouldn't be taking Joey with us.

I quickly got out of the car and made my way to the entrance of the school.

"BYEEEEEEEEE!" Joey stuck his head out of the window and waved like a maniac.

"Joey, knock it off!" Ben yelled, walking into school a bit behind me.

"B—" Dad pulled Joey by the arm back into the car and rolled up the window.

I felt like people were watching me intently, but the majority of high school people didn't know my delayed brother. I tugged at my skirt and walked into the school. It smelled just the same as usual; like sweat, old books and clothes, mold, and weed. Down the hall, I walked to my first period class. AP Bio. Not my favorite but I'd live. First day is usually just teachers telling you how much shit you're gonna have to deal with and what you need to bring the next day. I slipped into class and found a seat. Most of the kids in my class were in my class last year. The teacher was an old-looking lady with a big nose and glasses.

The bell rang. I sighed, and pulled out a notebook.

"Students!" This lady had an annoying-ass voice that I didn't know whether or not I could tolerate. "I am Ms. Roderico, your AP Bio teacher this year." She spoke with a tone that was so dull, yet had so much volume to it. She grabbed a clipboard and began to read off names.

"Nikki Biloti? Reagan Cunzair? Conner Evans? Benji Goldberg? Alice Green?" She went through the roll, and when she got to my name I said "present" quietly. The entire class was a big lecture. She talked limitedly about science and mainly about what we'd be doing and what her expectations were. The bell rang, I shoved my unused notebook into my backpack and walked down the hall and up the stairs to my history class. I sat down in the back again, there was an open table next to me that I hoped Leo could sit in, if he ever came. He darted into the room just before the bell rang. The teacher was sitting on her desk, using her phone.

"I'd hope this doesn't become a regular thing," she said to him without looking up.

"Oh, sorry. I have a boot and stairs are kind of hard to get up." Leo rubbed the back of his neck and smiled at me. He took the seat next to me and I smiled back.

Alice, Jackie, and Betty sat on the other side of me. Technically, Jackie sat next to me, Alice sat in front of me, and Betty sat in front of Jackie. Alice hates my guts and Joey's guts and I hate hers too. Jackie and Betty are nice, but fall victim to Alice's manipulation a lot of the time. I looked around and noticed that Evan sat right up at the front, to the far left. Angel Mae sat behind him and he had his hand reached back and was rubbing her thigh. I also noticed that some of the nice theater kids sat scattered around the classroom.

"My name is Ms. Bobrosky, I will be your U.S. History teacher this year." She sounded so serious. "Pass these out please," she handed Evan a stack of purple papers.

"Aight." He stood up and began dropping them on people's desks. When he came around back, he skipped over me.

"This is the class syllabus. I will need this signed by a parent or guardian and turned in by tomorrow," she held up the paper like she was a model on those old game shows. I raised my hand. "Yes?" She looked over at me.

"I didn't get one."

She held out the one she was holding before and I walked up to the front to grab it and sat back down. She talked to the whole class about expectations and whatnot. Just like the last class. And quite frankly, the rest of the classes that day. By 6th period, PE, I was sick and tired of "Welcome to your class, I'm Mr./Mrs. blah blah and yada yada yada." In PE, our teacher had us walk a lap, so we knew where to run. Leo had a pass for PE but still had to walk the lap.

"So, how's your first day going so far?" He asked.

"Eh. I've gotten tired of listening to lectures." I laughed.

"Saaame!" We both laughed for a bit.

We talked about life, he tried to get into family life, but I avoided more personal answers like, how's your life with siblings? You have two brothers? That must suck. Stuff like that. I don't need him knowing that Joey's my brother. The bell rang at 3:00, and Leo and I walked to our lockers to put stuff away, and down out of school together. We talked most of the way, but parted ways about two blocks from my house.

"Bye!" I waved as he walked up to his house.

"See ya, Harp!"

* * *

Dad was just leaving as I came up to the house. Joey sat on the porch steps and opened and closed his legs.

"Where are you going?" I asked, walking up to Joey and placing my hand on his head. He grabbed my wrist with two hands and squeezed.

"I'm needed at Mr. and Mrs. Ramos's house. They need help with moving something . . . I'm not sure, they didn't specify." Dad stuck his hand out of the window and was holding a list, "I forgot to get this before school, can you and Joey head down to the grocery store and pick this stuff up?"

"Sure," I said, trying not to sound annoyed. "C'mon Joe." I decided I might as well just take my backpack, and shoved the list into my sweatshirt pocket.

He stood up, "Where we goin'?"

"Moon Mart." I grabbed his hand and we walked back down the street. In front of Moon Mart, there was an old homeless man. He stood out there every once in a while with this raggedy old cello. He couldn't play it very well, but it made him a couple dollars a day.

Joey and I had to pass him to get into the store.

"Why's that man so *diiiirty?*" Joey pointed to him and stared.

"Joey!" I grabbed his hand and held it down.

"Whaaaat?"

"Don't say that!" I said sternly, then turned to the man, "I'm so sorry." I fished through my pocket and tossed a quarter into his open cello case. He continued to play, not acknowledging my brother or me. He just played his crappy cello.

The air from a vent above the automatic door blew on my face. The smell of fish and flowers. Joey giggled and clapped his hands loudly when the door slid open and closed. I grabbed a basket and scanned the aisles for what we needed. I stopped in the cereal aisle, next to that was chips, which we needed too.

"Hey, Joey?" He turned to look at me, shaking his head to one side to get his bangs out of his eyes. "Pick out two (I held up two fingers) cereals that you want ok? And don't go *anywhere*. I'll be right over there." I pointed to the next aisle.

"Any cereal?"

"Two! Just two. I'll be back in a sec." I walked down the aisle and across to the other. I grabbed two bags of Lays and one bag of veggie chips. I held another bag of Lays, contemplating whether or not we needed another bag, when I heard someone scream from the other aisle.

I ran across to see Joey plugging his ear with one hand and holding onto some woman's wrist with the other.

"Get away from me you fucking creep!" The woman smacked his skinny arm. He pulled it back.

"Ow!" Joey rubbed his arm.

"What the fuck is happening?" I asked her, knowing that Joey wouldn't answer my question.

"This motherfucking psychopath grabbed my fucking hand like a fucking pervert or some shit!" She said "fucking" way too many times.

"Look, I'm so sorry about my brother. He didn't mean anything, he's just—" I stopped. He's just what? Playing? Pretending? Delayed? That's what he is and I wasn't about to admit it. "He didn't mean any harm." I said to her. Joey was biting his nails on one hand and the other wrist is in my closed fist.

"Right." She said sarcastically.

"He's—he's special." I whispered to her. She looked at me, then over my shoulder at Joey who was pulling on my arm and leaning forward, head and body turned away from us, looking down the aisle.

"Oh man, oh—oh shit—fuck—I'm so sorry I—I didn't mean any of that—I—I—" She stammered and went red.

"You didn't know." I didn't say "oh it's ok" or "it's not your fault" because it's not ok. People usually never say what they really mean, except if they're mad or drunk. She meant every fucking word of what she said, before she knew how other people would perceive it. People's thoughts generally are diluted by other people's opinions. They say and do whatever the fuck they want until people begin to disagree with them or get upset. I pulled Joey past her and he waved. Completely unaware of what he'd done.

"Do we need any adovocados?" Joey asked as we walked past the avocado stand.

"No . . . we don't need any avocados," I responded dryly.

In line, Joey wanted to look at the cakes by the chicken and pasta, but I refused to let him go anywhere. I paid with a $50 bill and got a quarter for change.

"Have a nice day!" The man at the cash register said too cheerily.

"You too," I replied and pulled Joey out of the store. He didn't laugh when the automatic door shut. We walked quietly. Joey didn't say anything and nor did I for a while.

"Why'd you grab the lady's wrist?" I asked, carrying the brown grocery bag. He didn't respond for a bit. "I thought she was you," he said quietly. The lady wasn't wearing anything remotely close to what I was, and her hair was a much lighter shade of brown than mine.

"Joey, I told you I was going to the other aisle and to wait there for me." I adjusted my grip on the bag when the paper handles began digging into my palms.

"Ohhh," Joey realized that I had indeed told him that I was in the other aisle. "Sorry."

"It wasn't your fault." Joey is the one exception to that line. It never really *is* his fault, he can't control his brain. ∎

Big Brown Boys Cry Too

PERSONAL ESSAY & MEMOIR

TOREY BOVIE, Grade 12. New Orleans Center for Creative Arts, New Orleans, LA.
Anya Groner, *Educator*; Greater New Orleans Writing Project, *Affiliate*; Silver Medal

Fighting, in my family, is like an ancient art form. We are taught to fight before we are taught to read, speak, clean, tie our shoes, or love. As a child, play fighting with my father was something that I was supposed to enjoy, something to take pride in, something I could look back on and smile. One weekday afternoon, all his friends who weren't really his friends sat around and watched us fight around our townhouse living room. They were not my father's friends because they didn't stick around long, whether it be because of arguments or things I was too young to understand. I aggressively threw my soft eight-year-old fist, and he gently threw his hard grown man fist. I started to feel a sadness that I knew my father would never feel. He smiled as he was presenting me to all the big men with tattoos and brown skin. My father needed a tough enough son to continue this fight that is in some ways hereditary for young black boys. Little black boys are taught by their fathers to conform to an image of toughness and masculinity. Black boys are told to shun emotional hindrances that will make them anything else than a man. If we do this to our black boys, then they will do it to theirs. We are preparing a role for young black men assigned to them before birth.

As we fought, I knew each soft punch he threw meant "You're mine so I'm going to teach you to absorb my roughness. Then, you can teach your little black boy to absorb your roughness." I know now that the sadness I felt wasn't meant to be sadness. It was supposed to mold me to take the place of my father's toughness. I couldn't take any more of this sadness that wasn't supposed to be sadness, so I let tears run down the side of my face. My small body wanted to beat my father into the carpet. I wanted him to stop loving me with his fists. I wanted my father to stop allowing me to show him that I wasn't as strong as he was.

"You really cryin' bruh?" he asked. He told me to go to my mom's room. My father's friends watched me get up and shuffle away in shame.

From as young as I could remember, I was taught that I was never supposed to cry. Big black boys like me were never given the space for tears. Being "weak" was always met with public humiliation, physical beatings, self-doubt, and ridicule. I had never heard of black people in my family speak of the black men or boys as if they could be vulnerable or had the ability to be in touch with this vulnerability. Allowing your softness to show was always a call for punishment or shame. My family knows much about this shame, shame that comes along with being honest, or sad, or struggling with the issues that we are supposed to pretend don't exist. I am now seventeen years old. I am forcing myself to remember and confront the past because of two authors: Toni Morrison and Kiese Laymon. I am a creative writing student, which has been an outlet for me to be less afraid of the past and my emotions. I came to the realization that I don't want to look back on my life and say I made others happy. I want to know that I lived my life as freely, openly, and honestly as possible. Toni Morrison's stories are gruesome in a way that makes me face the harsh realities of life while learning to find joy in all the pain.

At the end of my sophomore year, I had to complete an independent study on an author of my choice. When I chose Morrison, it was simply because my teacher approached me about it and seemed more excited than I was. I also had no reason to advocate for another author, so just like that, I was tasked with reading at least six of Morrison's novels. I had only read one of her books before the independent study, *Sula*. I had first read *Sula* at the beginning of my sophomore year, then twice in my junior year. My experience with the book was heavily associated with a classroom setting and it altered the way I thought about it. When I started the independent study, it gave me a chance to read Morrison on my own without tainted thoughts.

The first book I read on my own by Morrison was *Song of Solomon*. *Song of Solomon* is the story of a character named Milkman. The novel details his life and his battle with being spiritually dead. With the help of his aunt and best friend, he embarks on a journey that will connect him to his past and teach him his self-worth. This book was the first stepping stone on a journey I am just now beginning. I'm learning to walk through adversity and not be afraid to let my emotions flow out as they come, whether that be through yelling, crying, or writing. While writing this essay I did all three.

My first time reading Kiese Laymon I loved the fact that he was black. I loved that I was able to look at this black man write about what it is to be a black man and how we are taught to be black men. I loved Laymon because I felt like my dad would hate him. There was a connection between me and Morrison's words, but it was hollow. Not hollow in the way that something was missing, but hollow in the way that something just simply was never there. If something was never there, then it can't be missing. I am a black man and Morrison is a black woman. I have too much respect for Morrison to pretend that I understand her completely. I aspired to build characters like Morrison. I wanted her sentences to flow from me like we were the same person. I admired her accolades, her audience's reactions, but I didn't know how our identities could connect. I don't know what it means to be a single black mother and to write on the side, but I connected with Laymon because of who we were simultaneously. Not saying that that makes Laymon any better than Morrison or vise versa. I'm saying that Laymon filled in a lot of the hollow spots between Morrison and I.

I remember reading *Beloved* one night while neglecting to do a science project. The pulse-quickening storyline of a mother who kills her daughter to save her from slavery made me want to stop breathing, not out of shock or surprise, but more so out of familiarity. Last time I checked my mother never tried to kill me in attempts to save me from slavery, but I knew the scenario all too well. A parent doing what they feel is best and ending up with not only a damaged child but a damaged self. The pressure that a parent holds to protect their kids can sometimes lead them to do crazy things.

Sethe, the woman who killed her child, had a relationship with a man named Paul D. When Paul D finally realized what Sethe had done, he shamed her. While reading the scene, I had an unintentional flashback to one rainy night in front of the Target on Clearview. Me, my mom, my sister, and my dog had traveled from Mandeville after an argument had by my grandmother and my mom.

"What's wrong," I asked, unsure if I was ready to hear the answer or that I would know what to do once I got the answer. The passing of my grandfather threw everyone in a million different places. On the day my mom and my grandmother were supposed to view the body, I knew something was bound to go wrong. There was some family that was coming into town that day because they had heard about my grandfather's death. This family never came around on any other occasion, but they took it upon themselves to drive to my grandmother's house in Mandeville. Once I told my grandmother that there were people at her house, she told me she most likely wouldn't be back until they left. She figured she would go view the body while she was on that side of the lake anyway. She neglected to tell my mother that she was going, which opened a whole can of worms.

"She went to go see him without me! She took the only opportunity I had to have time alone with him. That bitch knew what she was doing," my mom screams as tears run down her face in giant puddles. I rubbed her shoulder resentfully. I wasn't sure how to comfort someone when I was never taught how to comfort myself. While I wanted with all my being and heart for my mother to be okay, I wanted her to know I meant it. I didn't want to give her my default comforting mechanism.

"She took it away from me! I just wanted to see him in private!" My mother cried so much she couldn't breathe. I saw her choking on all the anger she had been forced to keep in her heart. I see now that parents try to raise their kids the best they can. My mom tried her best, but that doesn't mean she didn't make mistakes. That doesn't mean she didn't neglect to ask me about my mental state on several occasions. That doesn't mean that I didn't cry when grown black men and women weren't watching me because my mom or dad wouldn't understand what I was going through.

We are complex, we are vengeful, we laugh, we cry, and it's our right to do so. Reading Morrison, I realized that my mother had every right to cry her eyes out the way she did. She also had every right to tell my grandmother "I love you" a week later, which she did. I felt refreshed by Morrison's characters. They were able to curse and yell at each other, but also embrace each other. Her characters were never made out to be crazy for simply being complex.

I remember the first time I finished reading *Heavy*, a memoir by Kiese Laymon. I closed the book and I wanted to cry, but I didn't. I knew being angry would give me much more satisfaction than crying. I loved the book and I hated how much I loved it. The book was too real for it to not be a reflection of myself that I watched get clearer and clearer each chapter.

I didn't read *Heavy* as part of an assignment. I picked it up and read it through on my own. Knowing that I didn't have to share these experiences with my classmates gave me a connection to the book that I hadn't had in a long time. Laymon gave me terminology for all the weight we carry, whether good or bad. The addition of "black abundance" into my vocabulary made me feel big. I felt like my abundance was what made me angry, but a good angry. The type of angry that handles business. This angry black abundance had enough courage to talk to my mom about how I was feeling. I decided to talk to her one weekday night in my room. I wanted my mom to know that I wasn't as okay as I had made myself out to be.

"You can't let yourself get down about this stuff, Torey. Don't let the stuff you read get you upset," my mom said.

"I'm not lettin it get me upset, I'm just sayin reading this makes me see that there are things that I let sit on my mind and they never really go anywhere."

"Like what," she asked me.

"Like stuff you and my dad did that I never really made a big deal of."

"Like what?"

"Like when you constantly call me stupid or when my dad tells me that my stress and anxiety is the devil and I need to have more faith in God."

"I'm sorry," she says with a confused look. "I never knew me calling you stupid had such an effect on you. Now that I know, I won't say it."

I find it interesting when our family members try not to hurt us instead of not hurting us, but I can't blame my mom for what she has impulses to do. I won't blame her for not remembering that she said she would stop calling me stupid in 2010, then again in 2012. During the conversation, I kept thinking back to the sentences from *Heavy*, "I found more ways to fail and harm my kids than I ever imagined." Here, Laymon is talking about the students he taught. Laymon details everything that he has been through in the book, from childhood to adulthood, but yet he still finds a way to let his students down. To me, it makes him even more human.

Laymon talked about how a Vietnamese student of his told him about her parent's deportation. He asked her if she would like to write an essay about it and if she knew when they would be back. I find that we often don't go the extra mile to hurt family or the people we intend to care for, sometimes we just do. Me making my family guess about why I was so closed off probably wasn't the answer in a lot of cases, but it's what I wanted to do at that time. I won't be silent and wait for myself to stop feeling emotions that will be there regardless. It's dangerous not to have a voice.

In *Song of Solomon*, Morrison wrote, "Wanna fly, you got to give up the shit that weighs you down." I read that sentence and tried my best to pretend that she wasn't talking to me. Of course, I knew, logistically, that Morrison did not intentionally write that sentence in hopes that forty-one years later I would read it. I knew that Morrison herself, not just her words, was saying something to me. I was holding on to all the shit that was weighing me down, all the anger, all the times I cried violently to myself, all the times I felt like I wasn't equipped to handle life in general, all the times I thought my parents didn't like me. I pretended to let everything go once I went to the ninth grade, lost a couple of pounds, started making new friends, started getting more compliments, started getting validation on my writing from people who I didn't need validation from, and forgot what it was like to be depressed. As I read the scene where Milkman tells his father that he is going on the main journey of the book, my mind flew back to a memory.

I was in the third grade and I had just started playing football. I hated football. It made my dad happy but it was just a chore to me. One night, during practice, I went to go tackle number six before he could score a touchdown. I wrapped my arms around him and attempted to get his body to the ground. I gave up after he had dragged me about ten feet. I saw my dad get up from the stands and stomp aggressively over to me. We looked into each other's eyes for a good thirty seconds. We used to communicate that way: his eyes full of rage and mine begging for mercy. I watched my father gear up for a tackle. His broad shoulders grew broader and his feet sprinted towards me. I felt his shoulder enter my stomach. My body slammed to the ground. I laid there and waited for him to pick me up. I waited and waited and wondered if this was what being a black man was all about, letting all the softness ooze out of you while you lay on a football field, to leave behind a hard shell. Each breath was hard to capture because my wind was cut. Gasping for air, I asked, "Why did you do that?"

"Cause that's how you're supposed to tackle."

I hate talking to my dad about memories like these because he never "remembers" anything. I tell myself that my relationship with my dad is fine, but I'm still letting the past weigh me down. We haven't talked about those things that I wish I could forget. I can't remember the last car ride I took with either of my parents where I didn't have headphones on. I've gotten good at avoiding conversations that make me uncomfortable.

Reading *Heavy*, I started crying onto my book and I was scared. I was scared because I realized that all the heaviness wasn't just on Morrison or Laymon, it was on me too, and I had been suppressing it for years. Milkman leaving behind his home, his friends, and his parents in search of something bigger was what I wanted to do. Not to get away from anyone but to go towards something the way Milkman did. The journey was so important to Milkman because he was doing it; he was leaving and growing.

I don't know what's next and I don't have an answer key to life. This is not a twelve-step how-to guide; it's me doing myself a favor. I'm dumping all the shit that's weighing me down here on this essay in hopes that I can move more freely. I don't know if this will be a revolutionary process that changes my life forever, but I'm willing to try. ∎

Reign of Silence

PERSONAL ESSAY & MEMOIR

SARA CORNELIO, Grade 11. Carlisle High School, Carlisle, PA. Sarah Clayville, *Educator*; Commonwealth Charter Academy, *Affiliate*; Silver Medal

For as long as I can remember, I have always been quiet. *Calladita,* my family called it. "Shy" was what my preschool teachers would say. Whatever people called me, the general consensus was that I would grow out of it, that I would eventually shed my so-called shyness and emerge from the metaphorical chrysalis that was my silence. Or so they thought.

As I grew, so did my silence. It was comforting, in a way. My silence was something I could rely on. It was a blanket I could hide under when everything became too much. It was always there. However, I soon found that as comfortable as my silence felt, it was even more confining. The blanket I was so quick to wrap myself in became a shroud of clouds looming over my head. And as I got older, it took less and less for the clouds to pour. My mother called it shutting down. Whenever I became overwhelmed, which most often occurred in social settings, I retreated, distancing myself from the outside world. I became unreachable, withdrawing further and further within myself.

When I reached my limit, there was no getting through to me. Though I felt powerless when this happened, I now realize it gave me the upper hand. No matter how hard they tried, no one could get through to me. While I truly had no control over how or when I shut down, there was something so gratifying to watching them fail to reach me.

I rarely talked in school and could barely bring myself to make eye contact with anyone. I vividly remember Mrs. Payne, my second-grade teacher, saying sternly, "Sara, look at me," as I painfully brought up my gaze up to meet hers. In the moment I hated it. I felt vulnerable, exposed. There was an intensity to eye contact that was too much for me to bear; it was *too* personal, almost violating. Yet, as much as I detested Mrs. Payne for subjecting me to the torture that was making eye contact with her, I cannot thank her enough for it. Eye contact, as I would later discover, can be a powerful tool. Even more powerful than words.

Attending school, unfortunately, only became more difficult as I grew older. My desire to learn was often the only thing that kept me in school, and sometimes, even that was not enough. I soon began to dread school so much that I employed a tactic that would plague me for nearly all of elementary and middle school: avoidance. For the first time, I began to shut down at the mere thought of going to school.

In fourth grade, we focused a lot on essay writing, which unfortunately meant reading our essays aloud to the class. Though I liked writing, I could not bring myself to read what I had written to my peers. The first time I attempted to read my essay in front of the class, I clutched my paper with trembling hands, my eyes glued to the words upon the page.

"Go ahead, honey."

I took a shaky inhale and opened my mouth to read what I had written, but no sound came out. Picture a bottle of soda. You can see the bubbles threatening to burst out of the bottle, but the lid keeps the bubbles at bay. That's how my voice felt. Though it tried to bubble up and escape the confines of my body, my anxiety kept it sealed firmly within me. I was a prisoner of my own body.

"It's almost like she's mute," I remember my puzzled teacher saying to my mom. "I've had a mute student before, and it's very similar."

Looking back, she was actually on to something.

Middle school was by far the worst. I went to a language magnet school, and in seventh grade, I tested into the more rigorous language track at the insistence of one of my Spanish teachers. I was fluent in Spanish, so I welcomed the challenge of having half of my classes in the language. Little did I know that entering the program meant so much more would be expected of me. The workload was far greater than the previous year's, to the point where I would often stay up well past midnight studying and doing homework. There was a greater emphasis on going "above and beyond," on getting the highest grade. But students, no matter how motivated, can only go above and beyond for so long before they start to burn out. Value was placed on students for their overall grade point average rather than their love of learning. This is extremely degrading and dehumanizing, especially for someone as self-critical as I am. This, coupled with the ever-present social component of school, soon began to take its toll, and I began to detest school again. I have always been one to see the good in people. I try to give everyone the benefit of the doubt, as naïve as that may seem. But, I can say with certainty that I was angry. Angry at everything and everyone. At school, the world, myself. I began shutting down more and more frequently, but this time, there was a spite to it. *You don't get to hear my voice, not after what you've done to me.*

Once in English class, in the midst of a shutdown, I had reached my limit. I felt the anger festering within me, threatening to let loose. Since my body rendered me voiceless, I had to find some sort of release. In a moment of pure desperation, I took a permanent marker and wrote *HATE* in angry black letters all over my forearms. There was something so satisfying about having the word etched into my skin. It manifested my anger in a way I couldn't do verbally. My English teacher, unfortunately, saw the words peeking out from underneath the sleeves of my sweater. When she saw my arms, her eyes widened.

"Who do you hate?" she whispered.

I couldn't answer. *Wouldn't you like to know?*

As the year wore on, I was brought to the office so many times for shutting down in class that the administrators became involved. There was one moment in the office that I will never forget. The counselor was there, among others, and everyone was still stumped as to why I wasn't talking.

Suddenly, the counselor pointed a finger at me and said, "I know what you are! You're a selective mute!"

Never in my life had I felt so degraded. I felt as though I had been branded, the label searing into my skin just as the word "HATE" had been before. Only this time, it was against my will. I was exposed.

What was even more painful, however, was how she felt the need to slap a label on me for her own sanity. It was like I was too much of an anomaly to try and figure out. Might as well put a name to it and call it a day. Problem solved. Good riddance.

That's what it felt like, anyway.

The thing is, selective mutism, or SM, as my shutting down is formally termed, doesn't go away by merely identifying it. It's often misinterpreted as disrespect or the infamous "silent treatment." What's worse is that the term "selective" implies that the silence is a choice, something you have power over, when it's really the exact opposite. At the root of SM is often extreme anxiety, so to successfully treat SM, one must find effective ways of coping with anxiety.

Public awareness of SM is still in its infancy; although it is a legitimate medical condition, it is often misdiagnosed by professionals in the psychological field. It is frequently mistaken for autism, as some of the surface-level characteristics of selective mutism may resemble autistic behaviors. Nearly all of the therapists my mom and I met with were unable to understand me and my condition. Many of them even went as far to assume that my silence was voluntary, which I will never forgive them for. Even after we found the right therapist and I began cognitive behavioral therapy, it took me one entire year before I could communicate verbally with my therapist. While I never said a word during that first year, she and I were able to communicate in other ways—through writing on a white board, nodding, making eye contact, and other nonverbal forms of expression. In fact, in that year, I experienced more personal growth than I ever had in my entire life. No therapist before had ever tried so hard to understand me as Stephanie had, and I can't thank her enough for her patience, professionalism, and support. During our work together, we even came up with a more fitting name for SM: "situational mutism." Above all, Stephanie taught me that there was power in my silence. A power I have only recently come to fully comprehend.

Although I have now overcome SM and it does not have nearly as large of a presence in my life as it used to, I still consider it very much a part of my identity. It shaped many of my experiences as a child, and I definitely would not be the person I am today if it were not for all the hard work I put into overcoming it. As frightening as it can be to try and control something that has dominated your life for so long, I can say with certainty that it is one of the most fulfilling and beneficial things you can ever do for yourself. In my experience with SM, nothing rings truer than a quote I once read from Brené Brown: "You can choose courage, or you can choose comfort. You cannot have both." In the end, I stepped out of my comfort zone and chose courage. And I my life has undeniably changed for the better because of it. ■

Loving Someone and Letting Them Go

PERSONAL ESSAY & MEMOIR

RIA MIRCHANDANI, Grade 10. John Burroughs School, Saint Louis, MO.
Michael Dee, *Educator*; Greater Kansas City Writing Project, *Affiliate*; Silver Medal

I began watching Indian soap operas at the tender age of four. I did not understand them at first. They mostly seemed to consist of characters living in beautiful houses, wearing colorful attire, who frequently raised their voices angrily at each other in a language I only knew a few words of. Nevertheless, I found it entertaining to watch my grandma (my Nanima) absorbed in the stories, providing kind and helpful suggestions to resolve the misunderstandings even when the characters involved clearly could not hear her. Often, she would glare witheringly at the villains of the show and tell the protagonists not to trust them, which they almost always seemed to do. My Nanima was a tiny woman with long shiny hair which reminded me of Rapunzel. Her stamina was astounding despite her age. She would wake up before sunrise each morning to make the family a healthy and hearty breakfast with complex blends of flavor. I did not know her well when young and only saw her as a member of the family who had always lived with me.

It was not until after my grandfather's (my Nanaji) death that I truly began to get to know her. I was eight years old at the time, and it suddenly struck me that she was the last living grandparent I had left. I saw how lonely she was without my Nanaji. I told myself that I would speak with her whenever I could during busy school days and say goodnight to her every day before I went to bed. I hoped that by doing this I could make her feel less alone. Every day after school, I would go to her room and sit with her. She would normally be watching her evening program, and I would watch it with her, interjecting a couple of times to ask what the characters were saying. She would patiently explain each show to me. I noticed that they generally seemed to have a common plot in which a young bride, initially disliked by her mother-in-law, would eventually win her over with goodness. The family would live happily together until another villain entered the show, perhaps an ex-girlfriend or ex-boyfriend.

You would think that after years of watching shows with extremely predictable plots Nanima would get bored and stop watching them, however, it was quite the opposite. Every day, at 4:30 p.m., she would turn on the television to see the next episode of the story, and I would join her. The plots, as well as the acting, were subpar almost to the point of being comedic. However, the more I watched the shows, the more I understood them, and soon I was able to speak broken sentences in the Indian language Hindi. In doing so, I was able to communicate more freely with Nanima, and our bond began to grow beyond the shows. I learned how fiercely independent she had been her entire life while balancing her career and family. She would wake up early to make my mom and grandfather breakfast and lunch for school and work, tidy up the house, rush to catch a train to work, and run up several flights of stairs in tall heels to make it to her office on time. I also discovered that we shared the same sense of humor as we would burst out into peals of laughter when witnessing certain situations such as when the villain in one of our shows was hauled away by the police while protesting his innocence.

One day as we were sitting together, I realized that I was no longer forcing myself to spend time with Nanima. I had more fun chatting with her about the shows and our lives than I did with my friends at school. I found myself telling her first whenever something good happened to me and crying in her arms after a bad day. She was "my person" who was always there for me no matter what. She stayed up late night after night even if she was tired to make sure I would go to bed at a reasonable hour. She also encouraged me to pursue my dreams and build a successful career so that I would never be dependent on anyone. Knowing of my interest in science, she encouraged me to apply for a selective university summer residential program for rising sophomores. She was thrilled when I was admitted and said that if I found my career path, I would be fulfilling her dream.

However, Nanima became very ill around the end of my freshman year. I remember sitting in the car and my mom telling me that the doctors had found a nodule near her lung. Because of her age there was nothing they could do to help her. The treatment option was palliative radiation which only seemed to worsen her condition and weaken her. I watched as the strong woman I knew slowly slipped away from me every day, withering like a leaf in the winter. Though we would still spend time together, our conversations lacked their easy flow, often filled with long pauses during which we would just take in each other's presence, as if trying to remember every part of each other. We continued to sit side by side and watch our soap operas together. However, there was less laughter and discussions.

I decided to withdraw from the summer program to be with her. When I informed Nanima, she was disappointed and said that she wanted me to attend. For the next few days, I kept going back and forth on the decision and spent sleepless nights wondering if I would regret it more that I had left her side in her final days or if I had left her dreams for me unfulfilled. In the end, the memory of her happiness when I received the admittance notification convinced me to go.

I remember sitting on the floor in my dorm the day before she passed after receiving a video call from home. Nanima looked much weaker. When I asked her if she wanted me to come back home, she nodded her head. My parents purchased a ticket for me to return the next morning. Just before my flight departed, I received another call from my mom telling me that Nanima had passed away. I sat there in silence and let out a deep breath of air that I did not know I had been holding for a long time. I did not cry but got on the flight and returned home for the funeral. My mind was restless and my heart was heavy in the days after.

A few months later, I was laying in bed when I recalled the tune of one of our favorite Indian television shows. It had been months since I had heard the sounds of dramatic Hindi music in our home. For the first time in years, it seemed the house was completely silent. As I recalled Nanima's weak face during her final days, a realization dawned that she had left me many days earlier than at her death. It had happened during the last few shows that we watched together when she was quieter and more withdrawn. Perhaps this was her beginning to pull away from me to make the loss easier. I remembered a saying that when you love someone, you set them free. Her pulling away and insistence that I attend the camp was her way of showing that she loved me, and in departing she had taught me yet another valuable life lesson. This lesson began many years ago with an Indian soap opera, and it seemed appropriate that it ended with the memory of one. It was in this moment that I found my peace in letting Nanima go just as she had let me. ■

More than Muzungu

PERSONAL ESSAY & MEMOIR

MIREMBE MUBANDA, Grade 8. Fieldston Middle School, Bronx, NY.
Emily Wright, *Educator*; NYC Scholastic Awards, *Affiliate*; Gold Medal, Best-in-Grade Award

In Kampala, I sat cramped in between two of my aunties on a small, leather armchair. My relatives peppered me with questions about grades, homework, and extracurricular activities. Until, someone remarked, "Mirembe, you have such light skin."

"You are a muzungu, mmm?"

"Aw, let her be, look at her father."

"But look at the mother, she is a muzungu."

"Mmmm."

Immediately, I became shy and started to pick at a crack in the leather chair.

In Uganda, I am a "muzungu," the Luganda word for a White person. But in the United States, I am Black. From a young age I was aware that my father is Ugandan and my mother has ancestors from multiple European countries. Although I am Biracial, for a long period of time I struggled to recognize my European ancestry. Most Americans who meet me perceive me as Black, influencing in how I think of myself. I, too, see myself as Black, because I have skin the color of coffee with milk and tight, kinky curls. When my Ugandan relatives called me muzungu, I used to brush it aside and innocently display my five-year-old smile. Now being called a muzungu annoys me, and I recently came to the realization that it touches something deeper: who am I? How do people see me? Similar to Kayla DeVault, I found that "when I was older, the questions came, which made me question myself."

Visiting my aunt, I flip through leather albums filled dusty daguerreotypes. Women in the pictures wear corsets and hats with large, black plumes. Back at home, I lie on my couch and try to memorize a family tree, filled with names with Dutch Jewish names like Elizabeth Boasberg, Hannah Exstein, and Rachel VanBaalen. Who were these women? Did they like to gossip? Did they have favorites among their children? Other days, I attempt to bake a soda bread, with a recipe attributed to Honora Wall, who emigrated from Ireland. During these activities, I am able to appreciate my ancestors from Ireland, Austria, and Holland. It reminds me that I am African, but also have European ancestors who have passed down recipes and photo albums. So I am better able to recognize other parts of me, not only the part the world sees.

Even when American people see me as Black, they might not envision what it means to be Ugandan. This summer, I visited my eighty-nine-year-old grandfather. Sitting on his back porch, which overlooked the hills of neighboring villages, he told me stories of my distant relatives. I would ask him questions about my deceased great-aunts and great-uncles, and supposedly royal third cousins. Spitting out tart jambula pits and chomping on crispy, roasted grasshoppers, he would explain how I was related to a solemn-faced woman in a black-and-white picture, kneeling with a large group of women in front of a mud hut.

Visiting relatives, I would often feel excluded as they spoke in rapid Luganda. The words seemed to fly so easily from their tongues, but I would have to repeatedly ask my father to update me on the newest topic of the conversation. One morning, as I sat sipping my freshly squeezed papaya juice, my grandfather's housekeeper approached me. She tapped my shoulder and handed me a dusty red pamphlet. She explained that it was an English-Luganda dictionary, filled with the translation of many useful phrases. I was ecstatic. For the entire day, I sat on the porch and read the little pamphlet from cover to cover. Later, in the evening, I asked my grandfather to give me a lesson in Luganda. He would say a word, then I would repeat it, and state the translation. While speaking around the toothpick in his mouth, he would correct my pronunciation, and tell me to enunciate the "n" in "nnabo" ("ma'am" in Luganda). Although many of my family members still call me a muzungu, I try to honor my Ugandan heritage by asking my grandfather questions.

In Uganda I am a muzungu. In the United States I am Black. But I am also Biracial. Now, I am able to ask the questions that help me discover many sides of my heritage, without letting people decide who I am. ■

Dear Transgender Youth

PERSONAL ESSAY & MEMOIR

DMITRI DERODEL, Grade 12. Frank Sinatra High School of the Arts, Astoria, NY.
Melissa Jean-Baptiste and Stella Lee, *Educators;* NYC Scholastic Awards, *Affiliate;*
Gold Medal

Pay attention to every inch of your body; you'll need it for the debate. You, unfortunately, *are* the debate. You are likely painfully aware of this fact already. It's probably attended a few of your birthday parties by now. Your zipper will clamor for the chance to introduce itself to strangers before your vocal cords can, but they should both say the same thing if you can help it: *I am not what you think I am.*

As for me, I want to say congratulations. I want to say I'm sorry, and I want to say I'm so proud of you, and I want to say thank you, and I want to say so much more to you, so many incredible things, but we are only so infinite. I'm so stuffed with ideas for what to tell you that they clog my mind's drain. No one can be sure of anything, but I'm sure you know that feeling.

I don't know your name. I know things about you that no one else does, things you wish you didn't have to know. Things you want your family to know, but know they shouldn't (or perhaps they don't deserve to). You may not even know this letter is for you yet. I believe that to embrace one's trans-ness is currently one of the most dangerous—and therefore, the most rewarding—methods of loving oneself. There are no forms of love that willingly seal themselves in a voice box, so this letter, while for you, cannot be *about* you. It's about me, sprinkled with assumptions of you (and I apologize again because I know how deeply assumptions can plague us, but it's as close to you as I can get). Maybe you needed this letter; maybe you didn't. I can only hope that our experiences and aspirations overlap enough for me to feel as if I can say "you're welcome" by the end of this and not be a liar.

Your birth was many things: an emergence, a preamble, and destruction of the freedom you had when you were nameless. Within your first breaths, every witness snuck their classifications into your lungs like cigarette smoke. You were expected to learn the lessons of whatever you were assigned until you didn't have to think about it anymore, every day descending into pure clockwork. Of course, for you, time slowed here. At some point, you felt as if you were trespassing in public bathrooms. You wished for your hair to crawl down your back or slice itself off. How people talked about you began to sting.

You resisted skirts. You struggled in derby shoes. Even when fully clothed, you felt exposed. It all felt wrong for some reason, but you knew everything technically fit you. So what was the issue? Your current reality wasn't what you wanted. While everything was according to plan, it was still as if something was off-script.

The truth is, it wasn't your reality, was it? It was someone else's fantasy—*everyone* else's fantasy. Every stranger who has assumed incorrectly is pretending to live in a world where everything is clear cut and straightforward, where they know things about others that they don't. You pretended to follow along in order to entertain their illusion, either to protect yourself or simply because you couldn't be bothered to burst their bubble. It may have taken you years to notice that the world has coerced you into fulfilling a role you never chose. It may have taken you just a few hours of web surfing on a whim. It may have even been nothing more than a split second where everything you thought was permanent snapped open. The outcome, nonetheless, is the same regardless of the obstacles that prevented you from reaching it, and it's in your hands now, pulsing. Your only true identity is the one you forge. This newfound awareness is both rejuvenating and life-threatening.

I was one of the extremely fortunate ones, which in itself saddens me, but I am also infinitely grateful for it. I know how much more brutally others—perhaps even you—have it. For me, the personal path to self-discovery was rather gradual and linear. I never had a stage of denial. While I don't have contact with the majority of my family, nor do I plan on changing that, the very select few who were informed about my self-made manhood were more or less welcoming of it and supported me. (While my gender is possibly the only thing my mother respects about me, I'll take what I can get.) I felt safe enough to come out to my high school teachers as both agender and then later as transmasculine, and they accommodated my new names (it's hard to find one that fits perfectly the first time!) and pronouns without so much as a second thought. My classmates, for the most part, treated it as no big deal. It was incredibly relieving. It was freeing. It was also an incredibly rare success. If I weren't living in such a large city as New York, I'm almost certain that what I have now would've been nothing more than a pipe dream as I counted dust bunnies in the closet.

That said, I still get reality checks: ones where the box is blood-stained, others that verbally maim you and defend it by claiming brutal honesty, some that start with hashtags. I've known trans men with bound chests and full-grown beards, and even they have been misgendered. This is not to discourage you if you wish to go through with hormone therapy yourself, nor a warning that people will know your secret no matter what you do. That isn't true. These men pass very well, virtually 99 percent of the time. This is not an admittance of defeat, nor is it an excuse for such disrespectful mouths. I've read anecdotes of cisgender folk who will occasionally be interrogated by strangers who, for whatever reason, refuse to believe they are cis. In the end, the ignorant mind thinks whatever it pleases. Such is life, at least for now. Try not to beat yourself up if someone foolishly tries to recreate you. It is not, nor will it ever be, your fault.

Assuming you haven't had this occur already, someone will eventually demand you prove how real you are. Many people will. I am going to tell you right now that this is impossible. Gender, at its very core, is a spiritual object, a bit like consciousness. The only evidence that matters (or is viable) is one's existence. It is as beautiful and natural and indefinable as love. We have existed for as long as civilization. If they don't believe you, then nothing you say will change that, and you will have to accept this and invest your energy elsewhere. You are not a topic of discourse. If not even God needs to prove his existence to his children, then neither do you. You are already a miracle. You are allowed to just *be*. There are infinite ways to do so, and there's always room for another.

And, assuming you haven't gone through this already as well, there will come a day in which you question everything you've accomplished. You will worry if people who don't even know you were right about you all along, that you're merely playing dress-up with your skin. It'll get in your head and constrict your spirit like clay sitting in an angry palm, a pearl too big for its oyster. "What if I *am* faking it?" you'll cry in your head. (By the way, you're almost guaranteed to misgender yourself by accident at least once. It happens to most of us. It doesn't mean your unconscious mind knows the "truth." Your previous designations have been ingrained in you for years, and breaking any routine will take practice—lots of it.) You will look in the mirror and gouge out your own eyes, searching for proof that this is not just a phase. Do you know what a phase is? Pain. And it will pass.

Even if you suddenly wake up one day and think to yourself, *I don't feel like myself like this anymore,* that does not mean you were ever living a lie. The truth just changed. You did not waste your time. You did not inconvenience the world. If you had a partner you loved with everything you had but eventually you grew apart, is the life you built with them now meaningless just because it's unfinished? Does it mean that you never loved them at all? No, it doesn't. That'd be ridiculous! Let's say an artist begins a project and—despite having poured their heart into the paint buckets—decides after a while that they don't like the idea anymore and want to move on to something else. Was all that progress for naught? Was all that time wasted? Does it mean that they never created that piece? Does it make them a liar? *No!* All experiences are ones to learn from, and the ones that made you happy in the moment are always ones to look back on fondly. You will be okay. You're allowed to change your mind if it ever comes to that. Being human is all about adapting to yourself.

I've suffered and recovered from countless episodes like these. I would ask friends to deadname and misgender me sometimes to "make sure" it still made me uncomfortable. Imposter syndrome is simply a facet of the human experience. Nobody thinks they're enough, and this is the most miserable lie anyone can ever teach us. Even as I was beginning my testosterone injections, I was anxious. And this was something I'd fantasized about for *years!* I was determined to get the injections. It's what forced me to keep living. I didn't want to die while neglecting what my body ached for so earnestly. I couldn't. But as I got closer to obtaining my first shot, tangibly close, the second thoughts began to creep up on me again like bashful ghosts. Who could blame me? Some parts of what I was signing myself up for would be permanent. It was a big decision. I wondered if I should wait (as if I hadn't already been waiting for long enough!). I wondered if what I wanted was worth it or if I was making a mistake.

And then I said "fuck it" and signed the consent form.

I was excited. I was nervous. At some point, you realize that nervousness is just excitement that's a bit more careful than usual, the same way fear is just your body's way of preparing to do something courageous.

Remember how I said there are infinite ways to be human? There are also countless ways to be transgender! Your experiences might be just like mine, but most likely they won't. You may want bottom surgery or no surgeries at all. You may enjoy your birth name enough to keep it. Your name may be the only thing you decide to change about yourself, adoring your body and the way you dress as they are. You might go on hormones for just a few changes you're looking for and then stop. You could decide to go by multiple names or more than one set of pronouns, rotating your labels like your wardrobe. You might declare yourself from the rooftops, or never disclose your trans-ness unless asked (and perhaps not even then). You might comfortably align with most of your gender's norms, or you might actively subvert them with reckless abandon. You may hate the fact that you're trans, you may love it, or you may not care either way. All of these are okay. No method is greater or lesser than any other. They just are.

I can't begin to *imagine* how different my life would've turned out if I was cis, or even if I had to stay closeted for a while. My trans-ness has touched absolutely every corner of my life, and it will continue to do so until I die.

What does that mean for you and your trans-ness? Nothing. It's as principal or as insignificant to your life story as you believe it to be. You may call yourself a trans person, or you may not. Regardless of your relationship with it, your trans-ness will—especially due to our current political environment—be an integral part of who you are as a person. But remember: you are a person first. To be trans is to figure out what you want from yourself, to regulate your reality, to curate the version of yourself that is the most comfortable. Yes, you are trans, and it's unlikely that will change, but before anything else—and I absolutely cannot stress this enough—you are *human*. You deserve to be treated as such. Never forget this. Never let anybody tell you otherwise. Ever. Please. Promise me this. You are human! Everything else is secondary.

Living as a marginalized individual of any kind is exceptionally difficult. Even when you're proud as a lion, people will want your head mounted on their wall. Even when you feel as if you're on top of the world, the world still hates you. And it hates you passionately, as much of a grim recognition as that may be. Self-love as retaliation is good. Self-acceptance, however, is essential. The world will try to convince you that you're on fire. When this happens, pretend your ears burnt themselves off so that you can't hear them, because this is a lie. You don't need to escape yourself. They were the ones who lit the match and tried to slip it into your hair like a bobby pin. When the system's steel grip tries to strangle you, grip its hands and breathe. When it complains that your lungs disrupt the "order" which it demands of its people, live disobediently. *Live.* Apologize to nobody for what you can't control. Don't let anybody drown you out.

Make sure your fly is up. Now, remember your vocal cords? That butterfly net for your voice? Do you know how vital it is? Use it to repeat after me: *I am breathing. I am breathing. I am breathing whether the world wants me to or not.* ∎

Recycling.

POETRY

CAMILLA CHAKIR, Grade 9. George Washington Carver Center for Arts and Technology, Towson, MD. Rebecca Mlinek and Nora Pierce, *Educators*; Baltimore Office of Promotions & the Arts, Inc., *Affiliate*; Silver Medal

When I'm gone,
empty of the life you filled me with,
bring me back to the forest.

Lay my old tired body in the grass.
Let butterflies come and roost in my stomach like they have before.
Let my blood flow like the rivers I've come to love.

Let those same butterflies feast upon that scarlet nectar.
Let snakes with their glittering scales wrap around my wrists
like the bracelets my sister made me.

Let flowers grow in my hair,
their roots not so different from my own,
and the flowers not so different from the crowns I make of them.

Let trees grow around me.
Let their heads be in the clouds as mine is.
Let them reach the stars,
those same stars I desperately dreamed to reach.

Let the names of those in my mind be etched into the wood
Let birds circle around my head like thoughts,
dark and bright and light feathers welcomed all the same.
Let them carry earworms in their beaks,
and every song ever loved in their throats.
Let me return the forest where we started.
Let me come to the earth where my grandfather lays.

Bring me back to the forest.
Let me be.
Let me be found.
Come and find me. ■

My Sunshine

POETRY

SOFIA KOROSTYSHEVSKY, Grade 9. New Explorations into Science, Technology and Math High School, New York, NY. Ellen Sands, *Educator*; NYC Scholastic Awards, *Affiliate*; Silver Medal

Another Sunday,
I'm sitting here again.
The dusty couch of memories.
I come here every week
To see her
The frail woman
Almost translucent skin
Snow white hair dyed brown
Hazel eyes and a smile of missing teeth.
Today I sit with what she calls a biscuit
Eggs and sugar, nothing more.
On another day, it would be apples.
"Great-grandma, tell me about your life."
"Of course, my *solnyshko*, my sunshine."
She clears her throat and begins,
The stories of positive things.
She remembers what she wants to.
We forget what we want to.
But there are unspoken horrors
That a textbook can't tell me
And from her I want to know.
The only story of pain I've heard
Is of my grandpa
Died in a plane crash
When my dad was a little boy.
Stories I wish to hear
Are buried deep in that brilliant mind
If not forgotten
Buried beneath memorized poems of childhood
And languages, codes that she learned
Morse code she prides herself in.

One day I heard
A slew of tangled memories
It was as if she was holding on to them
And she did not want to let go.
But I was only ten,
And now I'm scrambling to remember the blood and pain that she does not
speak of
Blood on the snow
The feeling
That someone's always watching you
But sometimes I feel like it's just my imagination
That she said nothing at all.
Suitcases rolled to a train platform
Smoke and shots fired into the air.
A train
Seized by Germans
Stolen jewelry
Death in trenches
Arrested for being a Jew
Her father
Captured and killed
Is it my imagination?
The generation
Is dying out
And I might never know the truth.
And I can't bring myself to force her to
There she is smiling
I take a bite out of my biscuit
And I listen. ∎

Au Revoir

POETRY

SARAH LANGER, Grade 10. Council Rock High School South, Holland, PA. Trish Verdi, *Educator*; Philadelphia Writing Project, *Affiliate*; Gold Medal

the bleeding sun's final stand
mirrors the glow of fading embers
as its tainted pigments spill over the horizon

draping ruby clouds catch lone rays of ochre
twisted streams of crimson and burnt sienna
pillars of gold crumble before your very eyes

a sunset is what you make of it
a surrender to dusk
or an opulent toast
with the glimmer and vivacity of champagne
with hints of rose and droplets of honey

smug in the face of the night's triumph,
or beautiful in the way that tragedy is

a sorrowful farewell
or a bittersweet promise

a quill has been bestowed upon you
so what'll it be—
a tale of woe
or bravery till the very end

thoughts will race in its wake
as the gasping sun drowns
as midnight's icy grip tightens around its neck
as its heaving lungs cloud with charcoal

because just like that, it is over
a sunset begs a question we have yet to answer
what to make of it
when the light dies. ∎

Heritage

POETRY

EMILIO ONTIVEROS, Grade 11. DeBakey High School for Health Professions, Houston, TX. Diane Franz, *Educator*; Harris County Department of Education, *Affiliate*; Silver Medal

I do not care for heritage.
I do not care for a past that attempts to control my future.
The beliefs held by those I descended from
Are in no way my own.
All I have inherited is my name
And my skin.

My philosophy has been defined by my experiences
Not by what I am told has been experienced.
Whatever my forefathers suffered
I did not get to.
Whatever they have spent generations working towards
I do not have in my sights.

I won't let the shackles that have been passed down for generations
Keep me chained to a line of thought paved on dirt roads.
When they thought they graced me with hopes and guiding lights
Were nothing more than my burdens to bear
Like carrying a cross across a never ending desert.

There is no pride to be found
In the blood flowing through veins,
But only what the mind has earned for itself
And what the heart longs to find.
Advice, I can appreciate,
But I won't let it define.

The regrets of grown women and men
Are not to be passed down to the children
Who still have yet to come up with their own.
To try to live vicariously through undiscovered identity
Is nothing more than a sin born from a pitiful pride.

I will gladly hear what the past has to say
But I will decide if it's worth listening to.
The fruits of labor that beared from the seeds
Only grown to stifle the hunger for sense of self,
Will fail to pass my lips.

I do not mean to disrespect ideals tried and true.
Don't assume however that it will work for me,
If it bloodied and soiled life for you.
I understand what I try for over and over,
Dream for in such ways that only dress me the fool,
Cannot be easily understood by those unwilling too.
I only ask for respect to be given and returned
Don't belittle the future for which I yearn. ∎

Accessory

POETRY

TURON PARKER, Grade 12. School of the Arts, Rochester, NY. Marcy Gamzon, *Educator*; Region-at-Large, *Affiliate*; Silver Medal

You wear your heart on your sleeve
for the whole world to see! It's too much
for me!

But baby, I wear my heart like
an accessory. A gold chain with
a name on it,

your name at one time. The cool
metal opposing the warmth
of my chest. Bustling with

love that I can no longer give
you. You stripped it from
yourself, and threw it back

at me. I was warned from the
jump that once I landed,
I'd be in pain.

I took my chances, thought
I'd stick the landing, but
dammit, I overshot it and

now I'm left to clean up.
I was the straw
that broke our back. ∎

El Inglés de Mi Mama

POETRY

ISABELLA RAMIREZ, Grade 11. A. W. Dreyfoos School of the Arts, West Palm Beach, FL.
Carly Gates, *Educator*; Region-at-Large, *Affiliate*; Silver Medal

i'm sitting on my mama's bed
and she's on the brink of a mental breakdown
over her homework
i can see the glint of a blinking cursor
tears glossing over her eyes
as her hands search for words in a language
all too foreign to her.

she said i could count in both spanish and english
by the time i was 18 months old
but it's taken her 21 years and counting to flatten out
the unruly kinks of her language

my mama's English
is a stubborn wine stain on a white dress
she scrubs at her twisted tongue desperate
to clean the spice, *el cilantro, la salsa*
that is her accent.
her accent is the tambourine she hides
in the back of her mouth
behind the ivory piano keys that are her teeth
she speaks a *merengue, bachata, ranchera, tonada*
that she mutes to make room
for her English.

my mama's English
gets told it's pretty good,
for being an immigrant
to which she replies
you've got some nerve
for being a *gringa*
because my mama wasn't a stay-at-home mom

for fifteen years to be told that her English
needed housekeeping.
the beauty of my mama's English
is that she doesn't need it
to knock your head off your shoulders
call her a *luchador*
cuz she can make you tap out faster
than you can say
her English isn't good enough.

my mama's English
is me correcting her at the dinner table
it's me laughing when she can't find
the right syllables and sounds
and the words don't fit quite right
in her mouth.
it's the downturn of her lips
at the expense of my smile
because her English is not
the punchline of a joke
that's gotten too old.

my mama's English
is the *piñata* she got me on my 10th birthday
big and bright and pink and purple
but hollow on the inside
it's her count to three
uno, dos, tres
as she spun me blindfolded
dizzy and facing the wrong direction
it's the swing and miss of my bat
and the candy and confetti that falls
in the final hit that breaks it open.
it's a game of pin the tail on the donkey
no matter how many times you play
you never just get it quite right.
it's the *quinceñera* I never had
overrated and stereotypical
distastefully too latina

it's the number birthday candles
that melt hot wax onto the cake
she made from scratch
it's the reason my birthday is not just
a happy birthday but a *feliz cumpleaños*
it's the reason that when i go to my friend's parties
i want to sing happy birthday twice
because mama never let us blow out candles
before singing *en Español.*

my mama's English
is the one dollar and 35 cent Cuban coffee
i drive her to get every saturday
itching at the back of her throat
bitter and hard to swallow
only sweet from the sugar left
in the foam she licks off her top lip
it's the reason she insists
the starbucks double espresso
doesn't have the same kick.

it's the reason i'm sitting on mama's bed
watching her eyes swell as she fumbles with the keys
it's the reason she got into graduate school at 42
why i help her with her homework before i do my own
it's why the bottom of her computer burns my lap
with each oxford comma and restructured sentence
and fixed grammar rule

it's why she doesn't end up crying
when i whisper that everything will be ok

my mama's English
is the reason i can tell her in two ways
that she is my everything, *mi todo*
because her love knows
no language. ∎

jackdaw goes undercover

POETRY

MIRACLE THORNTON, Grade 12. Interlochen Arts Academy, Interlochen, MI.
Brittany Cavallero, *Educator*; Kendall College of Art and Design, Ferris State University,
Affiliate; Silver Medal

but i plug my ears so i can smell him.
there is something in his body,
the way he claims it in the night:
the black brimmed hat, black empty
shouldered jacket, black undershirt,
black dreads tipping the black hat over
his eyes, shiny like a beetle back.
or maybe it's the black in his skin
and the black in his black beard,
how his face melts into a shadow,
too black. in the night, i see his fast
beating form around the kitchen
for a midnight snack, but in the day,
his odor smacks me back on the street,
behind the gas station counter,
in the clearance aisle, class discussion
of the 1960s, passing on watermelon
at the cookout, on the radio gagging
until it feels good, laptop screen
while i blurring pink. i smell him
when i call myself a white man's
woman and see my babies tanned
with light calling eyes, burn our scalps,
brag about my nonviolent dad
and drafted tongue and fat ass. i smell
a black church pew, racks of charred ribs
and black eyed peas, the bitter snap
of my grandmother's gum, box perm,
oil and liver, buttered crab and old bay,
my nana's car—or i smell
power and old white paint, slapped down

under his fingers. i feel heavy and
embarrassed by his unfiltered blackness,
how it rings in his laugh like a broken key,
slack jawed and dying to be heard. ∎

Waltz of the Pancakes

POETRY

LILY COADY, Grade 11. Hollis Brookline High School, Hollis, NH. Lauren Grosse, *Educator*; The National Writing Project in New Hampshire, *Affiliate*; Gold Medal

My parents used to make pancakes
For us on mornings
When only the sweet smell
Of butter and sugar
Could peel us from the dents
In our beds.

We'd run downstairs and sit
At the table and wait while
My mother would slice the *mamon*
And prepare the *silog*
For my father to fry
And bring to life.

They danced around the kitchen
Moving to the rhythm of
Oil sputters and pan searing
A melodious partnership
Each step perfect in time
His pale fingers twirling my
Mother's golden browns
Enchanted—

The music so loud
Their minds so wandering
Almost far enough away
From the food.

My mother puts down a plate
Before my small head
And my father puts down
The *silog*, the *mamon*
And the pancake:
"Sorry, little one,
It's a little burnt on one side."

I flip the fluffy white top over
To the smoky brown underside
And I am not upset.
My heart is warm
Because it looks like my hands. ■

sestina to a publix supermarket

POETRY

LYDIA WEI, Grade 12. Richard Montgomery High School, Rockville, MD.
Molly Clarkson, *Educator*; Writopia Lab, *Affiliate*; Silver Medal

no one knows that ancient gomphotheres once roamed
this publix parking lot. we could unearth eons of history
if we demolished the tarmac pavement, bare hands
scooping out dirt to find scarred, speckled fossils.
every time i push a shopping cart across the lot, my neck
tingles: my strands of hair come alive, sweat gathering.

nonetheless, i'm a careful shopper, gathering
buoyant kale, siamese cherries, mild guacamole. i roam
through aisles for black beans, neck
up: the cheapest cans are always on the top shelf. history's
mastodons died in gales of arrows so i could choose between two fossils,
bush's or goya, and i almost cry. i take goya in my hands.

but all this is merely prelude for something else: my hands
on the shopping cart handle, teriyaki samples gathered
in little paper cups, smart shoppers' coupons clipped—i want to create a
fossil.
no one would understand this but you, miocene dawn roamer
of fort lauderdale streets; you, restless amber-eyed historian,
graphing the intimate records of an arching neck.

so hollywood beach starts and ends at the nape of your neck
and after half-awake extinctions i reach instinctively for your hands.
you told me woolly mammoth tusks reveal history
in wobbling rings; at your collar, eupatagus shells gather
like love letters. i bought salmon, your favorite, a romp
through the recipe equating fillet with fossil.

and what exactly am i trying to prove with this fossil?
that we loved each other? that our love carbonized in necklaces
of film? that we sat down for dinner? i can't think that we roamed

this earth without remains. when i passed you the rice, our hands
brushed; i could already see the oil gathering
at the bottom of your bowl, whatever that meant to cenozoic history.

for now, though, i see gleaming phosphenes of historic
meliorchises. the supermarket radio plays fossils
of 2012 pop hits and i feel oddly sentimental: i want to gather
checkout aisle kinder eggs close to my heart. the cashier bends her neck
to punch in keycodes on the glowing screen, her hands
darting about; i imagine each finger as a kyptoceras on a starry roam.

the fossils are humming, or perhaps the air conditioner; i gather
my groceries, hands aching like an arthritic mesohippus neck.
tonight i'll roam the empty parking lot, heart holding secret histories. ∎

Glimpses of a Better World

FLASH FICTION

PRIYA DALAL-WHELAN, Grade 12. Perpich Centers-Arts Education, Golden Valley, MN. Shannon Hannigan, *Educator*; Minnesota Writing Project, *Affiliate*; Gold Medal

Part I: Here

In our world, two vans arrive in a village called Nyoaga and people pile out. Four of the people are from a place called America. One of them is from a place called India. Three of them are from an in-between. They are all *mzungos*. (Swahili for white people, brown skin and black hair notwithstanding.) They come bearing large plastic water bottles and suitcases full of medicines and are greeted with overwhelming screams of joy. When the meetings begin, bodies fill plastic chairs in a cracked concrete room and joy gives way to overstated gratitude laced with need that will not be filled.

The children are supposed to be gathering water to wash the classrooms when they see the mzungos walking down the road. They form a procession, chattering and excited, and march down towards the lake behind them. The chatter is 50 percent curiosity and 50 percent hope that they might walk away from this parade with a little money or soap or a piece of candy.

The lake is called Lake Victoria and the children wade in to gather water. The mzungos shy away; they've been told not to touch this water. They shift uncomfortably and finger their plastic bottles of better-water. They marvel at the boats sitting on the sand, at the lights in the distance which are the fish farms and make the boats all but worthless. They talk of the hyacinth and the fish that used to be.

Lunch is in another concrete building. The Lou women gather to roll out chapati and pluck a chicken that had been running around in the yard a half hour before. There are also pots of tough beef and rice and a thick pasty meal called *ugali*. The food is warm and heavy in the stomach and coats the top of the tongue thickly.

The Indian woman helps roll chapati and politely declines the meat. The Lou women laugh at her. Lunch is served and the mzungos eat in the staff bedroom, the others in the kitchen.

Each night the mzungos pile back into the vans and tumble an hour away and halfway up a hill. The hotel is behind a gate and stacked further up the hill in tiers overlooking the lake. White staircases and rounded platforms, running water and mosquito netting and electric lights. They eat dinner and leave a nothing-tip, which is grasped with such gratitude.

The small mzungo boy enters the bathroom to find a roach staring at him and cries and cries. The next day, the vans leave for the last time, trailing candy bar wrappers and a small handful of promises.

Part II: There

A young woman from Surat, India, arrives in Nyaoga, Kenya, for a well-deserved vacation, her graduation present to herself. She has studied hard for the past four years, a double major in Gujdrati literature and engineering made for a heavy course load. She comes alone, as many college kids do the summer after they graduate, a moment of pause before the world of possibilities opens up before them. Sometimes, the kids fall in love with the places they visit and stay for a while. Sometimes they get homesick and return to their home countries within weeks.

She eats gourmet dinners along the lakeside, they bring her plates and plates of fish that could only be found in Lake Lollwe. The fishermen are sure they will catch more the next day, and more the next and the next and the next and the next day until the end of time. The university kids from Kisumu come every so often with all kinds of fancy instruments and clipboards and T-shirts that proclaim them "population monitors." Each time, they inform the fishermen that fish populations are stable. The fishermen simply nod. They know.

The woman tips 20 percent without a second thought; the waitress accepts likewise. She takes late night walks on the beach and is delighted that local teenagers seem to hang out here around bonfires and cheap, sweet bottles of wine and the gentle lap of the waves. Every so often, a few of them will suddenly decide to go swimming and run into the lake, shrieking when the water hits their bellies as if they just remembered it would be wet. For a week, the young woman watches. The next week, she joins them.

She stays in an old wooden farmhouse. The family who owns the farm lives on the other side of the fields. They invite her over for lunches and she strolls through their green fields of cassava and cabbage. The first time, they serve her warm, buttery ugali and vegetables and beef, which she declines politely. She insists that a meal can be flavorful without meat, and insists that the next day, she will cook. When they don't have any of the spices she needs at the local market, she calls her mother and asks her to ship her curry and cardamom and a few spices that don't have names in Swahili. When they arrive, she proves herself correct by transforming a mountain of lentils into steaming spicy yellow soup, a bag of flour into something like a crackling bread, a collection of vegetables into a brightly colored curry.

When she leaves, they make her agree to return one day. She promises. ∎

Tired

FLASH FICTION

ALYS GOODWIN, Grade 12. Maggie L. Walker Governor's School, Richmond, VA. Lisa Williams, *Educator*; Visual Arts Center of Richmond, *Affiliate*; Silver Medal

The biting air leaves a natural blush on my cheeks and nose. The cold is seizing my hands even from within my coat pockets. My coat slinks down to my knees, meeting the rims of my heeled boots. My curls bounce delicately on my shoulders, as crimson red slips from my lips to my teeth. I feel the paste plaster to my teeth, and make a conscious effort to fix it once I'm sitting down. I hurry down the steps and turn toward the Seventh Avenue Line. The frigid temperature and musty underground air create a bitter cocktail that presses down my throat and makes it hard to breathe. The doors open with a thud and I step inside. I'm greeted with warmer, no less musty air. The car is nearly empty, leaving a fine selection of stained and cracked seats to choose from. I find my place in a corner, where I can rest my head as I examine the hodgepodge of humanity around me.

There's a man to my right, whose wrinkles and tanned skin give him the appearance of a weeks old clementine. His hair hangs black and greasy over his face, obstructing my view of his eyes. A battered guitar case rests against his legs, covered in colorful markings and peeling stickers that hint at a long life brimming with stories. His fingers are rifling through the inside of a hat, only landing on pennies and nickels, with the rare and coveted quarter surfacing occasionally. He is tired.

My eyes shift to the young girl across the car. She sits with her legs crossed and back straight in the guise of composure, but her eyes are watermarked. Her well-tailored dress wrinkled, her lipstick dulled, her hair tangled at the ends. A bag sits next to her, spilling its contents onto the surrounding seats. Courier font stains my vision. After what audition did she stop smoothing out her dress, reapplying her lipstick, combing through her hair? She is tired.

Another woman is slouched further down the car, not even bothering to cross her legs. She sports a tour company logo and tattered puffer coat. Even the too long sleeves can't hide the paint splotches on her hands, the too long body can't hide the colorful stains on her jeans. She is tired.

All these people are tired. The weight of living with a dream deferred has taken its toll. And I want to stay on this subway car just a little longer. I want to stay tucked snugly behind this facade, wearing this coat, this makeup, these curls. I want these people to look at me and see a woman who exudes superiority. But then again, people in pain have a way of sniffing out others with the same ache. Do they all know? Can they all tell? I am yanked from my reverie when the car screeches to a halt. This is me. Wall Street. My workplace. The sun is low in the sky and the self-proclaimed "overworked" husbands are flooding the streets, looking for somewhere to displace their frustrations before walking through the door to kiss their wife and snuggle their children. For the right price, I can be that place and more. Situated in my open air office, I shed my coat. The air hits my bare skin like a frozen wall. The force makes me wobble on my heels, but I quickly find my perch, a perfect mixture of sultry confidence and helpless longing. You never know what your clientele is looking for. From my perch, I adjust my skintight skirt, fluff my curls, and coat my lips one last time. My dream deferred scratches at my heart, but there is no time. I'm open for business. I'm tired. ■

Stranger at the Window

FLASH FICTION

PRISHA MEHTA, Grade 11. Millburn Senior High School, Millburn, NJ.
Minaz Jooma, *Educator*; Newark Public Library, *Affiliate*; Silver Medal

Nothing's certain anymore, not when it comes to Stephen. Some days, he flings open the door and greets me with a firm smile and a clap on the shoulder, and it's then that I remember him as he used to be. The student who worked hard and earned good grades, the son who gave up his chance at college to take over Dad's shop, the brother who stayed with us for years after Danny enlisted. Solid. Steadfast. Always there.

Other days, he looks at me and thinks I'm Dad, or Uncle Evan, or even Danny. Ruth says we're lucky he remembers our names at all, this far into the disease. She's been doing a lot of research from the beginning—even more now that he's moved in with her. Personally, I don't see where the luck comes in, what with him getting dementia at the ripe old age of forty-eight.

Ruth's place is nice, a cream-colored house tucked onto the edge of a side street. With its worn lemony shutters and its white wooden porch, it's the kind of place you could call quaint. I'm his brother and Ruth's only a cousin, but we both agreed he'd like it better here—at least, better than my cluttered, cramped apartment in the city. It doesn't make me a bad person, I don't think. I mean, at least I drive up to visit him once or twice a month.

Today, he's outside when I pull into the driveway. He's wearing an old T-shirt and baggy pants, shuffling towards the edge of the yard with a pleasant smile on his face. I almost don't want to interrupt him—he looks more peaceful than I've seen him in a while, but Ruth says that when he tries to run away, it's better to divert him early on. Before he gets lost and upset.

There's a white picket fence in front of me. I need to get over it—I need to go home, back to Mom and Dad and Danny and Michael. Where . . . what am I doing here? I need to go home. Home. I need to—

I slam the car door shut. Dammit, where's Ruth when you need her? She's much better at dealing with him than I'll ever be. I walk up behind him and tap him on the shoulder. He turns around, raising an eyebrow. I force a warm smile.

"Stephen? Stephen, hi."

Someone taps my shoulder, and I blink. Another tap, and I turn around.

A man stands behind me, shifting from foot to foot. I don't recognize him. He has wild graying hair, muddy green eyes. His brow is furrowed in concern. Something about him seems familiar, but I can't . . .

He stares at me blankly. He starts to turn around, and I reach out and grab his wrist.

"Stephen, you need to go home. We're going to go home now, ok?"

He frowns and tilts his head.

He's saying something now, but it's as if his words are bouncing off of my mind. I can't catch them, can't understand them. He says something about home . . .

"Home? That's where I'm going. I'm going home."

I shake my head and point towards the house.

"Home is that way."

The man shakes his head. No, home is that way?

What? What is he saying? I turn and look. A strange house looms over me, stiff and cream-colored. No, no—he can't make me go there, I have to go home! Who is he? What does he want? No, he can't make me, I won't go, I . . .

He follows my gaze and a change comes over him. His brow furrows, his muscles tense, and he wrenches his arm out of my grip, his eyes wild. I take a step back. I swallow and hold up my hands.

"Stephen, come on. Come inside. You know me."

He squints at me, and I can see the anger slowly draining from his face as he forgets.

"Dammit! Stephen, you know me!"

Where am I? The man in front of me . . . do I know him? He looks like my father. "Dad?"

He pauses and stares at me for a moment. Dad? I'm your brother, I want to say, but it's hopeless. I know it'll only upset him, but I have to bite my tongue to prevent the words from coming out.

Something is off; my father's hair has always been cropped close to his head, and his eyes are brown. Still, the resemblance is so clear . . . who else could it be? "Dad?"

"Yeah. It's me. I'm Dad. Stephen, let's go inside, ok?"

The man hesitates, but he finally nods. Yes, it's him.

He lets me guide him across the lawn and towards the door.

Relief mingles with the uneasiness in my stomach, but I push it all aside as he guides me towards the house.

I glance towards the window and see another man on the other side. He looks like the first, but he's older, and his hair is shorter. He wears what seems to be pajamas—an old T-shirt and a baggy pair of pants. He's thin and weak, in dire need of a shave, and confusion darkens his eyes. I almost feel sorry for him.

"Who's that? Who's that inside the house? I don't know him."

He freezes suddenly as we pass the window, and his brow furrows again. He's staring at his own reflection. ■

Atta

FLASH FICTION

ARIVUMANI SRIVASTAVA, Grade 10. Greenwood High School, Bowling Green, KY.
James Davis, *Educator*; Southern Kentucky Performing Arts Center (SKyPAC), *Affiliate*;
Silver Medal

The blistering heat of the Punjabi summer struck Ranbir's skin like a bullet. Papa hobbled alongside him, his cane trembling as he picked it up with every step.

"How are studies in Allahabad *beta*?"

"They're going well, Papa."

"When is your train back?"

"Tomorrow."

"*Acha, acha.* Good, *beta*. Could you get the door for me?"

Ranbir opened the screen door and propped it open. He grabbed his father's arm and helped him up the stairs and through the door. His father looked back out at him.

"Ranbir, please be careful at Jallianwala Bagh, the army is supposed to be there."

"When have I not been careful?"

"I know *beta*, I just can't spare to lose both you and mummy."

"Yes, Papa. Do you need me to pick up some *atta* on my way home?"

"Please."

"Okay, I'll be back by six, Papa."

"Take care, *beta*."

Ranbir shut the screen door behind him and waited for the click of his father locking it. Convincing his father to let him go to independence demonstrations had always been a chore, but his documentation of the growing independence movement with Professor Reddy was invaluable. Allahabad University was a center of revolutionaries, and Professor Reddy had recruited him to record the demonstrations planned at the garden.

Ranbir turned down a narrow alleyway to escape the boiling heat from the summer sun. Stalls selling *pani puri* and *chaat* dotted the edges of the path, and the bustle of farmers hauling in flour from the previous year's harvest season filled the center. He zigzagged his way through the crowd, and eventually made it out of the narrow backstreet. Ranbir, who had always been obsessed with time, checked his pocket watch. *5:30, I'm going to be late, dammit.*

He ran to the narrow entryway to Jallianwalla Bagh and entered the vast garden. He heard the chants of nationalist protesters and the screams of British soldiers to back off. He pulled out his pocket notebook, pulled back the flimsy band keeping it shut, and began writing furiously. He documented every part of the demonstrations, from the villagers who had traveled to Harmandir Sahib to celebrate *Baisakhi,* to the university students and independence movement leaders who led rallying calls against the Britishers' arrest of freedom fighters. Ranbir checked his pocket watch again before he began sketching. *5:36, I need to hurry to be able to stop at the market for atta.*

Ranbir began scribbling on a new page, depicting a courtroom-like sketch of the freedom fighters and the opposing line of pale soldiers wrapped along the fringes of the wall of the garden. He began to draw the bushes dotting the garden when suddenly a loud pop and screams erupted from the crowd.

Chaos ensued. The once jubilant and righteous crowds of protesters now ran towards the exits, which appeared to be blocked. Ranbir stuffed his notebook in his pocket and sprinted towards the main entrance in panic, feeling the flesh of the wounded under his sandals as he stampeded along with hundreds of others towards the only way out. Hundreds of rounds seemed to fire off from the guns of the British, and Ranbir watched as bodies around him erupted in a red burst and dropped to the ground. To his left, the wall of soldiers was now covered in a veil of smoke from their rifles. To his right, he watched in horror as people jumped into the bagh's well, figuring that the possibility of death from the fall is better than being shot by a Britisher.

Ranbir continued his sprint toward the narrow gate, but the crowd around him seemed to be thinning. The stampede that had previously been hundreds had now been reduced to a few dozen, and the beautiful green grass that had covered the garden was now coated in red. Ranbir had almost reached the exit when suddenly, a bullet ripped through his skin, and the pool of blood splashed as he hit the ground. His notebook flew out of his pocket, the pages newly stained with red. The sound of his precious pocket watch crystal shattering was a mere whisper among the rounds of ammunition being fired and the screams still engulfing the garden.

Papa checked his watch. *6:05, Ranbir should be home anytime.*

He placed the *tawa* on the stove and pulled out the rolling pin in preparation for dinner. He limped back to his lounge chair in the parlor and sat down, resting his elbows in the indentions of the arms from years of sitting and studying. He picked up his copy of the *Times of India* and continued reading from where he had left off, waiting patiently for Ranbir to return with *atta* for tonight's *chapati.*

Papa turned his gaze to the grandfather clock in the corner of the room. *6:20, where is Ranbir?*

He pushed against the chair, grabbed his cane, and shuffled to the door. He gingerly opened it and looked out at the empty road, waiting for the familiarly heavy footsteps of Ranbir, straining under a hefty bag of *atta*. Instead, he was met with an unusual silence, interrupted by the howl of a stray dog in the distance. ■

Midnight Death Trap

FLASH FICTION

BRAYDEN BURGE, Grade 8. Wilson Middle School, Carlisle, PA. Jess Rauhauser, *Educator*; Commonwealth Charter Academy, *Affiliate*; Gold Medal, American Voices Medal

Scott struggled to get up, still half tied into his sleep, but alarmed because of the sharp ringing that pierced through his delayed brain and gave him an urge to wake. Everything was cloudy, wisps of smoke curled around his room, glowing from some sort of light that he couldn't yet identify. It seemed rather pleasant to be honest, still confused he didn't mind the presence of this unknown substance as he drifted further into sleep. Suddenly something snapped, and Scott realized he was in his room, and exactly why it appeared to him in this way. His house was on fire.

Adrenaline kicked into overdrive, and Scott shot from his bed, ripping the covers from there place and scattering on the floor. His body jump-started into survival mode, and his first thoughts were to open the door. Dashing for the door, he grasped the handle, but recoiled in shock and agony. The steel handle was scorched, and as he pulled away ribbons of skin peeled from his melted palm, cooking on the searing door handle. Scott winced, ripping off his shirt with his good hand and wrapping it over the fresh burns, now glazing over. Adrenaline now took over his body, surging from his upper legs up through his body, sending explosive chills through his body and simultaneously dimming the pain of his burns. Now able to understand the fire was most likely clawing at his door, Scott ran to the window. Smoke continued pouring in from the slit underneath his door, filling his lungs and stabbing into his eyes. He fell to the floor, choking and wiping at his eyes to relieve the tears. Staying low to the ground, with strength draining, he smashed the window, glass raining over his head as he continued to rasp for breath on the floor. Victorious, he grasped the window railing and pulled himself up to crawl out, perhaps wait on the roof for help. Instead, as he reached to grasp over the other side of the window, he was met by the wiring of the metal screen built in, something he hadn't even thought of. His strength gone and his morale exhausted, he collapsed to the floor.

Scott blinked. He saw nothing. Or rather, faded shapes here and there, but mostly, dim everywhere. His hearing and sense of smell came back to him, Scott realized he was still in the raging inferno he once called home. Feeling the back of his head, he discovered a trickle of a warm liquefied substance, which he presumed to be blood. Trying to get up, he managed to find the rail to the window, and was interrupted by a short coughing fit. As he crouched low to the ground, his attention was drawn to the ceiling, as a large "whoosh!" surrounded him. Looking up, he saw the most beautiful death trap imaginable. Flame had found the ceiling, and spread rapidly across the surface. Flame rippled and intertwined with itself, creating intricate patterns that crackled and snapped as bits of glowing hot plaster fell free from the ceiling and rained down on him.

Moving quickly, Scott grasped his antique hat rack, one of the few objects not scorching hot or already burned in his room. Hooking it to a wire in the screening frame, Scott's adrenaline took over again. Emergency fuels pumped into his arms and legs as he pulled on the rack, straining against the resistance from the frame. The frame fought back in an epic tug of war, letting out its groans and creaks. The door was rapidly disintegrating, and larger bits of plaster and wood rained down from the ceiling. It too let out loud sighs as the increasing deterioration became too much for the foundation of the room to bear. In an instant, the web of blazing plaster would win. And two thousand pounds of blazing wood and plaster would fall onto Scott. His muscles burned, ready to give in, and he turned to his last reserves of strength, ripping the wooden rack back towards himself. With that, the screening gave in, tearing itself from the wall with a final scream of anguish. Wasting no more time inside this death trap, Scott threw himself out onto his first story roof, and dove into a nearby bush in his garden. Looking up at where his room used to be, now all he saw was flame, leaping up and dancing its evil rituals into the sky. Scott escaped death by seconds, but his home and old life he remembered was gone forever. ∎

Standstill

SHORT STORY

MAPLE BUESCHER, Grade 11. Cleveland Heights High School, Cleveland, OH. Donna Feldman, *Educator*; Cleveland Institute of Art, *Affiliate*; Gold Medal, American Voices Medal

The world has always moved very quickly for Adiaba Lawal.

When she was two, three, four years old, the long days spent playing under the baobob trees seemed no longer than seconds. When she was a little older—seven, eight, nine years old—the elementary school weeks slipped by in the same amount of time that fidgety Njideka felt their math lessons took. And when she was older still—twelve, like now—she could never seem to get as much housework done as she'd like to because the days just went so fast.

Time really is a funny thing; Adiaba always seems to think it goes faster than other people do.

The other girls in camp, for instance. They describe when they were taken as moving slow as molasses, time slowing down as they froze in horror as men bore down on them. Most of the girls say it happened when they were out alone, running errands or walking home. Zikora had gone to fetch the doctor for a girl who had a seizure in class. The doctor made it to school; Zikora did not.

Zikora described in harrowing detail what had happened, and Adiaba was amazed because every intricate nugget she remembered made it sound like it took hours. It felt like that, Zikora told Adiaba; that one horrifying minute felt like days. She is baffled when Adiaba says it felt instantaneous, a blink, and then it was over and they were here.

Even here the time flashes by. The first day was a lightning flash. The men told them they must learn quickly, and so they did. And every day their hands work faster, and every day the clock speeds up. After a week, the days of stuffing ball-bearings into canisters and vests and bags blur together, all just second-hand ticks on the clock of Adiaba's life.

The months she stays at the camp zoom by. More girls arrive, and some of the girls suddenly disappear. Adiaba knows all about what happens when they leave, even if she's never seen it. The girls are celebrated, praised, even applauded—and then they are strapped to an explosive vest and shoved into the middle of a crowded market and ordered to offer themselves to Allah.

It used to go without a hitch almost every time. Then, though, the national police force caught wind of it. Girls were running up to officers, screaming about the bombs they were strapped to, begging the officers to save their lives. And the police force responded. They defused the bombs, freed the girls, took them away. Adiaba has never heard from a girl who has escaped, but she can just imagine them standing in front of her, her whole body heaving with her absolutely terrified breaths as a police officer carefully snips a few crucial wires. Adiaba is overwhelmed with a sense of longing for that to be her. The men who run the camp she works in are infuriated by the very thought.

Adiaba has heard their ranting and raving every time a girl is sent out and there is not a mass murder. She's heard their fury every time a girl runs away and her life is saved. She's heard their plots, too, seen the inventions they have made to take control back.

They have remote controls now, disguised as things innocuous as car keys, and they send men out to follow the girls. And if the girls don't detonate their bombs themselves, the supervisors point their car keys at the girls' chests and press a button, and the children are no more, and neither are the few dozen square feet surrounding them. But even this new move, it seems, has somehow been countered by the police. Adiaba has heard whispered stories of signal blockers, of high-tech devices that can disrupt the explosive waves in midair and stop the suicides before they happen. Adiaba has heard rumors of girls' lives being saved this way. It's funny, Adiaba thinks, the constant back-and-forth, like a game of cat-and-mouse with a high probability of both animals ending up dead.

Time continues to move quickly. She overhears conversations every week, and it seems that what she remembers like yesterday was actually months ago. She doesn't sense the days passing; she stuffs vest after vest after vest, not knowing who will wear them, not knowing who will die.

And then one day she makes her last suicide bomb.

In a movie, Adiaba thinks, this process—like any other "last"—would be slow-motion, underscored with dramatic music. But making the vests has gotten so easy that she processes it as little more than a blink.

And then she's taken. They take the bomb she just made with her own hands and they strap it to her. Apparently she's not one of the trustworthy ones, because an older man goes with her, fidgeting subtly with the car keys in her hands. She shivers. She is suddenly overcome with longing to live in a country where a man dangling car keys in a teenager's face is a reward and not a death threat.

They walk and walk until they are close enough to a building that Adiaba can tell that it is a police station. He gestures for her to move forward, raising an eyebrow with a murderous smile, and fingers the car keys again. She takes a few faltering steps. Her heart is screaming. She knows what she needs to do, and the world moves so quickly that if she doesn't do it now she will never get a chance.

She is still too far from the police station to make any real damage if—god—if she blows up now. If she stops she'll be suspicious, if she advances any further she'll be within range. There is not a second to spare.

And she begins to scream, hollering for mercy, begging with all of her soul for help. She sinks to her knees on the sand, trembling so violently she is sure she will throw up, and she screams. *"Help me!"* Adiaba wails, tears coursing through the dirt on her face as she allows herself to desperately hope that someone will listen. *"Help me, please!"*

And her chest does not explode. Her supervisor screams, hollers, curses at her to move forward, get closer, so she can be blown up and take other people with her. But there are officers flooding toward her now. It is all happening so fast, and the sights and sounds and smells and emotions are overloading Adiaba's brain. It is all happening at once, so quickly, and there is no time to stop and think.

An officer sprints in front of the crowd. He glances up at the terrified teenager, at the man brandishing car keys, and he puts it together instantly.

Adiaba's supervisor grins. There are plenty of officers close to his girl now; she could explode and take dozens of them with her. It isn't the plan, but it's close enough.

The world is flying by in Adiaba's field of view, and every second is whizzing by—blink and you miss it. But she doesn't blink, and she sees everything perfectly.

She sees the officer's hand slip into his pocket.

She sees her supervisor point the car keys.

She sees the officer pull out a signal blocker.

She sees two fingers jab two buttons in one instant, the supervisor to explode her, the officer to block the explosion.

And for a moment—just an infinitesimal sliver of a moment—the world stands still. ∎

Exodus

SHORT STORY

ADITI DEY, Grade 8. Sycamore School, Indianapolis, IN.
Emilie Molter and Beth Simpson, *Educators*; Clowes Memorial Hall, Butler Arts & Events
Center and Hoosier Writing Project at IUPUI, *Affiliate*; Gold Medal

The year was 1971. I lived in Bangladesh, a country that Pakistan held as their property. The Freedom Fighters had been revolting against the Pakistani army, trying to free us from their grasp, but with what seemed to be minimal luck. Every day, hundreds died. Lined up in a street and shot down or killed in an uprising. Women and children were shown no mercy. Villages near us were completely obliterated while we could do nothing but hide. Pakistan held so much power that it barely seemed to matter to me if we hid or not. Would it really matter if just one more person died? Maa said it did, but I did not know.

The Pakistani army was reported to be passing through that day. Rimi *mashi* told us it was on the radio. She had come down to tell Maa after she had gone down to the village's communication office. Usually, Maa would have offered her some tea, or maybe a snack, but there was nothing in the house. Usually, Rimi *mashi* would have expected her to. But these days, nothing was usual.

Maa had been preparing to leave the house for a while now. She had packed up all the rice and lentils into light, clay pots. Baba was at the market that day to make some final arrangements with his friend and wouldn't be back until late, around when the troops would be patrolling. Maa had said that if we were to leave, we would leave as a whole. While Maa and Rimi *mashi* talked, I called over my siblings, in hopes that one would come. None of us were in the mood for games, but we had to spend the time somehow.

We weren't to leave the house in fear of the troops, and we never wanted to anyways. The flora outside remained green as ever. The fruits and flowers still bloomed in the yards, and the bushes still held their same emerald tones. No matter though; the village spirit was drained. Drained enough to pull every last trace of color out of the greenery, leaving only the crimson splatters of dry blood on each living leaf.

Night came before Baba returned. Rimi *mashi* had left and Maa had pulled all six of us children out to the back of our clay house, a kerosene lamp in her hand. She had taken the pots of rice and grains and handed them to us to carry on our way. She walked out into the jungle and took us down a twisting path. We remained silent as we struggled through the trees, quietly untying each of the sharp branches that caught and tore our clothes as we followed Maa's dim lighting. We were careful not to wince or cry even as the jungle sliced thin cuts into our skin. We all were anxious, hoping desperately that our younger brothers, Ramesh and Naveen, would not make a noise. They were twins and only five, after all, and still loud and playful. Even the slightest sound might make the army catch on to us, and we couldn't afford to take a chance. All was silent. Through the sultry night air and the sounds of the jungle, I thought I heard a distinct clink of metal in the distance. A shiver ran down my spine as my brothers clung tighter to each side of me. I helped them over the shrubbery, praying they would not cry out. My sisters, Jayati and Mita, walked not too far behind us. Chitra, my eldest sister climbed on ahead of us, next to Maa. The trees tangled more and more as we hiked further into the woods, and, finally, after tripping over innumerable tree knots, Maa stopped. She kneeled down to search the ground, peeling back thick leaves off the earth, scattering handfuls of dirt as if she were digging to find a precious treasure. At last, she uncovered it. A rusty, metal handlebar in the ground, buried under grime and weeds. Maa called us to dust off some of the soil that covered the rest of the underground door, which already had shrubs and dirt stuck onto it for better camouflage. With the help of Chitra, she heaved the handle up to reveal a small hideaway. The walls were dirt inside and a few clumps fell as Maa and Chitra pulled up the wooden door. My mother went down the narrow steps, beckoning us to follow. Ramesh and Naveen, who, until now, had remained silent, chose this time to whine.

"But Maa, I don't want to go down there! It's dark and there are things crawling around in it!" Ramesh complained.

"Yeah, why can't we go somewhere else?" Naveen followed.

"Quiet!" Maa snapped, "If you don't stay silent we'll all be dead before you know it." The panic was evident in her eyes.

My brothers pulled harder on the hem of my dress, widening the holes already present in it. I snatched the fabric out of their hands and ruffled up their dark, curly hair. Plastering a smile on my face, I whispered to Ramesh to hold my hand, and Naveen to hold his. I took the lamp from Maa, and the three of us walked down into the dirt cellar. Jayati and Mita followed close behind, each carrying a clay pot of grain. Chitra climbed in and pulled the inside handle down.

Naveen and Ramesh buried themselves in between Maa and Chitra. Across from them, Jayati and Mitra sat on two sides of me, and the clay containers of grain sat along the side of the small space.

"Will Baba come soon?" little Naveen asked.

"I don't know, stay quiet," Maa replied in a hushed voice. She stared blankly at the earth wall, her long, dark hair looked messy as it tumbled out of her usually-well-kept bun. I could practically hear her saying, "I don't know if he even will come."

The night was probably the longest of my life. Maa had turned out the lamp, and it was pitch black. Twice, I heard a gunshot, and even the rustling of the leaves above us made my blood curdle and my heartbeat quicken. Another time, the army passed right above us, the sound of their thundering footsteps echoed into our hiding spot, and we prayed with all of our beings that they would not find us. Jayati and Mita grabbed tightly to each other in the dark, and I could just barely make out Maa's eyes which remained wide open throughout the night. I desperately wanted to reach out and hug her, but Ramesh and Naveen were asleep on my shoulders, and movement could be fatal.

* * *

The sun peeked in through the small cracks in the wooden cover of the dirt hole. We hadn't heard footsteps in a while, but in our hearts we all wondered if the army were just above us, waiting quietly for us to come out. I suppose Maa had had enough of the what-ifs, because she pushed the door straight up, making a creaking sound so loud that it woke up my brothers.

"Maa!" they whined as they rubbed their eyes.

My sisters and I all flinched at the sudden flood of light. Maa climbed out silently.

"I hate this stupid journey," Jayati mumbled. "It's like a storybook except it's bad and the antagonist wins while we all run and hide."

"At least have some hope." Chitra squeezed her arm. "The Freedom Fighters aren't doing that badly, you know."

"We might have a chance," Mita patted her sister's shoulder.

"Let's go, before we're late," Chitra started up the grimy, wooden ladder, and we followed.

I passed the pots of grain up for Jayati and Mita to carry, and climbed out last, pushing the door down as I went.

* * *

We reached the edge of the jungle, where the greenery ended and the river began. The water was the familiar greenish-blue that I had loved ever since I was small. An old man sat in a boat by the shore, waiting to take someone across the river. There was no money in the small wooden box that he kept at the head of his boat, and he seemed to be beaten up. Maa approached him.

"Sir, can you take us to the city across the river?" She pulled a few small coins out from a pouch in her saari. "There are seven of us."

"Of course, my child, but keep the coins," he smiled and folded the coins back into her hand.

"Climb in!" he gestured to my siblings and me.

As he helped us climb in, Maa looked around behind her one last time, before hurrying in behind us. I wonder what she was thinking when she looked back. There was nobody there. Except maybe Baba.

As we crowded into the small boat and pushed off into the river, I looked back into the jungle which now grew further and further away from me. I saw my house, with its red-tinted clay walls. I smelled the freshly cooked fish coming from my mother's kitchen, which I hadn't had for so long since the war began. We were forced to sell all our fish, our animals, our fruits and vegetables, just to live a barely decent life for the past few months. I felt the cool splashes of the pond in our backyard that my siblings and I used to play in so often, and I looked down at the green water of this river that we now floated through. I dipped my fingers into the calm waves and swirled my hand around. Would I ever get this back?

"Maa, are we close yet?" Ramesh asked the question we had all been wondering.

"Maa, how far even is India?" Naveen chimed in.

"Far," Maa smiled, "but we'll stop at your uncle's house in the town past the jungle across this river. He'll keep us for a while, and Baba might be there, too," she ran her fingers through their hair.

"Baba!" they exclaimed, causing the wrinkles on the boatman's face to crease into a smile.

Maa was the first to climb out when we reached the other side of the river. She helped each of us out and we all said thank you to the boatman and bid him farewell as he made his way back across the waters. It was early morning now, and the sun was still rising slowly above us, painting the sky orange and pink. The horizon reflected off the leaves, tinting our faces a pale magenta as we began walking through the jungle. It was less dense than the one we were in the night before, but for some reason, even in the open, with daylight shining through the trees, it felt more unsafe. The shrubbery rustled every now and then and my pulse sped up whenever I heard it. Our footsteps became more and more silent each time a leaf rustled.

We arrived fairly close to the city. I could see it in the distance through a thick bunch of trees. The colorful buildings and the market. They seemed quiet from afar, but I knew when we would get there it would be full of life. A bush fluttered its leaves behind us, and Ramesh, who seemed to be getting quite jumpy, spun around at the speed of light. Mita was just about to pat his back to turn him back around, when a dark flash jumped out of the greens. Two men stood there, in full uniform. They wore helmets and each held guns bigger than both my brothers combined. I knew who these people were. They were the very ones we had dreaded for so long. Each day in my village for the past few months had been pure misery because of these men. Each hour I spent, I anxiously waited for their attack on my hometown. Each minute, I watched my siblings with the never-ending fear of losing them. Each second, I wondered how my mother had stayed so calm through all of it. And now, I did all of it again, my feet planted on the earth's floor, unable to move. My veins were practically popping out of my skin in fear and I could already feel my vision begin to blur with tears.

"Don't move a muscle unless you wish to be killed," the soldiers spat, moving closer as if their guns couldn't already reach.

"As if you won't kill us anyway," my mother scoffed.

"How dare you!" one of the soldiers exclaimed, walking up to her and grabbing her by her neck.

I couldn't help but look over. All I could do was stand and watch as my mother's face began to turn red, then purple. I knew, at that moment, that these men would not let her go alive. She tried her best to turn to me and her eyes widened as they met with mine.

"Run," she choked out in Bengali.

I picked up Naveen in one arm, and grabbed Ramesh's hand with my other. I flung around, almost twisting my little brother's arm, and I began to run. Chitra snatched Jayati and Mita and pulled them into the jungle. We ran about fifty feet before I tripped on some thick tree roots. I pulled Naveen close to me as I fell so he wouldn't get hurt, and I felt a branch dig its way into my skin, leaving nothing but a piercing sensation as I lay on the ground, paralyzed.

"*Didi*!" Ramesh cried. He had not fallen with me, and now he leaned down and began to shake my arm.

"Ramesh, I don't think I can get up . . . go on," I whispered, the pain in my side making it hard to move or speak. "Go, please."

"No, we can't! You have to come with us!" Naveen had untangled himself from my arm and stood up. "We'll go to Uncle's house all together!"

They worked together, struggling to help me off the branch. It was working. They had managed to lift me off the branch and set me on the dirt, my side facing the forest floor in an attempt to stop the blood. I tried to stand, panicking and falling over again as I saw the silhouette of the two soldiers grow in the distance.

"Come on, *didi*. Please get up," Naveen begged, tugging my arm with all his might.

"We have to go, I can see them coming," his brother continued.

"Ramesh. Naveen. Listen to me. Follow Chitra to your uncle's house and don't look back. I'll be okay," I said softly, fighting for strength just to speak.

The soldiers were only a few feet away. My brothers still stood over me, and I could see tears forming in their eyes. They yanked at my arm once again, but I swatted them away.

"Go!" I yelled one last time as the soldiers drew even closer.

They finally listened. A gunshot rang through the air and I felt like I was falling even further, falling straight through the floor of the earth. I saw a shadow of a man loom over me as my vision dimmed and another shot blew through my frail form. I could taste metal on my tongue as my life flowed out of me. As my head tilted to the ground, I watched my brothers run into the forest, their innocence shattered as their bodies half-heartedly carried them out of sight. Out of sight into the lively green of the trees, while I remained on the ground, dressed in lifeless red. ■

Bakaak

SHORT STORY

ASHER JAFFE, Grade 12. Hunter College High School, New York, NY.
Daniel Mozes, *Educator*; NYC Scholastic Awards, *Affiliate*; Gold Medal, American
Voices Medal

The average human spends a third of their life asleep. A waste of time, really. Luckily I don't have to deal with it. The doctor said I have to look on the bright side, so that's what I'm trying to do. Someone with my condition has about six months left. Rapid onset, the doctor said. But I get more out of those months than anyone I think, because of my condition. Silver linings. My day is one and a half times as long as the average human's, and those black hours when the rest of the world sleeps have become an important time to me. From two to four a.m., I'd say, is the best time for me, the quietest, when I'm most alone with my thoughts. Everyone's asleep, but the world still talks, moves, breathes. Out in the woods, mice and rats scurry beneath the fallen leaves and owls catch the glint of the moon in their mirrored eyes. A fierce wind blows past my house, setting the timbers groaning softly; a lament. The shadows seem to take on a little more life, the house around me groaning, wheezing, whispering. Your thoughts echo off these sounds, magnify. I do most of my thinking during the night. During the day, I feel slower. The light dulls my mind, which is a nocturnal creature. I stare into the woods while it laps up puddles of darkness.

Initially, I didn't know what to do with all this new time I had. But staring out into the woods, I started to think of the movement in the shadows, the chirping of night birds and the shimmering call of the insects, and it sounded like music. The pumping of my heart became a drumbeat, and out of the woods a voice seemed to call to me, something ancient and aboriginal. People have been staring into the woods for thousands of years. What have they seen?

I work at an ad agency, a ways from where I live. Getting to work on time used to be a problem; I could never seem to wake up early enough to make the hour's drive into Green Bay. Not a problem anymore. After the beautiful velvet texture of the night, the way the darkness and sound seem to press close around me, the diurnal world seems thin, faded. My coworker, Sandra, says I look tired. Of course I'm tired, I tell her. Right, she says. I'm sorry. I forgot. Do I want a coffee? No thanks, I tell her, it doesn't seem to help anymore. She sits at the break room table and unwraps her sandwich. Tuna fish. My muffin sits sullenly in its waxed paper as I tear away chunks. What do you do at night, she asks. I look at her a moment, detecting pity, and a faint morbid curiosity. Why couldn't I have the decency to die of something normal? Her mother passed of leukemia, she knows how to deal with that. But this, it draws her fascination, makes her forget her manners. She realizes I've realized this, her expression shifts slightly; guilt. It's okay, I tell her, an understandable question. I've started work on a book, about the first European explorers who came here, and what they found. So it's historical? she asks. Fantasy. Of sorts. It's about the human psyche, what we see when we stare into the darkness. Some French fur traders find the woods around the lake haunted, not with quite the same demons they have at home, but similar. What lurks in the night here, I tell her (I've done my research), are what the Ojibwe called *bakaak*. Ojibwe? she asks. I chide her for her ignorance. Did you think we were the first here?

It's hard to concentrate on my work. The electric light of the screen seems jagged; the colors a razor's edge. I squint to stop the text from vibrating. I wonder if I should quit my job, just focus on my book. I should really spend as much time on it as possible. My day-to-day seems less and less important. Even here in the brightly lit cubicle (harsh, sterile) I feel the pull of the night, the softness of the woods, the notebook and pen where I scribble my ideas feverishly by the light of a candle. I like candlelight. It's easier on the eyes. Rustic. And the French didn't bring lightbulbs with them when they came here so many years ago, plying the misty lake, looking for beaver.

The sun sets while I'm making my way home and I turn on my high beams for visibility. The roads out where I live have no light but the stars. Something flits through the night ahead of me and I slow. The deer's eyes catch the light and throw it back to me. It heads off into the trees slowly, and its body is consumed by the darkness. The eyes shine still. Bakaak have glowing eyes, so say the Ojibwe.

I wish I had a quill pen, for maximum authenticity, but ah well a ballpoint will do for now. Jean Lebesque, I think, a good, strong name for an explorer of brave new territory. The woods sing to him in a way they hadn't back home in France. He's separated from his company and finds them dead in the woods, arrayed in a circle, bellies torn open. Their livers are gone. Why? I can explain, the woman says, moonlight catching softly on her skin. Her bare feet pad across the forest floor and her hair shines. She wears very little, a simple shift for a simple people. Does she have a name? I'll figure it out later. Bakaak are thin, she tells our protagonist; they fold themselves up to hide in holes, behind trees, above us, around us. She takes his hand. They will come for you while you sleep, with their heavy clubs and invisible arrows. I will help you build a fire. We can watch the night together.

Sandra's lunch today includes ham slices, wrapped in plastic. I ask her if she thinks about the animal before it goes in the wrapping and she tells me she tries not to. It's easy to forget, I observe, because it loses a lot of its vitality, its essential meatiness, in this form. Plastic, not skin. Bloodless. We're so far removed from the squealing, the whoosh of the blade, the sound of the saws hacking limbs apart, the spurts of blood on the sterile white suits of the industrial butchers. Stop, she says, I don't like thinking about that. I understand, I say, it can be a hard thing to confront. Society seems determined that we not. The printer starts up, shooting out fresh white sheets, blinding, bleached. No sign of the tree that once was, all the sunlight it drank, or the animals whose rotting flesh its roots explored. We were not the first here, but our world is not the same as theirs. We've paved it over, drained the blood, packed it in plastic. From inside the city you can't see the stars.

The Ojibwe saw the stars every night, before the white people came, before there was electricity. An earlier people of an earlier time, a people of the dark. I am beginning to empathize more. I can no longer look at my phone; it's too bright. In the office I squint. On the drive back home the headlights of an oncoming car blind me; I close my eyes, I swerve, I miss the turn. I'm lucky, the doctors say, that it was only the leg I broke. The other guy, his head smacked right into the dash. Wasn't wearing his seatbelt. A neat circle of blood on the plastic. It's patterned, tackily, I think, to look like wood.

Dr. Unogwu says I shouldn't drive anymore, I should stay at home. Besides, I don't have that long left. I might as well enjoy it. She'll come visit me, she says, to make sure I'm doing alright. I will do alright, I tell her. I have something to work on.

Jean spins around, shadows dancing away from his lit torch. He hears the sharp cry of the bakaak, but he sees it nowhere. And then—something, over there! Careful, the woman says. No man can kill them. Maybe none of your men, he says, and lunges for the creature with torch and blade. It melts away before him, shrieking. He whirls around, it is nowhere. Is it dead? The woman does not know. It might have just melted back into the trees.

Sandra visits me, saying, I hope you don't mind. I found your address in the employee registry. And I thought you should know we're thinking of you. Flowers, a card signed by everyone in the office, some brownies Cheryl baked. Thank you, do you want anything? Tea, cocoa? It's cold outside. No, you're hurt, don't trouble yourself. I hobble to the stove anyway and she catches me and sits me back down. I'll fix us something myself. She admires the cupboards while she rummages around in them. Beautiful wood. Virgin growth, I tell her. This house is old, built back when you could cut down a tree older than the white man's roots in America and use it to make a shelf. Its age gives it character. Forest fires, beetle infestations, it's all marked in little blemishes. History laid bare, a cross-section. I've finally bought a quill pen (goose feather, long and grey and mottled) and she sees it on the table next to my leather-bound notebook and glass inkwell. You like history, don't you? All this old stuff. It's what makes us, I tell her, and it can unmake us.

I enjoy our conversation, but I am happier when she is gone, when I can lie back and let the shadows sing to me. My bedsheets are nylon, a product of science once unimaginable, but now ordinary because of the ministrations of generations of men, swinging their torches out against the dark. The bakaak shrieks as it leaps away, and this time Jean sees it recede into the tree, hiding deep beneath the bark. He lights a fire at the base of the tree and it spreads and grows taller, towering against the sky. The sparks pop and fly, the demon's dying eyes, and the explorer and the woman make love in the embers of the old world.

You can't keep the lights off all the time, says Dr. Unogwu, and flips them on. The light dances jaggedly, now brighter than ever before. The shadows have deepened too, by contrast. They do not vibrate as much as they sway, a hypnotic dance, all hips, and I respond. Dr. Unogwu asks if I am okay, and I respond truthfully, telling her that I am better than ever. She seems worried about something, but I can't imagine what. I'm better this way. When I sharpen my quill and miss a stroke and the blade cuts deep into my thumb I rejoice and suck the red juice. How else should I know I am alive? She asks me to answer a few questions and hands me a quiz. How severe are my symptoms? I have none. I had before, but the veil is now drawn away. She nods and retreats quickly. She is afraid of your potential, a voice says.

The forest is gone, burnt to ash. The ground is charred, but it is good, Jean explains. The charcoal will fortify the soil. The Ojibwe chief, he is not sure if his people are ready for this new way of life. The opportunities are limitless, our intrepid explorer says. The bakaak are gone, burnt away. I trapped them in the trees and now they are all gone, ashes. What if not every tree burned? Then we will cut them down one by one and use them to make great houses. None shall come for us then.

At night, the wind sets the timbers creaking, and I call out in response. The shadows sway, and I sway with them. Release me, a voice calls, a high-pitched call. I am trying to write. Release me! Release me! I bang my fist on the table and ink spills everywhere. I push my book out of the way so as not to lose all my hard work, and hastily attempt to clean up the mess. My hands are stained and I go into the bathroom to wash them. One of my crutches slips and I end up on the floor, hard scrabbling against the tile. The puddle of ink surrounds me, and I roll in it. When I pull myself up and look into the mirror finally, I see a gaunt face, emaciated, stained, staring back at me. The eyes glint. Release me! it says, release me and I will teach you to be who you were meant to be. I will show you how to swing a club and shoot an arrow and remove a man's liver while he sleeps. I will teach you to shriek and sneak and melt into the trees like the shadow you are. What do I need to do? There is an axe in the garage, the bakaak says, break the timbers, set us free! We will make the world over again, a new world, an old world. On my way back from the garage, I fall and the axe cuts my hand. I am bleeding, I can still bleed. I am not yet dead like the others. Inside, I let the axe crash into every surface: tables, cabinets, chairs. More! the voice cries, more! more! The heavy metal head smashes through plaster, through sheetrock, to the timbers that hold up the house. I step inside the wall and feel the splinters press close around me. This is the place, the truest darkness. I am at the bottom of a black velvet bag, and it holds me warm. No, not velvet, the pelt of an animal, fresh and stinking. Now you're getting it, says the bakaak, twisting its way out of the darkness. Its glowing eyes meet mine. What do you want? I ask. You. I embrace it, and I am whole. ∎

Quiet

SHORT STORY

MAYA SHADID, Grade 9. St. Agnes Academy, Houston, TX. Herman Sutter, *Educator*; Harris County Department of Education, *Affiliate*; Silver Medal

Our family was happy—Mom and Dad and me. And the cat, Pringles. We got Pringles when I was five. She was a little tabby with spindly whiskers and bean-feet. Her fur was pretty; it looked like gingerbread and smelled like grass. She shed a lot though; everywhere Pringles went, she sprinkled a trail of orange-red hairs.

I had just turned seven when Pringles disappeared. School started up and I had to wake up real early. Pringles was there that morning, I remember. She sat on my lap as I ate my cereal, and she shed all over me. I was almost late to school because I had to lint-roll all the fur off. Then I rushed out of the door, said my *I love you*s, and walked myself to the bus stop. I don't really remember school that day, just that when I got home later, Pringles wasn't there. Nobody ever told that she died, so she couldn't have, right? I mean Dad said she was "gone," but she could've just run away. I *knew* she'd come back; I could just tell. So, I waited and waited at our front window all the way until dinner—until Mom convinced me there was nothing for me to wait for. It all hit me at once. I cried and screamed and *hated* my mom for telling the truth. I didn't *want* the truth, I wanted Pringles. I ran up to my room and threw myself onto my bed. The sheets were stained, but I didn't remember spilling anything. At that point, it didn't matter. I sprawled out against those dark marks and that firm mattress and yelled as if it would bring back my cat. It didn't—couldn't. I felt alone.

When I was satisfied, I slowly sat up, blew my nose in my sleeve, and began walking downstairs. As I made my way down the steps, I overheard my parents whispering.

"I can't do this anymore."

"Shh, shh."

"No, she was so *sad*, Michael. I don't think she knows what she did."

And then they noticed me. There was this awkward pause, and then some *are you okay*s? and sad looks. Then Dad hugged me, only it was different. It was empty. And Mom, Mom wouldn't even touch me. It was like they were scared of me, and I didn't understand. I didn't *do* anything.

I don't remember anything else that happened that day. I don't remember a lot from back then. I'd be putting on my socks in the morning one minute and falling from the monkey bars the next. I had these lapses—they left me confused and angry. And every time I woke from one of these, the world seemed a little quieter. It was the kind of quiet that couldn't be heard—only felt. It was the kind of quiet that went like this:

We used to have squirrels outside our house—a whole lot. They clawed up trees and danced with their tails and squeaked—a whole lot. But as my memory glitched away more and more, the clawing and dancing and squeaking grew less and less. It seemed like every time I "lapsed," one more squirrel disappeared. And then there were no squirrels left. It took a few months, but then they were all gone. I don't know where they went.

The quiet also came in other forms. My parents began withdrawing themselves from me ever since Pringles left. They started acting like I was fragile—like I'd hurt them. I didn't understand any of it. The only thing I did the night of Pringles's disappearance was cry. I knew they weren't afraid of crying, because mom had done that every night since. I wasn't supposed to notice, but I did. She sat in bed with her rosary pressed against her palm and sang quiet sobs—"It's my fault," and "I made her like this." She never explained those late-night whispers. What did they mean? My family wasn't so happy anymore, and I had a feeling it was my fault.

And there were still stains on my sheets, no matter how much we washed them. Sometimes, I even found little red cat furs, which was . . . weird. Pringles had never been allowed in my bed.

A little while later, on Christmas, my aunt Jackie surprised me with a new pet; this time it was a singing bird. I guess the gift surprised Mom and Dad, too—they seemed upset and uneasy. They tried to say no, tried to give it back, but I started crying. I wanted it—bad. Before my sobs could escalate any further, Dad picked me up, and Mom assured me that I could keep it. I was happy, sure, but something felt . . . off. They had never given in to me before—it seemed like they were afraid to say no. They had never been afraid before.

We put the bird in the living room. Mom and Dad made sure that the cage was real high up, and that the locks were all tight, and that nothing could get out and nothing could go in. There the creature sat, looking sort of majestic and omniscient, despite being trapped. I loved that bird—at first. But all through breakfast, it whistled and whistled and whistled. And right when I came back from school, it whistled and whistled and whistled. And as I closed my eyes at night, I heard a faint noise from walls too thin to conceal—whistle, whistle, whistle. One of those nights, I couldn't fall asleep. The tweeting was a quiet yet never-ending bell. I let out a groan of irritation; how long could I stand it? And then my memory flickered. I don't remember what happened. All

I know is that suddenly, everything was pulsing, and the whistling was loud, so loud, so loud. It was next to my ear, urgent, pleading, helpless. Screaming! Why was it screaming? Why was it loud, so loud, so loud—why was it . . . quiet? It got quiet, suddenly. I was startled, but what could I do? It was *quiet*. For once. And I was so tired. I felt a bit uncomfortable for some reason, like my pillow wasn't fluffed up right, but I was too exhausted to care. I shut my eyes and embraced a cloudy sleep.

Waking up refreshed for the first time in ages, I got out of bed, did a little stretch, and started getting ready for school. After my teeth were brushed and my uniform was on, I decided to make my bed. I fixed the under sheets, and then the blankets, and then I moved on to fluff my pillow. I lifted it up—and I saw something. I saw, I saw feathers? No, those weren't just feathers. I let out a scream, and my parents rushed to my room to see what had happened. Needless to say, I didn't go to school that day.

The bird died. It suffocated after being pinned under *my* pillow. My parents said it wasn't my fault, but the fear in their eyes told the truth. They blamed me. It couldn't have escaped its cage alone. It couldn't have found my bed alone. It couldn't have died without . . . help. But I didn't *remember* doing anything. I didn't want it dead; it couldn't have been me. The awful sound of whistling was traded out for the even worse sound of a therapist chattering on. I didn't *need* a therapist—I didn't do anything! But my parents said it would just be for a little bit, and I didn't want to fight with them. The first session was strained and uncomfortable. It began with introductions, promises of confidentiality, the usual. And then it *really* started.

(She clicked her tongue.)

"Do you want to tell me about that night?" Her eyes locked with mine.

"What night?"

(She clicked her tongue.)

"Come on, why don't you tell me about the bird?" Huh. The bird.

"Umm . . . oh. Well, there was tweeting, and then . . . I don't know . . . and then everything got loud, so loud, so loud. And then nothing." I could tell I was confusing her. She wanted me to explain, but I didn't know how. That night always played over the same way in my head.

Tweet (followed by) Something (which prompted the) Screaming (and then there was) Nothing. Tweet. Something. Screaming. Nothing.

And then the bird died, and . . . and *my* mom sent me to therapy, so who *really* lost?

"I don't know—I don't know anything. It all happened so quickly," I said.

(She clicked her tongue.)

"Hmm," she paused and thought for a moment, "Alright. How about you tell me about the cat, then." I froze.

"W-what do you mean, 'the cat'?"

(Click)

"Your parents mentioned something about an incident with a cat; Pringles, I think it was? Yes, Pringles. An incident."

An incident? Did she mean . . . ?

(Click)

No, no, no—she had *no* right to bring that up. What did she mean "incident"? I suddenly felt dizzy, nauseous, and the lights started flashing, and *why* was the AC loud, so loud, so loud? At that moment I realized why my parents had become so distant—why my sheets were stained that rusty color, what I had been doing each time my memory froze.

(Click)

Why couldn't I remember? All I wanted was to be normal. All I wanted was to stop forgetting. All I wanted was to know that I was at school that day instead of . . . This wasn't me; I didn't *want* this. There was a monster in my mind, and it hadn't always been there—only it decided it couldn't leave me alone anymore. What had I done? I tried to stand up, and then I was falling—I was stumbling and then falling, and my vision kept cutting out.

(Click)

"Hey, hey, I need you to calm down, okay?" Everything was muffled. (Click). And then suddenly she grabbed my shoulder. (Click). I hated the way she held me, I hated her soft voice, I *hated* her. So much. (Click). I would've been fine not knowing; I would've been at peace if she hadn't spelled everything out—if she hadn't been so insensitive. (Click). And that sound she kept making—it echoed in my head (Click), everything ached (Click), my mind was throbbing, my brain was pounding and I—(Click), I—(Click), I couldn't think! (Click). I wanted her to *leave me alone,* for her to—(Click).

I don't remember what happened next. ∎

Hundred

SHORT STORY

ANDREW GONG, Grade 11. Harvard-Westlake Upper School, North Hollywood, CA. Jocelyn Medawar, *Educator*; Region-at-Large, *Affiliate*; Silver Medal

Industrial steel beams whirred through the air above a blank roll of paper. As it unfurled onto the cold metal, it was cordoned off, sliced into bill-sized pieces with bureaucratic precision, and stamped with the smug green face of Benjamin Franklin, who seemed to declare, "I am invincible." Embossed on the corners were four 100s in bold official lettering. The little individuality the paper had before—the imperfections, creases, folds, and even the sterile white smell—had all been hydraulically pressed away, leaving a crisp rectangle with the distinctive odor of financial value. The only thing that now set it apart from the billions of twins it had been newly assigned was an eleven-digit serial number: *AG 052503881*.

The bill was first introduced to its brethren in the back of a crowded armored truck. It saw green stacks sway like anemone as the truck jostled over speed bumps, swerved around street corners, and finally pulled into the parking lot of a bank. Here, it rested in a vault as days and then weeks passed by, until finally, it felt itself being dropped onto a mechanical conveyor belt, squeezed through steel rollers, and deposited into the open air, where it was promptly snatched away by a man's hand at the mouth of the ATM. The bill wasn't accustomed to this new environment. It had grown acquainted to the bleak, hard metals of the vault and the production line, so the tough, calloused feel of the man's squeezing hand was a rough awakening into the life that lay ahead of it.

The bill soon arrived, tucked into the folds of the man's leather wallet, at a restaurant. At the end of a hearty meal, it was handed to a bustling young waitress, who hastily tossed it into a cash register and slammed the drawer shut to the tune of rattling coins. All night long, the money-filled chamber of the cash register opened and closed in a flurry of human activity, with dollars and coins constantly being dropped in and fished back out in a whirlwind of exchanges. The bill watched this commotion, uninterested, until at last it became the target of the hand that reached into the dark crevices of the register to rummage for cash. And thus began the life of a $100 bill, rudely injected into the American economy.

From the cashier's hand, the bill was first passed to a young woman who carried it purposefully to her neighborhood car dealership. She held the bill and waved it tantalizingly in front of the salesman, who had been stretched to quite the breaking point by her incessant bargaining. At last, he acquiesced, and snatched the bill, along with a stack of 100s, from her hand. The bill was laid to rest in his cashbox, until, after a long day of hard work, the salesman reached for it and grumbled and sighed his way to the bar. It was handed to the bartender in exchange for some shots and beers, which were downed by the salesman worryingly swiftly. The next day, the bartender, along with the bill which as now nested in his wallet, was cornered in an alley by a mugger, who coaxed the wallet away from him at gunpoint. The mugger introduced the bill into a new, darker environment—over the course of the next year, it was whisked off to facilitate hundreds of thousands of illicit black market transactions, each one more heinous and devious than the last. As the bill passed hands from criminal to criminal, the crispness of its composition faded, the once-perfect 90-degree corners rounded themselves away, and the straight-bodied bill buckled and wrinkled with the burden of constant handling.

The cycle of financial villainy was finally cut short when one criminal, with the bill clutched nervously in his right hand, went to a jewelry store to buy a wedding ring. He had been planning his proposal for months, and finding the perfect ring was the last missing piece. The only reason he had been trading on the black market, committing crimes, and endangering himself for the past few months was for *her* and the life they could have together—and once he bought this ring, it could all come to an end. The jeweler, of course, understood none of this, nor did she know of the vile history of the $100 bill she was being handed to pay for the cheap wedding ring. That night, she packed up the shop, and in her haste, accidentally let the bill glide out of her purse and come to rest on the sidewalk outside the jewelry store. A few hours later, a man wandered by in tattered clothes with no possessions aside from a dirty red shopping bag pockmarked with holes and grime. He was once a wealthy entrepreneur with a bright future and an inexhaustible supply of potential, before his parents fell ill and he sank his fortunes into their medical attention. Death, however, was unstoppable—his mother was the first to die, and his father went next. Money dwindled, and he was left wandering the streets homeless and hungry, until that day, he noticed a tinge of green on the ground out of the corner of his eye. Stooping lower, he saw the creased and fading 100s, one on each corner of the bill. Cradling the bill in his arms, he sank to his knees and cried tears of joy. They washed over the emerald ink like a melancholy waterfall.

* * *

Years passed. The endless exchanges became routine. The bill had by now facilitated too many new loves, saved too many lives, and broken too many hearts to count. If the bill had any crisp cleanliness left, it was gone and replaced with wrinkles and dirt. The bill found itself in a vault hidden deep in the heart of a military bunker, meant to safeguard valuable assets in dire times. Bombs rained from the skies and burrowed themselves into the ground around the bunker like jet black maggots. There was a brief moment of stillness, and silence hung precariously in the shelter. Then, explosions thundered and shook the musty air, grinding the bunker down into the dry earth. Tendrils of fire crept through the cracks of the vault, licking the treasures with their jealous snake-tongues. Towers of money toppled and burned, gold melted and bubbled at the floor, coins tumbled and danced like chaotic ballerinas, and through it all, the bill, tucked in a distant corner of the safe, survived. Yes, the tongues of flame lapped at its edges, singeing away the delicate green ink of the "100"s and leaving Benjamin Franklin's face a charred mess, but the bill persisted nonetheless. It seemed invincible.

The fires died down and bombs stopped raining. In the radioactive hazardous mess left by the third world war, survivors rummaged for food and resources. One man happened upon what looked like the decrepit and long-gone ruins of an American military stronghold. He picked his way carefully through the crevices with the seasoned eye of one who has had to scavenge for food in a previous life. Among the piles of debris and slabs of aged metals, a small slip of paper caught his eye. He stooped down to examine it, and he saw the now-empty white notches where 100s were once emblazoned in proud green lettering. He remembered when he once cried of happiness because he found a $100 bill outside a jewelry store, holding nothing but a tattered red shopping bag. With a gentle smile, he stooped to pick up the bill and wiped away the grime covering its weather-worn surface. The Benjamin Franklin, the emerald lettering, and the crisp edges with perfect 90-degree corners were all gone. All that was left was a slip of paper with a barely noticeable serial number printed in small font: *AG 052503881*. The man folded the bill in his palm, used it dab away the sweat and dirt that peppered his forehead, and tossed the dirty banknote back to the ground where he had found it. ∎

There Is a God

HUMOR

SAANVI BHATIA, Grade 9. East High School, Westchester, PA. Christine Bland, *Educator*; Philadelphia Writing Project, *Affiliate*; Gold Medal

There is a God. He rules with kindness and benevolence and takes pride in his subjects' happiness. He ensures that they are shielded from danger, and that death comes as a necessary finale rather than a record scratch in the middle of life. He rules with equity and peace and works so that every being can move in harmonious freedom.

God has a daughter. His daughter's name is Cassie. Cassie is a no-good, mostly incompetent alcoholic. It is Cassie who looks over Earth.

She was awarded the planet on her birthday, which didn't feel as much of a present as it did a burden. It was supposed to be an honor, but to be honest, Cassie had two goals in life and they were to be free of responsibility and to do a back flip, neither of which seemed possible in the near future.

The privilege of directing a planet was given with age and demonstrations of leadership and kindness. She received hers because of her father, who had gone on a spiel about how it was her turn to step up and maintain the reputation of her family. She hadn't really paid attention until he snapped (it took a while) and told her that if she didn't do this one thing, take care of this one planet, she would have to kick it in the streets. She couldn't remember the last time she saw someone homeless in heaven, and being the first seemed like it would take a lot more work than simply looking over the planet, so she grudgingly agreed.

The present she faked her joy for on her birthday, then, as he explained, was a new one with recent life that they'd just discovered. It was basic, covered with single-celled organisms and surrounded by planets with no life at all, so there was virtually no way to mess it up.

Virtually.

To be fair, she started off pretty well. The creatures on the planet were simple enough. All she had to do was watch over them and maybe sprinkle down some water and grow some food if they weren't already doing a fabulous job themselves.

Then, the worst thing that could have ever happened to Cassie happened. An unexpected evolutionary change and there it was. Intelligence. The planet kept filling up with more and more beings that could learn and play and communicate with each other. Her life had been hard enough when she had to deal with those algae things but beings that could use tools? Critically think?

No way. There was no telling what they would be able to do once they really got started. Cassie was panicking at this point. She had just downed an entire bottle of her elixir and it had made her really paranoid, so she summoned an asteroid, slammed it against the planet, hoped that it would get rid of all life, and fell asleep.

When she woke up, there were humans.

What headaches. Every second she looked away, they'd done something new. She needed to yawn, and they'd mastered fire. Needed to brush her teeth, they'd started farming. Needed to go to the bathroom, and they'd started building! They'd made structures out of material that was supposed to stay on the ground, their dislocation jumbling this nuisance of a planet around, tearing it from its natural oasis, and making it harder for Cassie to maintain balance.

With a crisis at its absolute finest and a killer hangover, Cassie decided the only logical thing to do to ensure the survival of this almost godforsaken planet—which included preventing overly smart beings from murdering the place—was to kill them off. So she sent disease after disease, disaster after disaster, and still, they survived. They recovered over and over again, and many times, they came back stronger.

This was enough. Cassie couldn't do this anymore. She pulled the strongest weapon out of her arsenal, one that she knew would make them destroy themselves from the inside out, one of the strongest bans that existed in the planet rulebook. She gave them religion.

Oh, how they fought. The most violent of the life-forms yet. They slaughtered each other and sacrificed themselves over their theories of Cassie's identity. It became a sort of competition to get as many followers as possible, because they believed they would win more of Cassie's affection. She felt flattered, but also, she didn't care. The fights were fun to watch and it kept them busy, but when Cassie got bored, she did what any other person would do. She went out.

When she came back, almost a day and a half later, they were gone, and so was everything else. In their place they left exactly what she was supposed to prevent: a planet left unusable, unmalleable, something that she couldn't interfere with or improve upon. They'd somehow activated a lockdown button and she had to watch the planet's slow, deteriorating death silently, unable to interfere.

Cassie wailed. She wailed and she cried and she crumpled to the floor, sobbing uncontrollably over this dreadful loss. She did this mostly because her father was standing right next to her. When he left, after Cassie had performed a pretty believable monologue on her innocence in the matter, she shrugged and leaned forward, glancing over the post-apocalyptic planet.

Temples towered over everything else, the highest level of extravagance and majesty that she could see. She observed candles and vigils and bodies dead in prayer, clutching necklaces, their plea still on their lips. There were crushed temples collapsed on thousands of bodies, craters born through explosions, and desperate bargaining buried within the bodies surrounding them.

She didn't know what had happened, but she chuckled over the blind devotion given to her. What fun. They had prayed like she was sober enough to care.

And she had gotten exactly what she wanted, too, with the bonus that she had seemingly tried the best she could. She smiled as she leaned back, taking a swig from the bottle on her bedside. Now, for the flip. ■

Start Your Keyboard Now

HUMOR

MAX MUNOZ, Grade 8. Hofius Intermediate School, Klein, TX.
Kionna LeMalle, Megan McCarthy, and Angie Young, *Educators*; Harris County
Department of Education, *Affiliate*; Silver Medal

NOOOO!! Why do you keep copying? Oh my gosh, bro. Can you chill out with all the copying of your homework, man?

Can you stop trying to access the dark web on a school computer?!!!

Why did I have to be the keyboard for this kid? Out of all the kids in the school, why him? I wish he could hear me, so I could tell him all the mistakes he's making.

"Like stop looking at your grades! Just looking at them isn't going to change them."

So, pretty much let me catch you up. I'm a keyboard, and I don't have a name, because, well, I'm a keyboard for this great, amazing, fantastic piece of . . . society.

Yeah, he's great. He's always on his computer, never lets me go to sleep, and guess what? He never does anything productive either. He's always playing games, or he goes to the dark web. Just a reminder: he's on a school computer, but he hacked it with me!! So, that's the person I'm dealing with. I bet you're like, this keyboard has it all. I do, I got this inspirational person controlling me on everything.

Man, when I was a new keyboard I had such high hopes for my life. I was going to be the next big thing, like free Wi-Fi. Instead, I got stranded in a middle school with this horrible person who can't even type the alphabet right, but can still somehow hack a computer.

Today he watched the stupidest video of a song called "Babies" by Justin Beaver. It made me want to cry just from it being typed, and I can't even hear it. Not only that, but he also tried watching a "Poodeepie" video just because he was bored. Just a reminder, he's on a school computer. That is his everyday routine listen to bad songs, watch "Poodeepie" videos, and then dive into the dark web again.

Whoa, isn't this your 115th time copying this school year? Oh my gosh, why you copy so much? This is so annoying. Why don't you have an imagination? Why do you have to use other people's ideas? For example, just last week you had to do a paper on the impact of recycling, and you tried to copy and paste the whole web page on "recycling basics" from the U.S. Environmental Protection Agency. Way to recycle that one.

Dude, this kid has to write an autobiography about himself. I wonder how that's going to go.

Wait, hold the phone! You're finally doing your homework? No way! I would've never seen that coming in a million years. I always thought you were just a loser who couldn't do anything.

Oh, never mind. I was right because all I see is a life that you WISH you had, but you don't have a life because you spend it all on me. Instead of writing the autobiography, you copied and pasted a Wikipedia entry about some billionaire who's named "Pill Bates" who owns a software company call Micromax. Man, I can't believe you, kid, and neither will your teacher.

My experience of being this kid's keyboard is an experience I wish I never had. I wish I had never been invented. I have to work with a kid who doesn't know what he's doing, who never actually does his homework, he just copies it from the internet. He eats over me, leaving crumbs stuck in between my body parts, and he stinks. I hate it so much. I can't go anywhere because I'm stuck with him. My biggest hope now is that he will spill water on me and I'll malfunction, and he'll have to replace me. That's the plan I'm working on.

If you find this note, it means I'm gone. Just know that keyboards have feelings, too. ∎

An Educator's Guide to
The Best Teen Writing of 2020

Prepared by the National Writing Project

Use the works of these National Medalist teen writers to inspire discussion and guide writing exercises with students.

1. **Short Story**

The relationship between setting and mood— *35 minutes*

Goal: Students explain how authors establish mood through details of setting (time and place).

Activity: Choose a story for review that contains many evocative details of setting (time, place, weather, etc.). Ask students to read with a highlighter, making note of the plot elements.

List on the board.

Discuss: What would it feel like to be here? Why do you think so? Choose a "favorite element." How did that particular detail add to your feeling about the place?

Revising for mood: Students choose a story they are working on, or a story from *The Best Teen Writing*. Add details of setting to enhance the mood being conveyed. Share with a partner for response.

2. **Short Story**

Writing with focus on characterizing the narrative—*35 minutes*

Goal: Students restructure a narrative with another narrator, creating the same story with a different perspective.

Activity: Ask students to take on the voice of one of the other characters and tell the story from that point of view, filling in blanks that the original narrator left. Challenge students to use important characterizing details in the reading to give color to their entries.

3. Poetry

Writing with focus on form—*30 minutes*

Goal: Students write using different structural techniques.

Activity: Have students write two poems on one topic of their choosing. Begin with a prose poem, in which they write freely on that topic; then have them write another poem on the same topic with a focus on line breaks to emphasize changes in rhythm or highlight specific phrases. Discuss the differences after sharing the results.

4. Personal Essay & Memoir

Writing with a focus on structure and pacing—*45 minutes*

Goal: Students write an organized and coherent memoir imitating the format of a *Best Teen Writing* piece.

Activity: Select a Personal Essay & Memoir from the anthology to read out loud with your students. Talk about the format in which the memoir is written. Discuss the choices made and how those choices are inherently personal, therefore inherently suited to convey a personal essay.

Ask your students to write their own memoirs modeled after the memoir you have selected. Have the students share their work and discuss choices that each student makes, including how those choices convey something personal to the reader.

5. Genre-Shifting Exercise

Blackout Poetry—*40 minutes*

Goal: Students explore form's relationship to function by distilling the language in a single piece of prose into a piece of poetry.

Activity: Have the students choose a page of prose in *The Best Teen Writing*. Students then scan the page for words that are interesting and lightly circle or underline those words with a pen. Next students read the page from top to bottom, looking for more interesting words, or words that might relate to the circled words. They should circle these, too. Finally, students begin to black out all the words on the page that they aren't using, in a sense "whittling away" the words that aren't part of the poem they've found within the text.

6. Blog Exercise

40 minutes and homework time

Goal: Students use critical-thinking skills to offer critiques and analysis of specific works or the anthology as a whole.

Activity: Ask students to write a blog post expressing thoughts about a specific piece of their choosing. Posts will be sent to the Alliance for consideration to be included on the Alliance blog.

• Students should express their opinions, offering positive feedback or constructive criticism, on a specific work in *The Best Teen Writing*. Alternatively, they may discuss the anthology as a whole.

• Posts may be emailed to **info@artandwriting.org**, with subject line "*The Best Teen Writing of 2020* Student Blog Post."

Educators: Continue the discussion! Explore with your peers even more ways in which *The Best Teen Writing of 2020* can inspire students in your classroom. Feel free to share new ideas about how to use *The Best Teen Writing* by sending your ideas to **programs@nwp.org**.

Works Cited

Tiffany Onyeiwu, "The Role of Black Girl Magic in Intersectional America"
Works Cited

Abdul-Kareem, Maryam. "Here's Why We Should Care More About Equity, Not Equality." Muslim Girl, muslimgirl.com, 5 January 2018. Web.

Carter, Charly, and Carol Lautier. "Taking Our Seat at the Table: Black Women Overcoming Social Exclusion in Politics." Demos, Demos, 20 November 2018. Web.

Chavers, Linda. "Here's My Problem with #BlackGirlMagic." ELLE, Hearst Magazines, 11 October 2017. Web.

"Cornrow Braiding Originates in Africa." History of Cornrow Braiding, Web.

Crenshaw, Kimberlé. "Transcript of 'The Urgency of Intersectionality.'" TED, TEDWomen 2016, Web.

ELLE. "Watch This Documentary on Braids and Appropriation in America | ELLE." YouTube, YouTube, 27 December 2017. Web.

Flake, Ebony. "As #BlackGirlMagic Turns Four Years Old, CaShawn Thompson Has a Fresh Word for All the Magical Black Girls." The Community for Black Creativity and News, Blavity, Web.

Ford, Ashley. "There Is Nothing Wrong with Black Girl Magic." ELLE, Hearst Magazines, 11 October 2017. Web.

Ginzberg, Lori D. "Elizabeth Cady Stanton." The New Yorker, The New Yorker, 19 June 2017. Web.

Gonzalez, Christian Alejandro. "The Illiberal Logic of Intersectionality." Quillette, Quillette Pty Ltd, 13 May 2018. Web.

"How Dr. Yaba Blay's 'Professional Black Girl' Captures the Creativity and Artistry of Black Girl Culture." The Black Youth Project, The Black Youth Project, 9 April 2019. Web.

Lewis, Maya. "As a Black Woman, I Wish I Could Stop Code-Switching. Here's Why." Everyday Feminism, 12 April 2018. Web.

Mayblin, Lucy. "Intersectionality." Global Social Theory, Global Social Theory, 5 February 2016. Web.

Michals, Debra. "Mary Church Terrell." National Women's History Museum, 2017. Web.

"Minority Rights: Do Members of Minority Groups Enjoy Equal Opportunity and Treatment in the United States?" Issues & Controversies, Infobase Learning, 11 March 2013. Web.

Norwood, Arlisha R. "Ida B. Wells-Barnett." National Women's History Museum, 2017. Web.

Putman-Walkerly, Kris, and Elizabeth Russell. "What the Heck Does 'Equity' Mean?

(SSIR)." Stanford Social Innovation Review: Informing and Inspiring Leaders of Social Change, Stanford University, 15 September 2016. Web.

Staples, Brent. "How the Suffrage Movement Betrayed Black Women." The New York Times, The New York Times, 28 July 2018. Web.

Virk, Kameron, and Nesta McGregor. "Blackfishing: The Women Accused of Pretending to Be Black." BBC News, BBC, 5 December 2018. Web.

Chloe Duren, "Arming Teachers: A Fatal Solution"
Works Cited

Alfonsi, Sharon. "Stoneman Douglas Student Tells *60 Minutes* Why Arming Teachers Is 'Stupid'." CBS News. CBS Interactive Inc, 18 March 2018. Web.

"Arm Teachers? The Facts to Argue Against It." VPC. Violence Policy Center, 22 February 2018. Web.

Bump, Phillip. "The Economics of Arming America's Schools." Washington Post. The Washington Post, 22 February 2018. Web.

Dailey, Ryan. "Commissioner: Arming Fearful Florida Teachers Will Make Black Kids Targets." USAToday. USA Today Network, 28 February 2018. Web.

Givens, Amy. "Missing the Mark: School Personnel Should Not Be Armed." Udayton. University of Dayton, 2014. Web.

Sit, Ryan. "More Children Have Been Killed by Guns Than U.S. Soldiers Killed in Combat Since 9/11." Newsweek. Newsweek LLC, 16 March 2018. Web.

Alex Lu, "Essential and Unforgettable: What *Calvin and Hobbes* Teaches Us About Our Daily Lives"
Works Cited

Watterson, Bill. *Calvin and Hobbes*. Los Angeles Times. 26 April 1990.

Watterson, Bill. *Calvin and Hobbes*. Los Angeles Times. 2 November 1990.

Watterson, Bill. *Calvin and Hobbes*. Los Angeles Times. 11 September 1992.

Watterson, Bill. *Calvin and Hobbes*. Los Angeles Times. 15 December 1992.

David Wang, "Is Space Travel Worth the Cost?"
Works Cited

Etzioni, Amitai, and Eli Etzioni. "Humanity Would Be Better Off Saving Earth, Rather Than Colonizing Mars." The National Interest, The Center for the National Interest, 25 August 2018. Web.

"Global Poverty Rate Drops to Record Low 10%: World Bank." CNBC, CNBC, 19 September 2018. Web.

Weindling, Jacob, et al. "Point/Counterpoint: Is Space Travel Worth It?" Pastemagazine. com. Web.

Gia Shin, "Shining a Light on the Dark Side of K-Pop"
Works Cited

Benjamin, Kathy. "The Disturbing Truth Behind K-Pop Music." Grunge. Web.

"BTS Jin and Jimin Reveal the Extremely Unhealthy Diets They Had to Suffer Through." Koreaboo, 2 November 2017. Web.

Bruner, Raisa. "Here's Why K-Pop Group BTS Is Taking a Break." Time, 12 August 2019. Web.

Chua, Jessica. "The Extremes That Koreans Take to Become a Kpop Idol: Entertainment: Rojak Daily." Entertainment | Rojak Daily, 27 January 2017. Web.

Han, Sang-hee. "Is There a Solution for Slave Contracts?" KoreaTimes, 11 August 2009. Web.

Herman, Tamar. "2018 Sees K-Pop Claim Space in Global Markets While Looking Toward Future." Forbes, 30 December 2018. Web.

Hong, Euny. *The Birth of Korean Cool: How One Nation Is Conquering the World Through Pop Culture*. Simon & Schuster, 2014.

Kim, Min Joo. "Sex Scandals Stain the Clean-Cut Image of South Korea's K-Pop." The Washington Post, WP Company, 5 August 2019. Web.

"K-Pop Band Six Bomb 'Celebrate' Plastic Surgery with Before and After Videos. BBC News, 17 March 2017. Web.

Mak, Henry Prince, director. BTS on How Much Money a Kpop Idol Makes (Truth from an Actual KPOP Idol) | STORYTIME. YouTube, 27 January 2018. Web.

Malleta, Kimg, and Carl Samson. "Why Korean Parents Give Their Kids Plastic Surgery as Graduation Gifts." NextShark, 13 March 2019. Web.

McKirdy, Euan. "Jonghyun: Fans Mourn Death of SHINee K-Pop Star." CNN, Cable News Network, 19 December 2017. Web.

Russell, Erica. "BTS Member Jungkook Nearly Collapses from Exhaustion in 'Burn the Stage' Documentary." PopCrush, 29 March 2018. Web.

Stone, Zara. "The K-Pop Plastic Surgery Obsession." The Atlantic, 17 September 2014. Web.

Tai, Crystal. "The Cutting Edge of Beauty: Male Plastic Surgery in South Korea." South China Morning Post, 20 July 2018. Web.

Joshua Yang, "Unraveling the Narrative"
Works Cited

vanityfair.com/magazine/1997/02/brenner199702

theguardian.com/sport/2016/jul/27/olympic-park-bombings-atlanta-1996-richard-jewell

atlantamagazine.com/great-reads/presumed-guilty/

columbia.edu/itc/journalism/j6075/edit/readings/jewell.html

retroreport.org/video/richard-jewell-the-wrong-man/

Major Supporters

 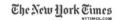 

For the National
Student Poets Program:

 INSTITUTE *of*
Museum *and* Library
SERVICES

THE
ANDREW W.
MELLON
FOUNDATION

The Wunderkinder Foundation

P O
E T
R Y
FOUNDATION

academy of
american poets

Partners: National Writing Project, NAACP ACT-SO, NAEA, The New School (Eugene Lang College of Liberal Arts, Parsons College of Design, and Parsons at Open Campus)

The Alliance for Young Artists & Writers, presenter of the Scholastic Art & Writing Awards, is a 501(c)(3) nonprofit organization that relies on supporters to empower creative teens nationwide by providing recognition, publication, exhibition, and scholarship opportunities. Their generosity is key to our success, and we are most grateful to them. Join us in supporting the next generation of creative minds by becoming a donor.

To make a tax-deductible contribution, visit **artandwriting.org/donate**.

Made in the USA
Las Vegas, NV
05 March 2021